A LM IA CERAMIC KILN
IN SOUTH-CENTRAL CRETE

Hesperia Supplements

Hesperia Supplement 30

A LM IA CERAMIC KILN IN SOUTH-CENTRAL CRETE

Function and Pottery Production

Joseph W. Shaw
Aleydis Van de Moortel
Peter M. Day
and
Vassilis Kilikoglou

with a contribution by Louise Joyner

The American School of Classical Studies at Athens
2001

Out-of-print *Hesperia* supplements may be purchased from
    Swets & Zeitlinger
    Backsets Department
    P.O. Box 810
    2160 SZ Lisse
    The Netherlands
E-mail: backsets@swets.nl

Library of Congress Cataloging-in-Publication Data

A LM IA ceramic kiln in south-central Crete : function and pottery production
/ Joseph W. Shaw . . . [et al.]
        p.   c.   — (Hesperia. Supplement ; 30)
    Includes bibliographical references and index.
    ISBN 0-87661-530-2 (alk. paper)
1. Crete (Greece)—Antiquities. 2. Excavations (Archaeology)—Greece—Crete.
3. Minoans—Greece—Crete. 4. Pottery, Minoan—Greece—Crete.   I. Shaw, Joseph W. II. Hesperia (Princeton, N.J.). Supplement ; 30.

DF221.C8 L59 2001
939′.18—dc21
                                            00-050416

CONTENTS

ILLUSTRATIONS

TABLES

A LM IA CERAMIC KILN
IN SOUTH-CENTRAL CRETE

INTRODUCTION

Kommos is a Minoan and Greek site located near the southern end of a long strip of north–south shoreline of the Mesara Plain in south-central Crete. Excavation by the University of Toronto through the American School of Classical Studies at Athens, with the cooperation of the Greek Antiquities Service, has been carried out since 1976, with pauses for study and publication.[1]

During the Minoan period there was a medium-sized town (MM IB–LM IIIB, ca. 1900–1250 B.C.) spread out over a hillside and hilltop and north of there for a still unknown distance. South of the town, and separated from it by a broad east–west paved road, were three large successive civic buildings ("AA," "T," and "P," respectively) of which the first two (AA, T) featured palatial central courts, like the one at Phaistos, for which Kommos was the harbortown. The third, P, comprised a series of six long, parallel galleries that may have housed ships of the Mesara fleet (Shaw and Shaw 1999). The kiln under consideration in this book was built within the South Stoa of Building T during LM IA (Fig. 1).

During the ensuing Greek period the character of the site changed, from that of a town with civic structures to a rural religious shrine of which the earliest of three successive temples ("A") was built ca. 1020 B.C. during the Subminoan period. It was followed by "B," ca. 800 B.C., and in turn by "C," ca. 375/350 B.C. All three, as well as other buildings connected with them, were constructed over the earlier Minoan remains. The Kommos site was deserted about A.D. 200 and was subsequently covered by drifting sand.

Publication has paralleled excavation. The most recent preliminary report is Shaw and Shaw 1993. A series of successive volumes is also emerging. The first volume, in two parts, contains studies of the Kommos area, its ecology, and Minoan industries, as well as the Minoan houses on the hillside and hilltop (*Kommos* I.1, 2). The second, by Betancourt, examines the Middle Minoan pottery from the houses (*Kommos* II), and the third, by Watrous, Late Minoan pottery and trade (*Kommos* III). In press is *The Greek Sanctuary* (volume IV), and in preparation is a volume on the Minoan civic area (volume V).

1. Financial support during the 1993–1995 period when the kiln was excavated was provided by the Social Sciences and Humanities Research Council of Canada (grants 411-88-0020-X6 and 410-94-1091-X1, 2), by the Institute for Aegean Prehistory, founded by Malcolm Wiener, and by the University of Toronto through the Vice President for Research and International Relations and the Dean of Arts and Science, as well as by Mr. Lorne Wickerson. A shorter, preliminary version of this monograph has appeared as Shaw et al. 1997.

Concerning the LM IA kiln itself, comparative study suggests that it is a type of cross-draft channel kiln popular during the Neopalatial period. As discussed by Shaw in Chapter 1, its good state of preservation allows us to speculate about its original internal layout and use, as well as about its roof.

In and around the kiln a large mass of broken pottery was found, which in all likelihood represents the waste of the kiln operation. A first study of this material is presented here in Chapter 2 by Aleydis Van de Moortel. It aims: (1) to provide the reader with a detailed understanding of the stratigraphy; (2) to give an overview of the vase shapes and varieties produced in this kiln; (3) to establish its date; and (4) to discuss evidence for some manufacturing practices and aspects of the organization of production that have become apparent thus far. More specifically, standardization of shapes and the relation of fabric texture to vessel shape are addressed, and peculiarities of vessel formation, surface finish, and decoration pointed out. Clues regarding the scale and mode of pottery production at this facility are investigated. Future research will focus on analyzing idiosyncrasies of the manufacturing process in greater detail. Since this is the first time that a large amount of Minoan pottery has been found in association with its production facility, we have the unprecedented opportunity to document the specific technological, morphological, and decorative profile of a body of pottery produced at a known locale. With this profile we might be able in the future to study the spatial distribution and consumption of Kommian pottery at other sites, and to reach a better understanding of the production decisions taken by the potter or potters of a single locale in relation to the available technology as well as to environmental, economic, social, and political conditions.

It will be argued here that the kiln was in use from mid to late LM IA. This date is bound to be controversial, because the kiln produced light-on-dark patterned pottery, traditionally associated with the Middle Minoan phases of Cretan ceramics, and there is no evidence that it ever produced vases with dark-painted motifs on a lustrous buff ground, which were dominant on Crete at the time. The kiln's date is established on the basis of its stratigraphical position and of the stylistic fit of the kiln vases and their associated pottery within the newly revised LM IA chronology at Kommos. This new chronology is based on the results of recent excavations in Building T and in House X, which have much expanded the number of stratified LM IA deposits at the site. Instead of the two LM IA stages distinguished in the past by Betancourt and Watrous, we are now able to identify three stages.[2] At present, these three LM IA stages have been established only at Kommos, and it remains to be seen whether they can be applied to other sites. We have decided to call these new stages early, advanced, and final LM IA. In doing so we eschew the terminology proposed by Warren and adopted by Betancourt, which distinguished a "Transitional MM III(B)/LM IA" stage in which light-on-dark patterned and lustrous dark-on-light painted pottery coexisted, from a "mature LM IA" stage dominated by lustrous dark-on-light painted vases.[3] Since at Kommos it now appears that light-on-dark patterned pottery was produced and consumed well into final LM IA, we prefer to adopt a strictly chronological dating

2. *Kommos* II, pp. 41–48; *Kommos* III.

3. Warren and Hankey 1989, pp. 61–65, 72–78; Warren 1991; see also p. 89, note 158 below.

terminology that does not make inferences about the stylistic composition of the assemblages of the various LM IA stages. The recently excavated LM IA deposits from Building T and House X are still unpublished, and it is felt that a detailed discussion of the new LM IA chronology at Kommos is beyond the scope of the present publication. It will be the topic of a separate article, which is currently being prepared by Jeremy B. Rutter and Aleydis Van de Moortel. At present, only a short description of the pottery characteristics of the three new stages will be given, and stylistic comparisons drawn with LM IA chronologies used at other Minoan sites and at Akrotiri.

The Kommos kiln was constructed in advanced LM IA—on top of an early LM IA destruction level—and its ceramic output as well as associated pottery fits stylistically into the advanced and final stages of LM IA. The ceramics also show specific links with "transitional" as well as "mature" LM IA pottery from other central Cretan sites and from Akrotiri. The absence of certain ceramic characteristics suggests that the Kommos kiln went out of use before the end of the LM IA phase, and thus within a generation or so of the volcanic eruption of Thera.

The excavated kiln structure with its associated pottery is a find of great importance for analytical ceramic studies on Crete. Its examination by an integrated program of analytical techniques is of value for our understanding of the technology and organization of ceramic production at the beginning of the Late Minoan period, for the study of pottery provenance and exchange, and ultimately for the design of analytical methodology.

In Chapter 3 Peter Day and Vassilis Kilikoglou present analytical data and interpretations pertaining both to the reconstruction of ceramic technology used in the production of pottery in the Kommos kiln, relating this to raw materials available in the vicinity, and to the establishment of a compositional control group. A combination of analytical techniques is used, including petrographic thin-section analysis, scanning electron microscopy, and neutron activation analysis. The characterization of the pottery has led to conclusions regarding the procurement and manipulation of raw materials, the decoration of the vessels, and their firing conditions. Both the clay matrix and aplastic inclusions have been connected to local geological deposits and other comparative pottery from the area of the Mesara. The variation in fabric according to shape and putative function is discussed. The range of firing temperatures has been documented by examination of vitrification microstructures and subsequent chemical analysis using the scanning electron microscope. These analyses show that the kiln was capable of firing in a reducing atmosphere, in order to achieve the iron-rich black decoration. Additionally, different firing regimes were found that are consistent with the typological groupings present in the pottery associated with the kiln. The latter finding implies the use of different firing conditions for various pottery types, either by different firing episodes or by the specific placement of vessels within one kiln firing.

Postburial alterations in elemental and mineralogical composition of the ceramics associated with the kiln have been investigated. These alterations have important implications for the study of pottery provenance by

chemical analysis, as they show the selective alteration of composition according to the technology, mainly as a function of firing temperature. A
detailed chemical and mineralogical study of this phenomenon and its
implications is presented elsewhere (Buxeda i Garrigòs, Kilikoglou, and
Day in press).

   We hope that our study may contribute to a better understanding of
Minoan kiln construction and use, ceramic technology, and the development of ceramic form and decoration in south-central Crete, and through
analyses of the clay provide comparative material for future studies.

The Authors   1 May 2000

CHAPTER I

The Excavation and the Structure of the Kiln

by Joseph W. Shaw

PROCESS[1]

During the 1992 season, in the process of searching for the southern limit of Neopalatial Ashlar Building T, a new excavation area was opened up to the southwest.[2] The first stage in the process was to remove by mechanical means the meters of deep, sterile post-Roman sand accumulation[3] from above the ancient levels (from ca. +9.17 m to ca. +4.80 m).[4] A single trench then located the western end of Ashlar Building P's Gallery 6 as well as the southern, east–west, wall of Building T (see Fig. 1, bottom, center).[5]

In 1993 we learned that this latter wall was the southern wall of what has come to be called T's South Stoa (Figs. 2–3), with six columns. It faced a similar one, the North Stoa, across the north–south length of the Central Court of Building T. During the same excavation season we discovered a pottery kiln, the subject of this monograph, presumably built within the South Stoa after it had been abandoned (see below). The eastern half

1. The authors would like to express their thanks to the trench-masters who were in charge of excavating the kiln, in particular Joseé Sabourin and Kate Walsh (1993), Gordon Nixon (1994), and M. C. Shaw (1995), also to Taylor Dabney for his photography and Julia Pfaff (assisted by Nicolle Hirschfeld) for the drawings of the pottery. Aleydis Van de Moortel, Jeremy Rutter, and Alan Johnston were responsible for pottery analysis. Barbara Hamann, Clarissa Hagen-Plettenberg, and Katharine Hall mended the pottery, which was inventoried by Niki Kantzios and Deborah Ruscillo. Giuliana Bianco drew the plans and sections. Thanks are also due to Doniert Evely, Julie Hansen, Ned Rehder, and Jennifer and Tom Shay, who were most helpful during various stages of the kiln study.

The kiln is presently covered with sand until a proper protective shelter can be built over it.

2. For Building T, see especially J. Shaw 1986, pp. 240–251. For the excavation of the south wing of T, see Shaw and Shaw 1993, pp. 178–182.

3. The nature of this sand accumulation is discussed by John Gifford in *Kommos* I.1, pp. 51–53, 64–71.

4. The "+" sign before a number indicates the level above mean sea level, as established originally in 1974 by topographer John Bandekas.

5. For LM IIIA2 Building P, the third of the monumental buildings in the civic area, see J. Shaw 1986, pp. 255–269, and Shaw and Shaw 1993, p. 182, and also 1999.

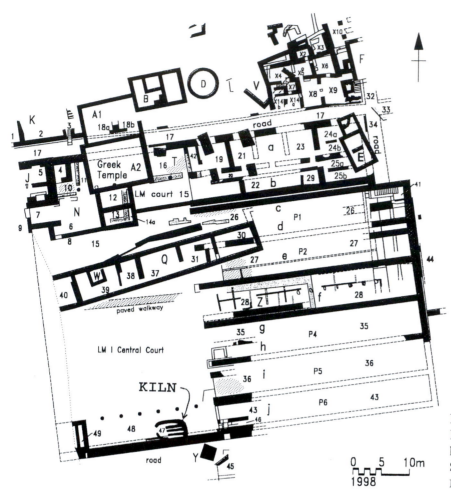

Figure 1. Plan of Southern Area of Kommos site, showing position of kiln *(lower left)* within the South Stoa of Building T. G. Bianco, M. Nelson

of the kiln was then cleared, as well as part of the northernmost channel or flue (channel 1 in Fig. 6).[6] In 1994 the western half of the kiln, including the firing pit, was excavated, as well as the second and fourth channels.[7] Kiln excavation was completed in 1995 upon the clearing of the third channel.[8] During excavation, dry sieving and wet sieving were employed extensively to recover small artifacts and, especially, any charcoal evidence of organic materials used to fire the kiln. Unfortunately, only ash was found, and determining plant/wood type without charcoal is extremely difficult.

6. Excavation of trench 87B revealed the northeastern sector as well as the channel mentioned in the text (July 21–August 12, directed by J. Sabourin). Trench 90C revealed the southeastern sector (July 28–August 5, directed by K. Walsh).

7. Trench 95A (June 29–August 12, directed by G. Nixon). Here the term "firing pit" will be used to identify the

pit within which the fires were set. "Firing chamber" denotes both the firing pit and the area with the channels/flues. The size of the firing chamber of the Kommos kiln falls in the mid-range of its kiln type (see Table 11, p. 107).

8. Trench 97F (July 20–28, directed by M. C. Shaw).

Figure 2. South Stoa area with kiln.

G. Bianco

Figure 3. Kommos, South Stoa of Ashlar Building T, with kiln *(center, left)*, from northwest. T. Dabney

THE STRATIGRAPHIC CONTEXT OF THE KILN

In order to understand the sequence of ancient activity in the kiln area, it is worthwhile summarizing various discrete stages of architectural use here:

1. Protopalatial period: A large civic structure (AA), the first of three in the southern area, is built upon a leveled platform. On the east, the general ground level is raised by means of walls that functioned like compartments to retain clay and earth brought in from elsewhere.[9]

2. MM III: Ashlar Building T is constructed early in the period. Its southern wall (the southern wall of the South Stoa) is set upon a wall of earlier MM building AA.

3. LM IA (advanced): The kiln is constructed. Since, as is proposed here (see below), it was covered by a roof, perhaps a domelike roof of clay, and the southernmost channel is tangent to T's ashlar wall, then the southern wall of the kiln, now destroyed, must have rested upon the ashlar wall, perhaps at the level of that wall as now preserved (as in Figs. 2 and 6) or a few courses higher. Therefore a portion of the southern wall of Building T here, as well as the colonnade, had probably already collapsed by the time the kiln was built, assuming that the stoa was actually completed. It is possible that the kiln's builders removed part of the still-standing ashlar wall in order to set the southern kiln wall upon one of the lower courses.

The kiln builders evidently created a low mound of earth and rubble, rising from west to east to +3.42 m (max.) (Fig. 8: section B–B). Upon this they set their eastern wall, the bottom of which is at +3.42 m, seen some 0.40 m above the floor level of the earlier stoa in Figure 12 (the scale is lying on the stoa's floor). A similar effect would have resulted if the kiln had been partially built upon the collapsed stoa remains. Entrance to the firing pit was on the west, in any case, from close to the stoa's floor level (+2.80 m). The kiln's bowl-like firing pit was excavated by its builders to some 0.40 m below stoa floor level.

4. LM IA (end)–LM IIIA1: Hiatus. Settlement continues in the houses north of the civic area,[10] but the civic area itself was used only

9. Shaw and Shaw 1993, pp. 166–170, fig. 10:b. In the area of the later South Stoa, a wide east–west wall directly under the Neopalatial southern wall, also built to raise the ground level, was set in.

10. House X, for example, for which see Shaw and Shaw 1993, pp. 131–161, and *Kommos* I.2, passim.

Figure 4 (*left*). **Kiln partially excavated, with superposed rubble fallen from south wall of stoa, from west.**
T. Dabney

Figure 5 (*right*). **Later LM III oven, from south (see also Fig. 11).**
J. W. Shaw

sporadically. Apparently the South Stoa remained unused (there is very little LM IB–LM IIIA1 pottery there), with the kiln abandoned, although there is a clear LM IB use level in Gallery P6 east of here. The leveling of the kiln (down to +4.00 m) took place between LM IA (the final use of the kiln) and LM IIIA2, when the court in front of the galleried building, P, was constructed.[11] The pottery immediately above the kiln collapse is of LM IIIA2/B date.

5. LM IIIA2–B: Construction of Building P in LM IIIA2, largely with blocks reused from Building T. During LM IIIB part of the still-standing southern wall of the South Stoa, south and southwest of the firing pit, collapsed to the north, over the pit and its entrance, as seen in Figure 4. Perhaps this wall collapse brought about the destruction of the kiln roof, but the latter may have collapsed earlier. The Central Court of T then became the West Court of Building P, with the court level raised significantly in the area of the South Stoa and kiln from about +2.80 m to perhaps as much as +4.00 m.[12] At some point during this period a series of clay ovens was built here. Two were set above the remains of the ashlar wall of the stoa (Figs. 5–6), and others on the slope farther south.[13]

6. LM IIIB–4th century B.C.: The kiln was gradually covered over by sand and alluvium. LM IIIB pottery in the South Stoa area, immediately above the kiln, is followed by Archaic and then 5th- and 4th-century levels with no LM IIIC/Geometric pottery, which can be found farther to the north near the temples. An Archaic slab platform and a shallow depression lined with cobbles are the only semipermanent features in the area until base Y, probably part of a statue base, was constructed during the 4th century B.C. on a rising ground level at +4.60 m.[14] Site desertion followed, ca. A.D. 200, and was accompanied by sand accumulation.

11. For various reasons Van de Moortel prefers LM IA as the time that the kiln was leveled (see below).

12. The floor of Gallery 6 of Building P, some meters east of the kiln, was at +3.60 m, below the level of the top of the kiln after it had been leveled. On the other hand, the same gallery was blocked by a rough north–south retaining wall, its top at +4.08 m. Thus someone entering P6 from the west would have stepped down from the level of the court into the gallery.

13. For those on the slope, see Shaw and Shaw 1993, p. 182, fig. 15 and pl. 43:a. For the type, see M. Shaw 1990, passim.

14. For Y, see Shaw and Shaw 1993, p. 183.

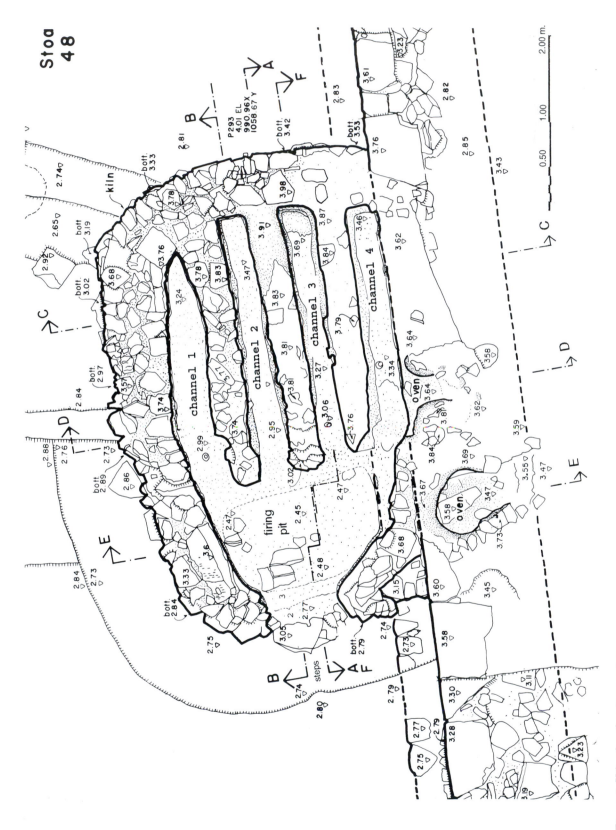

Figure 6. Kiln plan showing sections.

G. Bianco

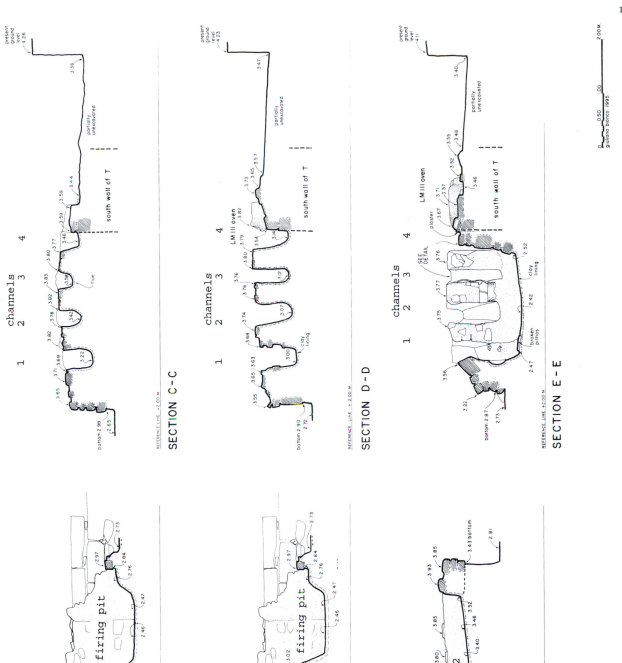

Figure 7. Kiln sections. G. Bianco

TABLE 1. APPROXIMATE DIMENSIONS OF THE KILN

	East–West (max.)	North–South	Pres. Height
Kiln	4.20 (int.) 5.40 (ext.)	2.70 (int.) 3.20 (ext.)	— —
Firing pit	1.00	1.30	1.23 1.00 (to east end of channels)
Channel 1	2.70	0.25	1.00 (west)* 0.67 (east)*
Channel 2	2.90	0.25	0.94 (west)* 0.44 (east)*
Channel 3	2.70	0.24	0.83 (west)* 0.40 (east)*
Channel 4	2.80	0.25	— (west) 0.45 (east)*

All dimensions in meters.

*Measurement down from horizontal plastered surface between channels 2 and 3 (at +3.91 in Fig. 6, a in Fig. 14).

THE KILN

In plan, the kiln is oval, and approximately 5.40 m east–west by 3.20 m north–south (Fig. 6; see Table 1 for kiln measurements). Its north–south orientation is 8°40′15″ west of grid north, or 10°10′15″ west of magnetic north, the same orientation as Building T, since the kiln reused the wall of the South Stoa. Its exterior walls, 0.70–0.80 m thick, were composed of a variety of rubble limestone blocks stabilized by clay mortar. To accommodate the firing pit on the west, with adjacent channels rising from west to east, the kiln was more deeply founded there, as can be seen in the sections and photographs.

The firing pit had an opening on the west, which was ca. 0.50 m wide. There were three rough steps (Fig. 6),[15] which led down into the pit where the fire was set. Outside the kiln for some distance to the west, north, and east, discarded fragments of clay lining as well as pieces of rejected pottery formed an impressive dump, reddish yellow from the heat of the kiln (see Chapter 2, below). Like the channels to the east, the firing pit had been coated with a thin clay lining, which had fired through use to a consistent color. This same color had first led us to the identification of hearths and ovens elsewhere on the site. The firing pit itself is roughly oval, with incurving sides that are more vertical on the north and south than on the west, where the entrance is, or on the east, where the side slopes up to merge with the channels, which led the heat up and around the pottery that was being fired. Within the lower 0.15 m of the firing pit was a thick layer of ash without charcoal; above that point was an accumulation of brown burned clay and rubble.

15. The first, highest step, its top at +3.05, may be later, added as the accumulation built up around the kiln. The next two steps were covered by clay plaster, suggesting that they are original rather than secondary.

Figure 13. Excavation of channel 3, west end, with clay and rubble filling, right, and clay relining *(left, at a)*, after first pass, from west.
J. W. Shaw

Figure 14. Excavation of channel 3, rough stone filling after first pass. Note intact clay plaster surface at *a*, from west. J. W. Shaw

Figure 15. Excavation of channel 3, pottery and rubble in channel after second pass, from west.
J. W. Shaw

Figure 16. Excavation of channel 3, west end after second pass, from west. J. W. Shaw

Figure 17. Excavation of channel 3, west end after third pass. Note conical cup (*a*) in clay of relining, from west. J. W. Shaw

Figure 18. Two sides of clay/rubble mass from channel 2. J. W. Shaw

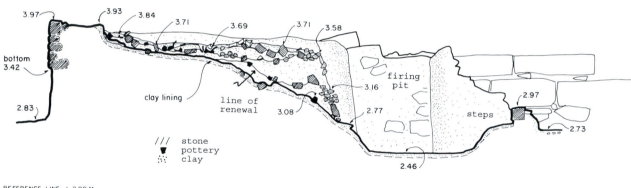

Figure 19. Archaeological section F–F of channel 3, showing stone, pottery, and lines of renewal, from north. G. Bianco and M. Shaw

The channels were found filled with an assortment of material. There was the usual reddish brown clay in the form of either powdery earth or thin pieces of fired clay plaster, some no doubt from the linings and tops of the channels. There were also coalesced lumps of material such as those shown in Figure 18, which in the third channel were more common at the western end, near the heat source. Some of the lumps were soft and blue gray, with short white "threads" that proved, upon close inspection, to be consolidated ash.[16]

In all channels there were small, rough, uncut, and uneven slabs of stone; these were particularly common toward the tops of the channels (see the section in Fig. 19; also, compare Fig. 14 with Fig. 15). Those from channel 3, totaling 0.066 m³ in volume, are seen laid out on a table in Figure 20. The first two rows in the foreground, shown in the same relative position of their discovery in the channel (west is on the left), are from the top of the channel. Those in the third, final row are from farther down;

16. As identified by Alain Dandrau and Peter Day.

Figure 20. Stone rubble found in channel 3. J. W. Shaw

Figure 21. Pottery in channel 2.
J. W. Shaw

17. For the pottery found within the kiln, see Table 2, p. 29.

18. The line of the original floor of channel 3 and at least one renewal can be seen in Figure 19, where the original floor is shown with a thicker line.

there was a significant accumulation of such stones at the western end of the channel.

In these channels there were also sherds and larger pieces of pottery, with conical cups predominating (Figs. 13–17, 19, 21), all without order.[17] Some of these cups, such as that in Figure 17, were found embedded within the clay plaster revetment applied to the channels during occasional renewals.[18] Most likely some of the pottery fell into the channels during the process of firing and was simply not removed when the kiln was being replastered.

USE AND FORM

Broadly speaking, there are two main types of Minoan kilns, which seem to be of different dates. The first type comprises structures that are hemispherical or circular, with or without a stoking channel; these generally date to LM III. The second type, normally found in Neopalatial contexts, comprises those with multiple parallel channels leading out from a firing pit; these function as cross-draft kilns, with the draft being drawn across the firing chamber.[19] In plan, this second type is rather like a hand, with the palm representing the firing pit and the fingers the channels. The Kommos kiln belongs to this second type, of which there are single examples in Crete at Gouves,[20] Aghia Triada,[21] Kato Zakros,[22] Kokkino Froudi,[23] Mochlos,[24] Phaistos,[25] and Vathypetro,[26] as well as four examples at Knossos.[27] The number of channels in these kilns varies from two to five. One of the problems in the past has been that it was usually unclear what actually had been fired in such kilns, for few wasters (with the exception of the Aghia Triada kiln) and no pottery dumps have been reported in connection with them. It has been suggested variously that pottery, lime, and even faience, glass, or metals may have been produced within them.[28] The use of the Kommos kiln is made clear by the pottery within it, by the pottery dump outside of it, and by wasters nearby. No traces of lime or metallurgical debris were found within it.[29]

How the upper portion of the kiln and the pottery to be fired within it were arranged, however, remains uncertain, although some proposals can be made. First, one of the wall tops between the channels (Fig. 14 at *a*), is,

19. For kiln typology, see Evely in press, pp. 298–312. Evely includes a third "type," a miscellaneous collection. Many of the kilns at sites enumerated below are described in detail in his catalogue on p. 304. I am most grateful to him for providing me with a prepublication copy of his text, and to Peter Day and Vassilis Kilikoglou for discussions about up-draft and cross-draft kilns.

20. Vallianou 1997, p. 337, pl. CXXXVIII:a.

21. Levi and Laviosa 1986; Tomasello 1996.

22. Platon 1977, esp. pp. 344–351; 1980.

23. Chrysoulaki 1996.

24. Soles 1997, p. 427.

25. Tomasello 1996. Of MM IIB date, this is the earliest of, and perhaps a prototype for, the Cretan channel kilns. Its firing chamber includes two supporting "islands" with channels alongside, and so differs from the later examples cited in the text.

26. Marinatos 1952, p. 270, and 1956, p. 298.

27. Hood 1958, p. 24, fig. 6:b; Warren 1980–1981. Recently discovered at Miletus were a number of kilns, of which two had channels (Niemeier 1997, p. 349 and pl. CXLVI:a). One (g), not well preserved, had at least four and as many as six channels. In plan the second, better preserved one (c), differs from the Minoan palm/fingers type being dealt with here, however, in that the channels are at right angles to the kiln's width and the firing pit is connected to the kiln's interior by a long, covered channel along one of its sides.

28. Evely in press, pp. 300, 309–311. He notes that the only reports of large amounts of wasters come from LM contexts at known or suspected kiln sites, but that these are unpublished.

29. This does not mean, however, that lime or metal could not, under certain circumstances, have been cooked or melted within the firing pit of a kiln such as that found at Kommos.

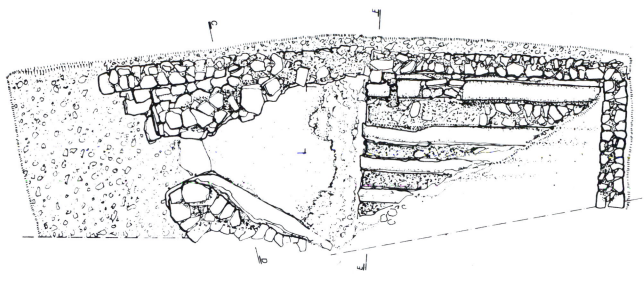

A

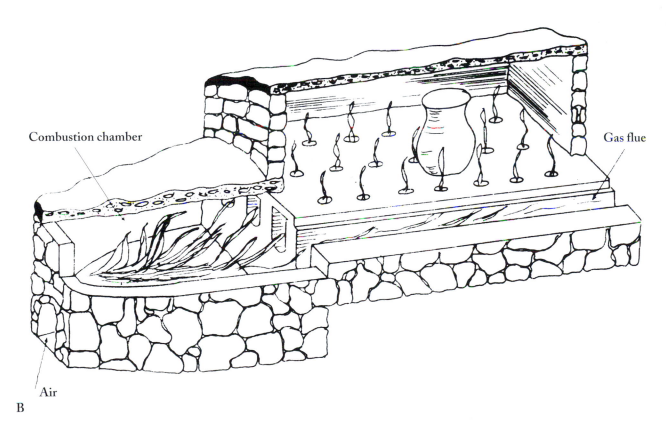

Combustion chamber

Gas flue

Air

B

Figure 22. Restored plan (a) and
reconstruction (b) of kiln at Aghia
Triada. From Di Vita, La Rosa, and
Rizzo et al. 1984, figs. 203–204

Figure 23. LM III pottery kiln at Stylos. J. Rutter

as mentioned earlier, covered by a uniformly smooth coating of clay plaster. We assume that the other wall tops terminated in a similar manner. On this basis one can argue that the pottery was simply placed on the wall tops between channels, or else spanned the channels, since there was probably not an upper floor or grate such as that proposed for the kiln from Aghia Triada, where a partial grate was found,[30] and as shown in the restoration by the Italian excavators in Figure 22:b.

It is possible, however, that some of the rough stone slabs recovered from the channels (Fig. 20) spanned them, as in the LM III kiln at Stylos (Fig. 23).[31] Also, some of the fragmentary coarse terracotta slabs or bats recovered from the kiln (C 10052, C 10073),[32] as well as some pithoi (below, **58**), basins (**54**, **55**), and large bowls (**27**), could have temporarily spanned the 0.25 m gaps, with other pottery stacked on top of them. Nevertheless it is curious that no spanning elements were found in situ, if they had been left in place by the potters, especially in the undisturbed area where the plastered upper wall (see above) is preserved intact. Also, since clay imprints were not found on the tops of the channel dividers, any terracotta or stone slabs placed there were apparently not stabilized by clay as were the slabs in the Stylos kiln.

At least some of the small stone slabs mentioned above were probably once built into the clay and rubble roof of the kiln.[33] While there is only indirect evidence to show that the kiln was "roofed," this must have been the case, as the analyses presented here show that the process of oxidation–reduction–oxidation was used certainly for the dark-painted vessels, as discussed below in Chapter 3. Such close control of the atmosphere of a kiln is not possible in one with an open top, perhaps covered only by broken sherds. The provision of an aperture at the eastern end of the roof would have guided the draft from west to east over the kiln load. Such a design makes much more efficient use of heat than do up-draft kilns.

Concerning the roof itself, while no definite fragments were found, the interior of the kiln above the channels was covered with a 0.10 m–

30. Levi and Laviosa 1986, figs. 5, 9. For further discussion and a new reconstruction see Tomasello 1996, pp. 30–32, figs. 4–5. Partial grates have also been found in smaller, circular Minoan kilns of Evely's type 1(c) at LM IIIC Kavousi (Gesell, Day, and Coulson 1988, pp. 290ff., fig. 5) and LM IIIB Stylos (Davaras 1973, p. 75, fig. 1, pls. 39–42, and our Fig. 23). See also below.

31. Some slabs may have fallen in from the upper parts of the channel dividers, as for instance from the top of the wall shown in Figure 14 where a slab is exposed, and others are clearly missing.

32. "C" followed by a number indicates a particular object of clay in the Kommos general inventory list. For these coarse slabs, see pp. 85–87 below.

33. A slight curve in the northern wall of the firing pit (Fig. 6: section E–E; Fig. 7) suggests that at least the roof of the pit curved inward.

Figure 24. Restored view of kiln from northwest. G. Bianco

34. Similar deposits of red-brown clayey soil have been found in Minoan kilns at Zakros (Platon 1977, p. 346) and Vathypetro (Marinatos 1952, p. 272), as well as in the Iron Age kiln at Torone (Papadopoulos 1989, p. 17). Both Platon and Papadopoulos have interpreted the reddish soil as remains of the collapsed superstructure.

thick layer of reddish and light brown clay,[34] and it is reasonable to suggest that this clay layer, as well as some of the reddish and brown clay fragments and stone found within the channels, is from a dome. The upper fills of the channels and the clayey layer in the firing pit included some earlier sherds, dating to MM IB/II, MM III, and early LM IA, as well as a worn lustrous dark-on-light patterned fragment (C 10307), which are not likely to have been part of the firing load (see below). Some of these may have been part of the superstructure; others could have been used as spacers separating the vessels being fired. Moreover, on the basis of the red clayey stratum found outside the kiln, the types of pottery found within it, and joins between that pottery and the pottery found within the kiln, it is argued below that here also may be remains of the dome, scattered to the sides of the kiln after the superstructure collapsed and the resulting accumulation had been leveled. The joins between the pottery in the kiln and that outside it suggest to Van de Moortel (Chapter 2, below) that part of the last firing load was removed and discarded on the kiln dump.

One must also inquire whether there was an intervening wall between firing pit and channels. There probably was not, for the western ends of the channels are so well preserved that part of such a wall would surely have been found had it ever existed. For that reason the roof shown in Figure 24 is made high enough on the west to accommodate the stoker/potter and high enough on the east for the stacked pottery, as well as for the potter who would enter the chamber to place and, later, remove the pots.[35] It seems clear that there must have existed a closeable vent on the eastern end of the kiln that would draw the draft through the kiln and could be sealed during the reduction phase of the firing cycle.[36]

From the kiln design, its pottery, and the analytical work presented below in Chapter 3, it is possible to reconstruct the steps that were likely followed in firing the pottery in this kiln.

1. Dried pottery was placed by the potters over the channels. Larger pots (perhaps bowls and basins) may have been placed upside down, spanning the channels, with other pottery placed carefully above this, and other vases may have been placed on some sort of temporary floor made up of slabs, bats, or large sherds. The unpainted pottery, which did not require as high a temperature, may have been placed toward the eastern end of the kiln.

2. The fuel was introduced into the firing pit and lit. This may have comprised brushwood, small pieces of wood, or olive pits.[37]

3. More fuel was added, and the kiln taken gradually up to its peak temperature, with the open vent on the east and the stokehole creating a strong cross-draft. The temperature was judged by eye, from the color of the kiln load.

4. When a reducing atmosphere was required, damp fuel was introduced into the firing pit as the temperature reached its uppermost, and both the stokehole and the eastern vent were sealed.

5. During the final stage of cooling, the kiln apertures may have been opened up again for the second oxidation stage.

6. When the kiln had completely cooled, the potters removed the pottery and discarded unwanted pieces on the kiln dump. At intervals the potter would have cleared out the firing pit and, as shown in Figures 13 and 19, renewed the clay lining of the channels whenever it had flaked off during use.

35. The dome height is reconstructed as greater than 0.90 m in order to accommodate the potter and also to allow for the baking of typical MM III/ LM I pithoi.

36. Van de Moortel also suggests that since the largest concentration of dump sherds was found east (rather than north or west) of the kiln, that there may have been a separate entrance into the firing chamber from the east such as in modern kilns at Thrapsano (Voyatzoglou 1984, figs. 14–17) and Kentri (Blitzer 1984, figs. 18-3, 4).

37. Recent work by Jeffrey Soles and Costis Davaras at Mochlos, on the Cretan mainland, has revealed an industrial area including two small LM IB kilns, both with firing pits "full of olive pits, a fuel which is still used in kilns today" (Tomlinson 1995, p. 68); see also Soles 1997, p. 427.

CHAPTER 2

The Area around the Kiln, and the Pottery from the Kiln and the Kiln Dump

by Aleydis Van de Moortel

A large mass of about 26,000 pottery fragments, weighing more than 450 kg, was found in and around the Kommos kiln, covering a large part of the South Stoa of Building T and spilling onto the court (Figs. 8, 13–17, 19, 21, 26–28, 30–31).[1] Several features of this deposit, apart from its location, indicate that the bulk of it represents waste from the kiln operation. First, there are more than 300 ceramic wasters distributed throughout the deposit, as well as small numbers of burned and overfired sherds and badly deformed vessels.[2] Some vases could not be fitted together properly, pre-

1. I would like to thank Joseph W. Shaw and Jeremy B. Rutter for permission to publish the kiln pottery. A warm debt of gratitude is due also to J. B. Rutter for his continuous guidance during the course of my pottery studies. The interpretation of the kiln pottery has also benefited greatly from advice given by Gloria London and William D. Glanzman. Needless to say, the responsibility for any remaining oversights and inadequacies is entirely mine. Professor V. La Rosa and Nicola Cucuzza have graciously given me permission to see the unpublished pottery from Seli di Kamilari. Cucuzza's dissertation on this pottery has been published jointly with La Rosa (La Rosa and Cucuzza 2000). The discussions of burned kiln superstructures, wasters, and coarse slabs owe much to information collected by Doniert Evely in his forthcoming book on Minoan crafts (part 2), and by Beatrice McLoughlin in her honors thesis (1993) on ancient Greek kilns. My sincere thanks to Cucuzza, Evely, and McLoughlin for permission to refer to their unpublished manuscripts. Finally I would like to thank the Classics Department at the University of Washington in Seattle for enabling my access to the University library.

2. A few much-deformed vases from the Kommos dump have been inventoried: C 10335 (trench 95A, pails 143, 144) and C 10294 (trench 95A, pails 119, 139, 143, 144, 150, 152). The term "pail" at Kommos refers to a basic excavation unit. The term "waster" is used specifically to refer to badly overfired sherds that are deformed and often cracked, are gray to black in color, and have surfaces marked by projecting inclusions or lime-spalling; occasionally the surfaces may have a shiny brown color. Wasters have been reported from elsewhere at Kommos, but always in small quantities. One was found in MM III–LM IA rubble located in and above Room CH 16 (*Kommos* II, p. 164, no. 1381). A second vase fragment dated to MM IIB is insufficiently overfired to be considered a waster according to the definition given above (*contra* Betancourt [*Kommos* II, p. 92, no. 416]). Its interior shows a grayish hue, whereas its exterior preserves a polychrome decorative scheme. Its shape is somewhat warped, but as a result of pressures applied when the handle was attached rather than from overfiring. Two other wasters are known from a LM I fill on the hill (*Kommos* III, pp. 4, 9, nos. 147, 152). Concentrations of wasters have been found in association with Minoan kilns at Aghia Triada (Levi and Laviosa 1986, pp. 18–28, figs. 17, 20, 23, 26), at Kavousi (Gesell, Day, and Coulson 1988, p. 291; McLoughlin 1993, p. 15), and elsewhere (Evely in press). Mac-Gillivray (1987, p. 276) reports seeing tens of thousands of wasters, mostly dating to MM IIIB and LM IA, with the remains of a kiln at Silamos, but because of the huge numbers quoted it appears that he uses the term "waster" to refer to general kiln waste rather than in the sense defined above.

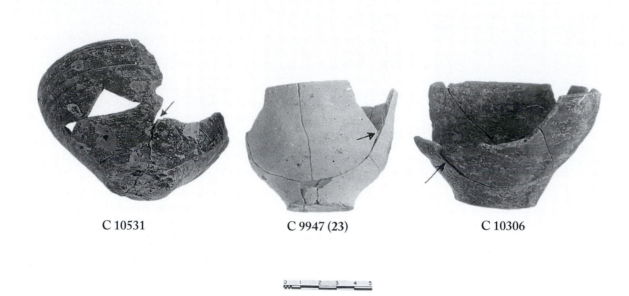

C 10531   C 9947 (23)   C 10306

sumably because they had broken during firing, and their parts subsequently had been warped (Fig. 25).[3] Second, the large majority of the pottery is highly repetitive in fabric, shape, and decoration, and it looks strikingly fresh, as if it had never been used.[4] Finally, even though the restorable vases represent common household shapes, the absence of mendable cooking pots, lamps, and braziers would be unusual for an ordinary household assemblage at Kommos, but fits well within the kiln dump interpretation (see below).[5]

   In the upper parts of the kiln and throughout the dump, small quantities of earlier sherds have been found, which are datable to MM IB, MM II, MM III, and early LM IA. These sherds are small in size and are worn at the edges as well as on the surfaces. Some may derive from the kiln superstructure (see above, p. 23), but most of them, since they were distributed widely and not just in areas of fallen superstructure debris, are likely to have served as fire supports. During the loading of the kiln before firing, they would have been set in between the unfired vases or between those and the clay-lined superstructure of the kiln to prevent them from

Figure 25. Vases thought to have broken during firing. Arrows indicate the warped areas, which do not join properly anymore. T. Dabney

3. Only three such examples have been recognized at present, but their number may increase as more vessels are mended. Two (C 10306, C 10531) are conical cups found inside the kiln, in channels 2 and 3, respectively. The third example is a bell cup (**23**) from the dump.

4. The fresh condition of most of the pottery is indicated by the minimal wear of surfaces and fractures, and especially by the absence of wear patterns on rims, handles, or the

undersides of bases that could be related to use. Another aspect of their fresh condition is the large average size of the sherds, as illustrated by their great average weight (see Tables 2–4 and Figs. 28, 30–31).

5. For MM III household assemblages from the Central Hillside at Kommos, see Wright 1996. According to recently developed chronological criteria (see below, pp. 90–91), a few deposits from this area may now be datable to early LM IA.

touching during firing.[6] During the emptying of the kiln after firing, these supports would have been discarded together with the broken pottery. These earlier sherds will not be considered in the present study.

The distribution of joins among the pottery pieces found inside the kiln suggests that these vases were part of the last firing load (see below, p. 28). If this interpretation is correct, the fact that pottery from within the kiln joins with fragments from the dump would mean that part of the last load had been thrown on the dump.[7]

Because of the substantial size of the deposit, only a preliminary study has been conducted thus far, and that is what is presented here. Its purpose is to establish the range and frequency of vessel shapes and decorative motifs within the kiln output, as evidenced by the finds, and to propose a date range for the kiln's operation. In addition, some aspects of LM IA pottery production at Kommos will be discussed. The catalogue includes representative examples of each shape thought to have been fired in the kiln (**1–59**). Shape frequencies have been estimated on the basis of countable diagnostic features, such as spouts, handles, bases, and rims (Tables 2–4).

Mending the kiln pottery was not as straightforward as it first seemed it would be. From the distribution of joining sherds it appears that parts of the dump had been moved about, while unknown portions had been carried off in the LM IA phase to be used elsewhere on the site (see below, pp. 40–41). These circumstances greatly increased the difficulty of finding joins, and as a result few vases could be restored to near completeness. For the purposes of this preliminary study, therefore, vase types have been accepted as kiln products on the basis of consistency in fabric, decoration, and state of preservation with the bulk of the vases in the dump and kiln. They include large fragments or restorable examples in a fresh condition, and each type is usually represented by at least five examples.[8]

Cooking vessels have been eliminated from consideration because they are very fragmentary and quite rare, representing only 6% of the sherds in the dump (by count). Also rejected were the highly fragmentary remains of some twenty vases of different shapes carrying dark-painted motifs on a lustrous ground (e.g., **62–70**). This associated pottery, not actually produced in the kiln, nevertheless had been thoroughly mixed with the kiln material, so it appears that the kiln dump had been used in antiquity for other kinds of ceramic waste as well.

6. For ethnographic examples of the use of sherds as fire supports, see Voyatzoglou 1974, p. 23; Blitzer 1984, p. 156; 1990, p. 696. Blitzer (1984, p. 156, note 39) stresses that the Kentri potters use spacers only to keep the pots from touching the kiln walls; the pots are allowed to touch one another. The same practice is found among traditional Cypriot potters (London 1989b, p. 221).

7. Such joins occurred in basins **54–55** (see below), bridge-spouted jars C 10490 and C 10567, cylindrical vase C 9957, and jar C 10591. None of the other presently inventoried vases from the kiln have joins in the dump, but it is likely that more joins will be discovered in the future as more vessels are assembled.

8. The only exception made to the last criterion is for three piriform rhyta, which in fabric, decoration, and condition of preservation are entirely consistent with the accepted kiln dump pottery (see Table 4 and p. 80 below).

POTTERY INSIDE THE KILN

The channels of the kiln were filled with reddish-brown clayey soil mixed with rubble and pottery (Fig. 8). This pottery did not exhibit any orderly arrangement or preferred orientation (Figs. 13–17, 21). The entire channel area was covered with a thin layer of clayey soil.[9] Clayey soil and rubble presumably represent the collapsed kiln superstructure (see above, p. 23). Immediately on top of the thin layer covering the tops of the channels was a thick LM IIIA2/B fill, which included the remains of small ovens (Figs. 5–7; see above, p. 9). This stratum continued over the entire pottery dump surrounding the kiln (Fig. 8).[10]

In the bottom of the firing pit was a stratum of loosely compacted, dark brown, and fire-blackened soil containing ash (Fig. 8). It was topped by a thick, brown, clayey upper stratum, presumably of collapsed roof material, which reached the elevation of the pit's entrance. Both strata contained uncontaminated kiln pottery.[11] They were covered by a thick layer of LM IIIA–B debris mingled with some kiln pottery, which in turn was topped by collapsed debris of the south wall of Building T.[12]

The pottery found inside the kiln includes many fragmentary as well as complete vases (Table 2). The loose dark soil in the firing pit contained highly fragmentary remains, heavily burned to a gray or black color. In contrast, most sherds from within the channels and from the clayey layer in the firing pit have fresh surfaces. Some sherds were covered with limey deposits, and a few suffered postdepositional water damage from exposure to rain, which caused surfaces to wear away and edges to soften. Similar water erosion also occurred in all strata of the dump.[13]

A study of pottery joins inside the kiln yielded remarkable results. Joins were found only between sherds from adjacent channels and from the firing pit (e.g., **28, 54, 55, 57**), but never between fragments found in more distantly removed channels. This distribution pattern would occur if the vases, before they fell, had been placed above the channels and on top of the dividing walls between them. Thus it suggests that much of the pottery found inside the channels represents remnants of the last kiln load.[14]

9. Channel 1 (northernmost): trench 87B, pails 90, 90A; trench 95A, pail 135. Channel 2: trench 95A, pails 101, 142, 172. Channel 3: trench 95A, pails 100, 174; trench 97F, pails 72, 73, 76. Channel 4: trench 95A, pails 131, 132, 133. The clayey layer on top of channel 1 had a reddish color (trench 87B, pail 81); the one covering channels 2, 3, and 4 was light brown (trench 90C, pail 87).

10. LM IIIA2/B stratum: trench 87B, pails 81, 85, 86, 88, 92, 94, 98, 100, 101, 103, 103A; trench 90C, pails 78, 79, 80, 81, 82, 83, 87, 88, 89, 91, 92, 93, 96; trench 91B, pails 43, 44, 48, 50, 56; trench 95A, pails 15, 16, 17, 19, 21, 22, 23, 24, 25, 26, 27, 30A, 30B, 31, 32, 40, 41, 42, 43, 47, 48, 49, 52, 57, 62, 63, 65, 66, 67, 69, 72, 73, 79, 80, 81, 85, 86, 90, 93, 96, 97, 102, 105, 120, 122, 123, 124, 125, 126; trench 95B, pails 108, 170; trench 95C, pails 113, 196.

11. Clayey stratum of the firing pit: trench 95A, pail 111. Fire-blackened soil: trench 95A, pails 114, 127, 130.

12. LM IIIA–B debris: trench 95A, pails 102 and 105. Kiln pottery: trench 95A, pail 103.

13. The larger average weight of the sherds from the firing pit compared to those from the channels (Table 2) is due to the fact that there is a higher proportion of medium-coarse sherds in the former area.

14. Scientific analysis of 19 vases from within the kiln has yielded quite a wide range of firing temperatures, from 750° C or less to 1080° or more (see Table 13, pp. 121–122). However, most of these vases in fact may have been fired within a pretty narrow temperature range, and only three were definitely fired at temperatures exceeding 1000°. Of these three vases, two were found in the firing pit (95/7 and 95/48) and may have fallen when the ashes were still hot. The third example (95/5) comes from the bottom of channel 1, and its proximity to the firing pit has not been recorded. It seems to me that the present evidence is not strong enough to rule out the possibility that most of the vases found inside the kiln belonged to the last firing load.

TABLE 2. ESTIMATED NUMBER OF VASES IN THE KILN[15]

Vessel Shape	Channel 1	Channel 2	Channel 3	Channel 4	Firing Pit
Conical cups,					
type C	5	10	30	2	3
type P	5	5	57	7	6
type Q	6	8	6	—	—
Bell cups	1	—	5	1	2
Side-spouted cups	1	2	4	—	1
Conical bowls	—	1	—	—	—
Kalathoi,					
fine	—	2	—	—	—
medium-coarse	—	1	1	1	1
Bridge-spouted jars,					
fine	4	3	2	4	3
medium-coarse	1	—	—	—	—
Collar-necked jugs,					
fine	—	—	6	—	—
Ewers,					
fine	2	—	—	—	—
medium-coarse	—	—	—	—	2
Oval-mouthed amphoras	—	2	1	—	1
Basins	—	1	—	—	1
Pithoi	1	1	—	—	—
Total	26	36	112	15	20
Wasters	1	—	—	—	2
Coarse slabs	—	—	1	—	2
Sherds (count)	406	262	374	211	214
Sherds (kg)	2.950	4.820	4.585	2.735	5.905
Sherds (avg. wt.)	0.007	0.018	0.012	0.013	0.028

Sherd totals include wasters and slabs.

Vases that were distributed over more than one subdivision of the kiln have been
   listed under the subdivision that contained the majority of the fragments.

15. In Table 2, shape frequencies have been estimated on the basis of diagnostic features such as spouts, handles, bases, and rims. For each vase shape the most appropriate diagnostic features were chosen, and fragments were roughly added to form "complete" features before they were counted. Frequencies of conical cups, handleless bell cups, and fine pedestaled vases were derived from the number of "completed" bases. Convex-sided, conical, and concave-flaring bowls as well as handleless basins and large closed jars were counted on the basis of the "completed" rims; the estimates obtained were checked against the numbers of "completed" bases. "Completed" handles were used to estimate the frequency of handled shapes, whereby the number of handles was divided by two for two-handled vases; the obtained estimates were checked against the numbers of "completed" spouts and rims. Frequency estimates of rhyta were based on the number of spouts and distinct body fragments, which were easy to recognize by their shape and heavy interior rilling. The number of coarse slabs was estimated on the basis of "completed" rim fragments and of distinct body fragments.

Sherds have been counted and weighed according to the method developed by Rutter for the pottery at Tsoungiza. For a description of this method and its limitations, see Rutter 1990, p. 378, note 7.

Counts and weights refer to all sherds recovered, including intrusive earlier and later sherds, as well as LM IA pottery not thought to be kiln products.

The extraneous material is estimated to represent approximately 3–4% of the sherds by count, and about 6% by weight.

Fragments of one large basin (**54**) were distributed over three adjacent channels, which may mean that it had been placed quite high above the channels. Unusually high concentrations of types C and P conical cups, as well as of bell cups and collar-necked jugs, occurred in channel 3, suggesting that vases of the same shape or type had been placed near each other in the kiln (Table 2).

The distribution and condition of the pottery found in the various parts of the kiln do not provide a clear answer as to what was the direct cause of the kiln's demise. The scientific analyses show that the decorated vases in the kiln underwent a series of oxidation–reduction–oxidation firing steps (see below), and thus it is certain that the last firing had been either entirely or largely completed. Since the last pottery load was not entirely removed from the structure before its abandonment, it is reasonable to suggest that an accident happened toward the end of the firing cycle, burying intact vessels below broken pottery debris and causing them to be left behind. There is little supporting evidence for such an accident, however. The fact that the firing pit contained many fire-blackened sherds but few wasters indicates that this pottery fell into the pit when the embers were still hot enough to burn the vases, but not to turn them into wasters.[16] This could have happened during the cooling phase, which is a risky part of the firing cycle, but it also may have occurred soon thereafter during salvaging or leveling operations (see below).[17] It is even more difficult to determine at what moment the pottery fell into the channels.[18] Furthermore, it is impossible to say when or how the roof of the kiln collapsed, or indeed to determine if it was actively demolished, since the mixing of roof debris and pottery within the channels, which is likely to have happened during salvaging or leveling activities, has obliterated the evidence. Whatever the scenario for the closing moments of the final use of the kiln, the fact that it was not repaired and reused suggests that, if not simply personal reasons, larger economic, social, or even political reasons led to its final abandonment, which is unlikely to have resulted from a simple accident.

Most of the smaller shapes found inside the kiln are restorable. These are conical cups, bell cups, and side-spouted cups (Table 2). Vases of somewhat larger sizes—conical bowls, kalathoi, bridge-spouted jars, collar-necked jugs, ewers, and basins—are fragmentary, but their fresh condition suggests that they are kiln products as well. It can be no coincidence that most of the larger vases had only their upper bodies preserved:[19] this may mean that they were in an inverted position when they were fired or after they fell. Their lower bodies would have been removed during the leveling of the superstructure debris, which most likely took place still within LM IA (see below, p. 39). Also interesting is the distribution of the joining fragments of a coarse slab (C 10073). Two fragments came from the firing pit, three others were found just west and north of the entrance, and one to three farther north at the edge of the stoa.[20] Their scattering might be the result of a partial cleaning of the firing pit after the last firing, perhaps during the salvaging or leveling operation. A similar distribution has been observed for large clusters of wasters (see below, p. 88; Figs. 28, 30). Also, a group of burned and overfired sherds located just west of the firing pit entrance may have been redeposited during this cleaning operation.[21]

16. For a similar interpretation of burned sherds found in the fire box of an 8th-century B.C. kiln at Torone, see Papadopoulos 1989, p. 21 (also McLoughlin 1993, pp. 12–13).

17. For a discussion of the dangers involved in a kiln's cooling cycle, see Blitzer 1990, p. 697.

18. All sherds found inside the kiln channels, including the fresh-looking majority of fragments, have surfaces marred by hairline cracks and scars, whereas such surfaces are much rarer among the pottery found outside the kiln. The scars and cracks of these sherds at first sight look like they were caused by exposure to excessive heat, which could mean that these vases fell into the channels when heat was still radiating from the clay-lined channel walls. However, the damage to their surfaces may also have been caused by postburial calcite formation. The range of firing temperatures estimated for the pottery found inside the channels does not provide evidence for excessive heat, since it is not significantly higher than that of the vases from the dump (see Tables 12, 13, pp. 112–113, 121–122).

19. I thank J. B. Rutter for drawing my attention to this point.

20. Trench 95A, pails 110, 111, 114, 140, 156, and perhaps pails 150, 166.

21. Trench 95A, pail 189.

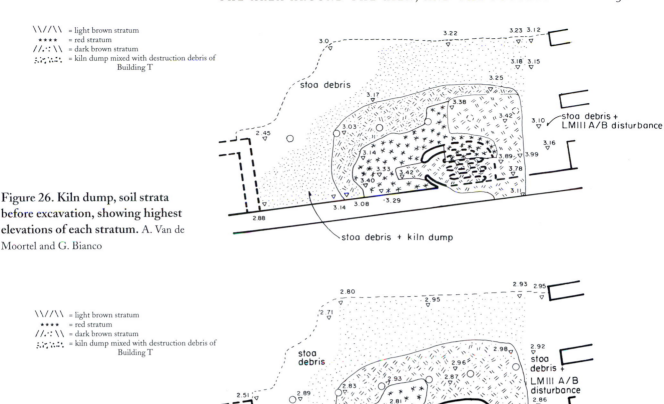

\\\//\\ = light brown stratum
**** = red stratum
//.·\\ = dark brown stratum
:.·::.: = kiln dump mixed with destruction debris of
Building T

Figure 26. Kiln dump, soil strata before excavation, showing highest elevations of each stratum. A. Van de Moortel and G. Bianco

\\\//\\ = light brown stratum
**** = red stratum
//.·\\ = dark brown stratum
:.·::.: = kiln dump mixed with destruction debris of
Building T

Figure 27. Kiln dump, bottom elevations reached. A. Van de Moortel and G. Bianco

22. Trenches 87B, 90C, 95A, and 97C. Pail numbers of the individual soil strata will be listed below.

23. Trench 91B, pails 45, 46, 47, 48, 49, 50, 51, 56; trench 95B, pails 121, 173, 175, 212; trench 95C, pails 168, 203, 206; trench 97B, pails 52, 54; trench 97C, pails 19, 22, 26, 31, 33. LM IIIA2/B contamination in trench 91B, pails 46, 48, 50, 51, 54, 56; trench 95B, pails 121, 173, 175; trench 95C, pails 203, 206; trench 97C, pails 15, 31. Pottery from historical periods was found in trench 91B, pails 46, 49; trench 95B, pail 121.

24. Kiln dump just north of firing pit: see below, p. 32. Wall fall north of firing chamber: trench 87B, pail 104.

25. Trench 87B, pails 107B, 111, 116C.

STRATIGRAPHY OF THE KILN DUMP

The dump covered a 14.5 by 7.5 m area stretching east, north, and west of the kiln (Fig. 27).[22] Farther to the north and east, kiln pottery was mixed with destruction debris of Building T as well as with LM IIIA2/B and historical material.[23] The dump was covered by the same LM IIIA2/B stratum that topped the kiln (Fig. 8; see above, p. 28). Below the kiln dump as well as to the west and east of it, excavators found debris of the ruined South Stoa (see above, pp. 5, 8). This destruction material differed from the kiln dump in that it was packed with stone rubble and with painted as well as unpainted plaster fragments. Stoa debris as well as some later accumulation formed the mound on which the kiln had been constructed. To the north, this mound appears to have projected 0.80 m beyond the wall of the kiln, as is indicated by the configuration of the kiln dump and of wall fall just north of the firing chamber.[24] On the east side, the kiln mound must have been narrower, because kiln dump pottery was found closer to the kiln.[25] A hypothetical reconstruction of the mound's east slope is presented in Figure 24 (p. 23).

THE THREE STRATA

The dump included three soil types distributed in roughly homogeneous strata (Figs. 8, 26–28, 30–31): (1) rather loose, mostly dark brown soil; (2) more compact, reddish clayey soil on top of this; (3) and light brown soil on top of the red clay.

DARK BROWN SOIL STRATUM

The lowest part of the dump deposit consisted of a matrix of rather soft, dark brown to gray-brown soil mixed with some stones (Fig. 28; see also Figs. 8, 26–27).[26] Pottery was densely packed and was usually in a fresh condition. Some water damage had occurred, mostly on unpainted conical cups and on medium-coarse sherds.

The dark brown stratum reached its maximum thickness (ca. 0.60 m) and highest elevation (+3.43–3.40 m) on the east side of the kiln, where it was about level with the top of the kiln mound (see Fig. 8: section B–B). It sloped down slightly to the south, spilling in part over the south wall of Building T.[27] To the north and northwest, the dark brown stratum showed a more pronounced downslope, gradually thinning to 0.10–0.25 m over an east–west strip beginning about 0.80 m north of the kiln wall. At the north edge of the stoa the stratum sloped up again, covering the two easternmost column bases of the stoa, and continuing over the court of Building T, which had a higher elevation (ca. +2.93–2.98 m) than the stoa surface (ca. +2.80 m) during the lifetime of the kiln. To the west of the kiln, the dark brown stratum maintained a thickness of 0.10–0.25 m, reaching a maximum elevation of +3.08 m near the western edge of the dump. The dipping of the stratum north of the kiln may be related to the existence of a walking track running parallel to the kiln, just north of the kiln mound. The pottery of the uppermost units in this area was unusually worn, perhaps as a result of having been trampled.[28] A similarly poor condition of the pottery, presumably as a result of walking activity, has been reported on the surface of the dark brown soil stratum farther to the north. In addition, patchy surfaces have been recognized in the east part of the dump as well as to the west of the kiln.[29]

The pottery of the dark brown stratum shows more evidence of disturbance than does that of the overlying two strata, and is therefore likely to reflect a different mode of deposition and postdepositional activity. It is

26. Lower brown stratum: trench 87B, pails 89, 105, 109, 110, 111, 111A, 111B, 111C, 111D, 112, 112A, 112B, 112C, 112D, 114, 115, 115A, 116, 116A, 116B, 116C, 116D, 116E, 117, 118, 118A, and part of 120; trench 95A, pails 69, 70, 71, 116, 134, 137, 143, 145, 146, 148, 161, 163, 164, 165, 166, 169, 178, 179, 180, 181, 182, 184, 187, 193, 194, 197, 198, 201, 202, 205, 207, 216; trench 97C, pails 40, 42, 50. Mixed units surrounding the kiln

dump and including a large proportion of kiln dump material: trench 91B, pails 45, 46, 47; trench 95B, pails 121, 173, 175; trench 95C, pails 168, 203, 206; trench 97B, pail 52.

27. The unit on top of the south wall of Building T (trench 90C, pail 100) represents the southern end of the excavated area. It contained a lot of kiln dump pottery, but included sufficient amounts of later material to indicate that it was near the south-

ern edge of the dump.

28. Trench 95A, pails 134, 143, 180, 182, 184, 187.

29. East part of the dump: trench 87B, top of pails 111, 111A, 111B, 111C, 111D, 112, 112A; trench 87B, top of pails 114, 116, 116A, 116B, 116C. Pottery joins found between these surfaces indicate that they have been disturbed. West of the kiln: trench 95A, pails 120, 137, 198, 199; trench 95C, pails 203, 206.

\\/ /\\ = light brown stratum
**** = red stratum
//.·: \\ = dark brown stratum
:·.·..·. = kiln dump mixed with destruction debris of
                    Building T
W = clusters of 10–17 wasters

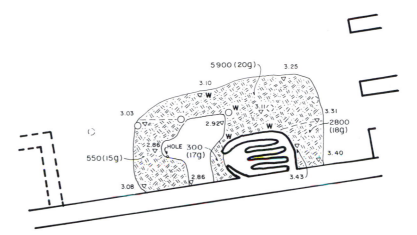

Figure 28. Kiln dump, lower brown soil stratum, showing highest elevations, number of sherds, and their average weight. A. Van de Moortel and G. Bianco

argued here that this layer is made up of the refuse of earlier kiln firings as opposed to the red and light brown strata, which represent the debris of the kiln collapse, as will be discussed below. In addition to the evidence for informal walkways, the lower dark brown stratum had fewer clusters of vessels of the same shape than did the upper strata.[30] The stratum was thickest and its sherd concentration densest in the area east of the kiln (Figs. 8, 28).[31] It is possible that an entrance to the kiln superstructure had been made at this end, allowing access to the space on top of the channels where the vases would have been stacked. The area just outside this entrance conceivably would have been a primary dumping ground for the potter emptying the kiln after firing.[32] A first study of pottery joins has shown that parts of the same vases were distributed over relatively large distances, the most remote ones ranging from the east to the northwest of the kiln (**20, 37, 60, 65**; C 10590). One of these vases (**65**) had sherds distributed throughout the thickness of the stratum east of the kiln. Thus it seems that the dumped pottery was subsequently moved, perhaps more than once, to the west and north, over the central part of the stoa and onto the court, ostensibly in an effort to manage overflow of debris.

The dark brown soil stratum was not continuous, but left a large area free to the west of the firing pit. This empty space extended the entire width of the stoa between its middle two column bases (Figs. 8: section B–

30. Conical cups of type C were clustered in trench 87B, pails 111, 112D, 116, 116B; trench 95A, pails 165, 179. Conical cups of types E/F: trench 95A, pails 146, 148, 179, 181, 187, 197, 198, 205; trench 97C, pails 42, 50. Dark-splattered conical cups: trench 95A, pail 116. Medium-coarse kalathoi: trench 95A, pail 180; trench 95B, pails 173, 175. Medium-coarse bridge-spouted jars: trench 95B, pail 173. Oval-mouthed amphoras: trench 95A, pails 145, 148, 161, 180, 187;

trench 95B, pails 173, 175. Large concentrations of medium-coarse unpainted sherds were found in trench 87B, pails 111D, 112A, 112D; trench 95A, pails 146, 148, 179, 201, 207; trench 95B, pail 121.

31. Since the dump was excavated in units ("pails") that varied in shape and size according to the excavators' needs, and the soil strata were highly irregular in shape as well, sherd density calculations must of necessity be approximate. The area east of the kiln

shows the largest concentration, having yielded 2,800 sherds as compared to the 5,900 sherds found in an area about four times this size to the north and northwest of the kiln (Fig. 28).

32. For descriptions of similar dumping behavior among present-day traditional potters in Crete and the Peloponnese, see Blitzer 1984, p. 154; 1990, p. 697, fig. 5, pl. 108:b; Fiandra and Pelagatti 1962, pl. VIII:2; Hampe and Winter 1962, pl. 21.

B; 28). Most likely this space was kept clear to facilitate access to the firing pit, and perhaps also to store fuel within easy reach of the kiln operator (Fig. 24).[33] It is also possible that a pottery workshop was located here, but the evidence is scant and its interpretation tenuous. At the west edge of this empty area, about 4 m from the kiln and 2.4 m north of the stoa's south wall, a small cylindrical hole was found (Fig. 29; Figs. 2, 8, 28).[34] It measured 0.20 m in diameter and was 0.10 m deep, reaching the pebbled floor of the earlier, Protopalatial, stoa at +2.68 m. It was filled with soft soil containing two undatable, worn sherds. This hole is of a size that could have housed the pivot stone of a potter's wheel, even though such a stone has not yet been identified with certainty at Kommos.[35] If a wheel had been located in the hole west of the Kommos kiln, it would likely have had a short axle, sitting close to the ground, since it would have been too far from any wall that could have held the lateral support necessary for tall-axled wheels (Figs. 2, 24, 28).[36] Unlike tall examples, low potters' wheels do not have a lower kick-wheel, but only the wheel on which the pottery is thrown. Ethnographic and archaeological evidence, supplemented by experimental data, indicates that such low wheels require the use of wheelheads or bats of at least 0.60 m in diameter in order to create sufficient momentum for throwing pottery.[37] Fragmentary coarse slabs of such size, which may have been used as bats for low wheels, were found throughout the Kommos kiln dump, but their identification is likewise uncertain (see below, pp. 85–87).

Further tentative evidence for the presence of a workshop is provided by the discovery of haematite and limonite encrustations on two small

33. For similar fuel storage practices among traditional potters in Thrapsano and Koroni, see, respectively, Voyatzoglou 1974, p. 23, and Blitzer 1990, fig. 5.

34. Bottom of trench 95A, pail 198A.

35. A stone with socket from the hilltop at Kommos has been tentatively interpreted by Blitzer as being the pivot base for a potter's wheel (Blitzer 1995, p. 487, pl. 8.62:F). It is larger than the cylindrical hole west of the kiln, but need not have been for a potter's wheel. No incontrovertible evidence for a potter's workshop was found on the Kommos hilltop (see below). Moreover, it appears that pivot stones for potters' wheels need not have been very large. Recently, several pivot stones, including two in situ, have been identified in the LM III potters' quarter at Gouves (Chatzi-Vallianou 1995, pp. 1050–1051, fig. 11, pl. 180; Vallianou 1997, pp. 335, 338). Being

roughly square or rectangular in section, these stones appear to range in width from ca. 0.13 to 0.16 m, and in height from ca. 0.6 to 0.14 m, and would fit the cylindrical hole to the west of the Kommos kiln. A pivot stone also has been reported from a LM IB–II potter's workshop at Mochlos (Soles 1997, p. 427). No dimensions have been published, however. The identification of other Minoan wheel supports from the Heraklion area and Vathypetro is uncertain, and no dimensions are known (Evely 1988, p. 117, pl. 20). It is worthwhile to point out that some ancient pivot stones from the Levant and Egypt, as well as present-day examples from traditional potters' workshops in Crete and India, are comparable in size to the Gouves pivot stones, ranging between 0.12 and 0.20 m in diameter, and between 0.05 and 0.10 m in height (Evely 1988, figs. 12–14; for the Cretan examples, see Hampe and Winter 1962, figs. 13, 14;

Fiandra and Pelagatti 1962, figs. 1, 3, pl. I:2; Voyatzoglou 1984, p. 134, fig. 17-1, pl. 14:D). Some of the latter stones project above the surrounding surface, as would three of the Gouves stones if placed in the hole at Kommos.

36. Present-day Cretan examples hold wheels with tall axles that are supported at a higher level by crossbars anchored in a wall. It is interesting to note that the two pivot stones found in situ at Gouves were also located close to walls (Vallianou 1997, pp. 335, 338, pl. CXXVI:c). Thus they may have housed wheels with tall axles. The pivot stones from the Levant, Egypt, and India mentioned in the previous note belonged to low wheels.

37. Evely 1988, pp. 112–115. Evely himself (1988, p. 118) prefers a low rather than a tall axle for the Minoan wheel, although without adducing any evidence.

Figure 29. Cylindrical hole (Depth 0.10 m, Diam. 0.20 m) found in surface about 4 m west of kiln (see also Fig. 28).

clusters of pottery found just east and northeast of the kiln. It is possible that this ochre had been used for the painting of vases.[38] In addition, a ceramic potter's rib has been tentatively identified in a mixed LM IA–B context on the hillside at Kommos, and could have come from a workshop connected with the kiln.[39] Apart from this possible tool, the ochre, the presumed bats, and the hole, which may have held a pivot stone, however, more definite clues for a LM IA pottery production facility—such as potters' wheels, pivot stones, tools, settling basins, or clay stores—are lacking. It is likely that most potters' tools then, as today, were made of perishable materials, and that whatever was still of use would have been removed when operations ended,[40] but this also means that we are unable to positively identify the location of a potter's workshop in association with this kiln or elsewhere on the site.

38. Pottery with ochre encrustations or stains was found in trench 87B, pails 106E, 107, 107C, 111, and 112 (including **4**, **8**, **9**, and **17**). The limonite was identified by Vassilis Kilikoglou and by Alain Dandrau. It is a hydrated form of haematite (hydrous ferric oxide), yellow (10YR 7/6, 10YR 7/8) to brownish yellow (10YR 6/8) in color. The ochre presumably had been dumped in these locations. Red and yellow pigments have been found in a LM IB–II potter's workshop at Mochlos (Soles 1997, p. 427). Abundant red and yellow ochre remains also were found in Early Chalcolithic pottery workshops at Hacılar (Mellaart 1970, pp. 30–31). Querns and mortars from Hacılar were found

covered with this material, and it is clear that this ochre had been used for painting pottery (Michaelidis 1993, p. 34).

39. Blitzer 1995, p. 521, C 5.

40. All the tools used by 20th-century traditional potters at Kentri are made of perishable materials, except for iron potters' wheels (Blitzer 1984, pp. 148–149). Reasons for the poor visibility of pottery production locations in the archaeological record are discussed comprehensively by London (1989a, pp. 73–78; 1989b, pp. 224–225). However, potters' tools and installations made of nonperishable materials have been identified in the Minoan archaeological record. These include potters' wheels or "mats," points, and spatulas, as

well as other small tools made of bronze or bone, stone polishers, stone palettes or slabs, stone mortars or querns, sunken settling basins, ceramic jars for clay storage, and remnants of raw clay and pigments. Various groups of such remains have been found at Myrtos Fournou Korifi (Warren 1972, pp. 18–20), Mallia (van Effenterre and van Effenterre 1976, pp. 81–82; Poursat 1983, p. 279; 1992, pp. 17–20), Chania (Tzedakis 1968, p. 425; 1969, p. 503), Zominthos (Sakellarakis 1989, pp. 168–171), Zou (Platon 1961), Vathypetro (Marinatos 1952, p. 272; 1960, p. 310), and more recently at Gouves (Vallianou 1997) and Mochlos (Soles 1997, p. 427). Cf. Evely in press.

TABLE 3. ESTIMATED NUMBER OF VASES IN THE DUMP STRATA[41]

Vessel Shape	Lower Dark Brown	Red	Light Brown
Conical cups			
type C	120	129	11
type D	3	4	—
type E	28	37	5
type F	33	41	6
type P	20	24	1
type Q	15	4	1
type V	12	11	2
Teacups	4	2	2
Straight-sided cups,			
narrow	12	2	1
wide	2	3	
Bell cups	4	7	—
Side-spouted cups	3	11	1
Convex-sided bowls	3	4	—
Conical bowls	1	2	1
Kalathoi,			
fine	6	6	3
medium-coarse	26	36	4
Bridge-spouted jars,			
fine	30	32	5
medium-coarse	19	12	1
Collar-necked jugs,			
fine	11	11	2
medium-coarse	11	12	2
Ewers,			
fine	8	10	3
medium-coarse	5	4	1
Rhyta,			
globular	13	6	1
piriform	1	1	1
Oval-mouthed amphoras	28	31	7
Basins	2	5	3
Large jars	5	—	—
Pithoi	4	3	1
Fine pedestaled vases	2	2	1
Total	431	452	66
Wasters	140	157	15
Coarse slabs	26	24	12
Sherds (count)	12,828	9,435	2,301
Sherds (kg)	227.640	158.248	49.250
Sherds (avg. wt.)	0.018	0.017	0.021

Sherd totals include wasters and slabs.

Vases that were distributed over more than one stratum have been listed under the stratum that contained the majority of the fragments.

41. For a description of the method used for counting and weighing sherds, see above, note 15. Percentages of extraneous material are higher in the dump than inside the kiln, approximating 7% by count and 12% by weight.

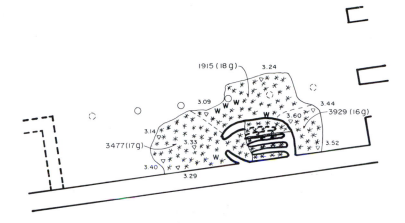

Figure 30. Kiln dump, red soil stratum, showing highest elevations, number of sherds, and their average weight. A. Van de Moortel and G. Bianco

The dark brown stratum contained a large range of vessel types, representing all the shapes that are thought to have been produced in the kiln (Table 3). Many lumps of clay have been found throughout this stratum as well. These could represent fragments of the interior lining of the kiln, which occasionally may have been replaced.[42] They may also be discarded remains of clay and mud that could have been used to seal the entrance to the firing pit and the presumed eastern entrance to the area above the channels during each firing.[43]

RED CLAYEY STRATUM

The second stratum of the dump had a reddish-brown clayey soil matrix mixed with occasional small stones, calcite fragments, and charcoal (Fig. 30; see also Figs. 8, 26–27).[44] It reportedly was less densely packed with pottery than was the underlying dark brown stratum.[45]

Covering a smaller area than did the underlying stratum, it was mostly contained within the stoa; only its northeastern part extended for a short distance over the court of Building T. West of the kiln, red-brown soil filled the hollow within the lower brown stratum in front of the kiln's

42. This practice was brought to my attention by a traditional potter at Thrapsano, in the summer of 1994. There is evidence for the replastering of the kiln channels at Kommos as well (see above).

43. For similar practices in traditional Greek kilns, see Voyatzoglou 1974, p. 23; 1984, p. 141; Blitzer 1984, pp. 153, 156, note 43; 1990, p. 696. In addition, all these kilns have temporary roofs partially made out of clay, so that the clay accumulation after each firing must have been more substantial than for the Kommos kiln, which presumably had a permanent roof (see above).

44. Red soil stratum: trench 87B, pails 81, 86, 93A, 96, 105A, 105B, 106, 106A, 106B, 106C, 106D, 106E, 107, 107A, 107B, 107C, 108, 113; trench 95A, pails 68, 76, 78, 92, 94, 95, 109, 110, 115, 117, 118, 119, 136, 138, 139, 140, 144, 147, 150, 151, 152, 153, 156, 157, 157A, 158, 160, 176, 188, 189, 191, 195. Pails 81 and 86 of trench 87B covered the northernmost channel.

45. Supporting the excavator's observation is the fact that the red stratum contained fewer sherds than the lower dark brown stratum (see Table 3), even though the soil volume of both strata may have been comparable, the red stratum being thicker but at the same time more restricted in area than the lower dark brown stratum.

firing pit (Fig. 27). Over most of its extent, the red-brown stratum was thicker than the dark brown stratum, and it had not one but two areas of exceptional thickness, located east and west of the kiln. East of channel 1, it was 0.30 to 0.35 m thick, with a top elevation of +3.66 m, remaining about 0.25 m below the top level of the kiln wall. It gradually thinned to the north, northwest, and south. West of the kiln, the red-brown stratum was thicker (0.40–0.50 m) than on the east, peaking at +3.40 m at about 4 m from the kiln, in the vicinity of the cylindrical hole discussed above. To the south, it ended roughly level with the wall of Building T as it is presently preserved. The bottom of the red stratum was marked by some fire-blackened patches west and southwest of the firing pit.[46]

This red-brown stratum is similar in composition to the reddish soil stratum found inside the kiln. Both include clay lumps with reed impressions as well as sherds and clay lumps covered with a limey substance (see above, p. 28).[47] Limey coatings are virtually nonexistent in the dark brown layer.[48] Because of these striking similarities it seems likely that the red-brown stratum outside the kiln, like the one inside, represents part of the kiln superstructure. Since it was sitting on top of the dark brown stratum and was only to a limited degree intermingled with it (see below, p. 42), it would appear to have been deposited after the kiln collapsed, and so is not the product of occasional dismantlings of the superstructure during the kiln's lifetime. As such, it should contain vases belonging to the last firing load of the kiln. This hypothesis is supported by the discovery of pottery joins between the red stratum outside the kiln and the fill inside.[49]

Like the dark brown stratum, the red stratum contained all vase types thought to have been produced in the kiln (Table 3). These were generally in excellent condition, there being no evidence from this stratum for wear of the type caused by trampling such as that attested on the pottery from the lower layer. As in the lower stratum, water damage occurred frequently on unpainted conical cups and medium-coarse sherds. Vases of the same shape tended to cluster more than they did in the dark brown stratum, suggesting that the red stratum, unlike the lower stratum, was the result of a single, relatively undisturbed depositional episode.[50] Sherds of several

---

46. Trench 95A, pails 157, 157A, 158.

47. All reported occurrences of limey deposits on sherds are in the western part of the dump: trench 95A, pails 94, 109, 110, 115, 117, 119, 138, 144, 156. They have not been noted for the eastern part (trench 87B), but all the pottery from that area has been acid-washed, and it is likely that this removed all traces of lime.

48. Limey encrustations occur in only three pottery units of the lower dark brown stratum. Two were situated just south of the firing pit entrance at the bottom of the kiln wall (trench 95A, pails 71, 161), and the other was excavated on the court (trench 95B, pail 175). All were associated with plaster debris, so it is likely that these encrustations are redeposited lime plaster.

49. See notes 7 and 66 in this chapter. All these vases include fragments from the red stratum and usually also from the dark brown or light brown stratum outside the kiln. The number of such joins is still relatively low, but is likely to increase in the future after a more thorough search. The joins with the dark brown stratum could be explained as a result of limited intermingling during the initial spreading of the red and light brown strata over the dark brown stratum, or as a result of later disturbances (see below, pp. 39, 42).

50. Conical cups of type C cluster in: trench 95A, pails 94, 117, 119, 138, 157. Conical cups of type E: trench 87B, pail 107; trench 95A, pails 109,

115, 118, 119, 188, 189, 195. Conical cups of type F: trench 95A, pails 109, 115, 118, 119, 188, 189, 195. Unpainted conical cups: trench 87B, pails 105A, 106B, 107B; trench 95A, pails 92, 95, 147, 156, 160, 191. Monochrome conical cups: trench 95A, pail 115. Medium-coarse side-spouted cups: trench 95A, pails 109, 110, 115, 157. Medium-coarse kalathoi: trench 87B, pail 106E; trench 95A, pails 92, 94, 95, 109, 110, 119, 144, 152, 156, 157, 158. Fine bridge-spouted jars: trench 95A, pails 147, 156. Wide-mouthed jugs: trench 95A, pails 95, 119. Ewers: trench 87B, pail 106D; trench 95A, pail 156. Oval-mouthed amphoras: trench 87B, pails 106D, 106E; trench 95A, pails 95, 157. Pithoi: trench 95A, pail 153.

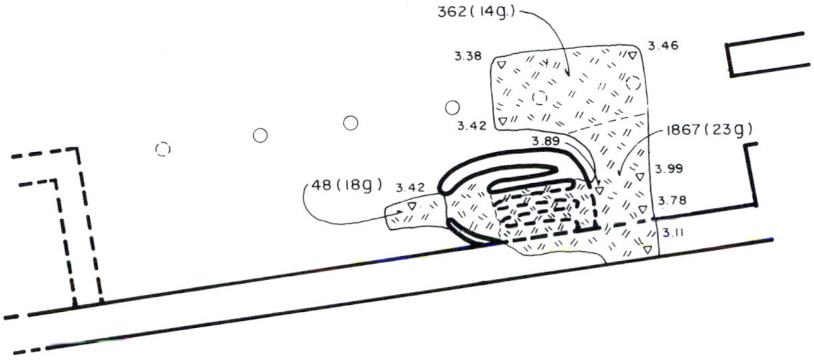

\\/ /\\ = light brown stratum
**** = red stratum
//.·:\\ = dark brown stratum
:·:·:·:·. = kiln dump mixed with destruction debris of
                    Building T

Figure 31. Kiln dump, light brown soil stratum, showing highest elevations, number of sherds, and their average weight. A. Van de Moortel and G. Bianco

vases in the red stratum were distributed east and west of the kiln, over larger distances than those within the dark brown stratum. This, and the fact that one of these vases (**55**) included fragments from inside the kiln, supports the interpretation of the red soil as representing part of the kiln superstructure, removed after its final collapse.[51]

It appears that the leveling of the kiln superstructure and the removal of part of the last kiln load took place still in LM IA. This is suggested by the absence of post–LM IA pottery in the red and blackened soil strata inside the kiln, other than a few LM IIIA2 contaminants in the southernmost channel, which are most likely traceable to later oven activity in that area (see above). Also, the hollow in the dark brown stratum west of the kiln as well as the top pails of the dark brown stratum, which would have been exposed until covered by the deposition of the red soil, is free of post–LM IA accumulations. Further support for a LM IA date for the dismantling of the kiln will be adduced below (p. 41).

LIGHT BROWN SOIL

The topmost discrete soil stratum detected within the kiln dump was a matrix of light brown soil mixed with small stones (Figs. 8: section B–B, 31; see also Fig. 26). A thin layer of this soil covered the three southernmost channels of the kiln.

The stratum continued east and north of the firing chamber, sitting atop the red clayey stratum, but being more restricted in area.[52] Like the red stratum it was thickest east and west of the kiln. East of channel 1, it had a maximum elevation of +3.99 m, rising slightly higher than the top of the kiln wall (+3.92 m). With a maximum thickness of 0.50 m, it was thicker than the red stratum. To the south, the light brown stratum thinned to 0.25 m. It spilled over the south wall of Building T, dipping down abruptly to the south of this wall. North of the kiln it tapered rapidly, remaining on the whole somewhat thicker than the red layer (0.15–0.20 m). Just west of the firing pit there was a small but thick (0.40 m) deposit of light brown soil, which continued into the firing pit. It was mixed with large cut stones representing LM IIIB collapse from the south wall of Building T (Fig. 8), and inside the firing pit it was contaminated with LM IIIA–B vase fragments (see above).

51. See below, **32, 35, 40, 55, 58, 70**; also C 10155, C 10553, C 10560, C 10562, C 10587, C 10588, C 10591, C 10595. Some include fragments from north of the kiln: **58, 70**; C 10562, C 10587. Others were distributed east and north of the kiln: see below, **20, 47, 50, 51, 59**; also C 10135, C 10426, C 10547. West and north of the kiln: C 10589.

52. Light brown layer: trench 90C, pail 87, covering the three southernmost channels; trench 87B, pails 99, 102, 103, 104, north of firing chamber; trench 87B, pails 80, 82, 83, 84, 93, 97, and trench 90C, pails 86, 90, 94, 100, east of the kiln; trench 95A, pails 104, 107, deposit west of firing pit; trench 95A, pail 103, inside the firing pit.

The pottery of the light brown layer is mostly fresh except for heavy water damage suffered by some conical cups and unpainted medium-coarse vessels. No limey coating has been reported. Sherd density was much lower than in the lower two strata (cf. Figs. 28, 30), but vase shapes are similar (Table 3). There are many joins with the pottery from the red stratum, including many examples that are distributed in the areas east and west, or east and north, of the kiln.[53] Vases of the same shape clustered together to a degree comparable to the clustering in the red stratum.[54]

The interpretation of the light brown stratum is less certain than that of the red stratum. Sharing many similarities and pottery joins with that stratum, and some joins with pottery fragments from within the kiln, it is likely to be part of the dismantled superstructure as well.[55] Its much greater extent to the east and northeast than to the west may reflect the fact that the roof over the firing chamber was much larger than that over the firing pit. Its light brown color suggests that this layer was less exposed to heat. It is difficult to explain, however, why the light brown stratum, if it were merely part of the dismantled superstructure, was sitting neatly on top of the red stratum rather than being intermingled with it.

It is argued here that this upper stratum represents kiln debris that suffered postdepositional disturbance. This is strongly suggested by the LM IIIA–B contamination of the light brown deposit in the firing pit and by the fact that inside as well as just west of the kiln, light brown soil was superimposed on small LM IIIB and LM IIIA deposits, respectively.[56] LM IIIB should thus be taken as the *terminus post quem* for the last disturbance. This particular episode must have been related to the collapse of the adjacent south wall of Building T, during which a group of cut wall blocks penetrated the light brown stratum (see above, p. 39). In the east part of the dump, on the other hand, the large expanse of light brown soil may have been disturbed during the building or use of the LM IIIA2/B Building P located just to the east, or even earlier. There is evidence of at least two major instances of disturbance that took place after the leveling of the kiln superstructure.

Kiln Waste Used Elsewhere

At a distance of about 50 m northeast of the kiln, a LM IA fill was discovered alongside the east facade of Building T; its upper level ran about level with the top of the krepidoma, and its lower reached close to the bottom of the krepidoma.[57] This fill contained several wasters as well as fresh-

53. Vases with joins among fragments from the light brown and the red strata: **17, 35, 42**; also C 10572, C 10598. From the kiln, the red, and the light brown strata: **55**. From the three strata: see below, note 66. Vases with fragments distributed east and west of the kiln: **32, 35, 40, 55, 58, 70**; C 10587, C 10595. Also **31** and C 10283, with sherds from the light brown and lower dark brown strata

only. Vases with fragments east and north of kiln: **47, 50**; C 10426.

54. Unpainted conical cups cluster in: trench 87B, pail 82; trench 90C, pails 86, 90. Fine monochrome bridge-spouted jars: trench 90C, pail 100. Kalathoi: trench 90C, pail 94. Pithoi: trench 87B, pail 83.

55. For the distribution of joining fragments, see note 7 above.

56. Inside the firing pit, pail 103 of

the light brown stratum covered pail 105, datable to LM IIIB. To the west of the pit, pail 104 of the light brown stratum was found superimposed over pail 117, which represents a small LM IIIA deposit including a kylix rim. All these pails belong to trench 95A.

57. Trench 88A, pail 37. The fill was roughly 0.20 to 0.25 m thick (from +3.39–3.44 m to +3.62–3.66 m). The bottom of the krepidoma is at +3.42 m.

looking sherds resembling material from the kiln dump. No fewer than five pottery joins have been found between this fill and the dump, confirming that part of the fill consisted of waste from the kiln dump.[58] Nearly all joining fragments, and also most nonjoining sherds—which to all appearances belong to vessels from the fill—came from the eastern part of the dump.[59] This distribution indicates that the reused kiln dump material found east of Building T was taken primarily from the area east of the kiln, which would explain why the eastern border of the dump is rather straight and terminates abruptly (Figs. 8: section B–B; 27).

Several vases with fragments in the fill east of Building T come from the red and the light brown strata of the dump. If these strata indeed represent the dismantled kiln superstructure, the sherds would have been removed only after the kiln had been leveled. Thus the fact that the fill east of Building T is solidly dated to LM IA strengthens the proposed LM IA date for the leveling of the kiln superstructure. Apart from this irrefutable example of the reuse of kiln waste, it is possible that sherds from the dump were used for other purposes elsewhere on the site.[60]

58. See below, **18**; also ewer C 10562; oval-mouthed amphora C 10595; strainer C 10491; fine conical vase C 10571. The latter two belong to rare shapes that may not be kiln products. The joining fragments were found in the following units: trench 87B, pails 106B, 108 (red); trench 87B, pails 109, 111, 116 (lower dark brown); trench 90C, pail 94 (light brown). The fill east of Building T contained 6,265 sherds weighing 56.125 kg. Kiln dump material appears to have made up only part of this fill, however, since most of the sherds of the fill differ in character from the kiln dump pottery. They are much more worn and, unlike in the dump, teacups, straight-sided cups, and cooking pots, are common shapes. In the fill, cooking vessels make up 15% by count, and medium-coarse pottery only 37%. The average weight of fine sherds is 0.004 kg, and of medium-coarse sherds 0.014 kg. In the dump, however, cooking pots represent only 4% of the pottery of the red stratum by count, and 7% of the lower dark brown stratum. Medium-coarse sherds make up as much as 51% of the red stratum by count, and 52% of the lower dark brown stratum, and 66% and 67% in weight, respectively. With an average weight of 0.007 kg for fine sherds, and 0.022 to 0.023 kg for medium-coarse fragments, the kiln dump pottery

obviously is less fragmented than are the sherds of the fill east of Building T.

59. Nonjoining sherds from east of kiln: trench 87B, pails 82, 89, 92, 93, 97, 105, 105A, 106D, 111B, 111D, 112, 115, 116C, 116E; trench 90C, pail 90. Northeast part of dump: trench 87B, pails 112, 112A, 112D, 116A, 116B; trench 91B, pails 45, 46. Northwest part of dump: trench 95A, pails 147, 148, 201). South of firing pit: trench 95A, pails 161, 164. Southernmost channel: trench 95A, pail 131. Some of the nonjoining fragments undoubtedly belong to bridge-spouted jar C 10490.

60. There are archaeological as well as ethnographic examples of the recycling of potsherds for use in the household or as building materials, but these practices have not yet been studied at Kommos. For pottery recycling at the Neolithic site of Nea Makri, see Pantelidou-Gopha 1991. For ethnographic examples from Cyprus, see London 1989a, pp. 76–77; 1989b, p. 221. The use of potsherds in the walls of Minoan ovens in the Zakros area is mentioned by Chrysoulaki (1996, p. 17). She also alludes to reused potsherds in Minoan pottery and metal workshops at Kokkino Froudi (Chrysoulaki 1996, pp. 20–21).

LM IIIA Disturbance

Six LM IIIA sherds have been found mixed in with the dark brown stratum, in the vicinity of the LM IIIA2–B Building P (see p. 9; Fig. 1).[61] One fragment probably dates to LM IIIA, and the five others seem to belong to a single amphora (C 9063), datable to the construction phase of Building P (early LM IIIA2). Parts of this amphora also have been discovered below the floor of Gallery 5 of that building.[62] Thus it appears that this particular instance of contamination is related to the construction of Building P. Perhaps at that time a need was felt to tidy up the dump, which was located in front of Gallery 6 (see above). A small, rough east–west row of stones, no more closely datable than LM IIIA2/B, was found in the same area, about one meter northeast of the kiln, and at an elevation of ca. +3.58 m, which is 0.15 to 0.60 m higher than the contaminating sherds.[63] The stones formed a retaining wall separating kiln dump pottery from LM IIIA2/B material, and may have been part of the same landscaping effort.

Mixing of Strata

Even though the three strata of the dump are fairly distinct, some degree of intermingling has occurred, perhaps during the initial spreading of the kiln superstructure over the dump or as a result of later disturbances. Small patches of dark brown soil have been found on top of the red stratum in the area of the firing pit as well as farther to the north.[64] At the edge of the stoa and over the court of Building T, displaced stoa debris, dating to early LM IA, was encountered on top of the dark brown stratum.[65] In addition, pottery joins have been found between the three strata.[66]

Because of the evidence for limited mixing of the strata, one has to keep in mind that not all the pottery from the red and the light brown strata may be the products of the last firing of the kiln. Only those vases that include fragments from inside the kiln may be accepted as certainly belonging to the last load. However, a rough calculation shows that most of the vases found in the red and the light brown strata could in fact have fit in the kiln. A more thorough search for joins between the pottery of these strata and that of the kiln should throw more light on this question.

61. Trench 87B, pails 111D (LM IIIA), 115, 116, 116D, 118. The fragments were identified by Rutter.

62. Trench 93A, pails 1b, 4, 5a, 6, 7/1, 10.

63. Dismantling of the row of stones: trench 87B, pail 94. Kiln dump units located to the south of it were: trench 87B, pails 80, 82, 83, 84, 93, all embedded in light brown soil. LM IIIA2/B units to the north were: trench 87B, pails 85, 88, 92.

64. South of firing pit: trench 95A, pails 70, 71 situated on top of pails 109, 156, 158. Over north wall of firing pit: trench 95A, pail 69. Stoa edge: trench 95A, part of pails 138, 139 on top of pails 150, 151, 152, 153, 188. North of firing chamber: trench 87B, pail 99.

65. In stoa: trench 95A, pail 139. On court of Building T: trench 95A, pail 134 situated on top of pails 145 and 146, which belong to the dark brown stratum.

66. Joins between fragments from the light brown, the red, and the lower dark brown strata only: **32, 40, 46, 47, 50, 58, 70**; also C 9439, C 10426, C 10579, C 10587. Between the red and the lower dark brown strata only: **22, 23, 26, 27, 34, 45, 48, 51, 59**; C 9443, C 9943, C 10135, C 10155, C 10277, C 10542, C 10547, C 10553, C 10560, C 10565, C 10569, C 10575, C 10582, C 10583, C 10588, C 10589, C 10590, C 10592, C 10596. Between the light brown and the lower dark brown strata only: **31, 53**; C 10283, C 10594. Between the kiln, the red, and the lower dark brown strata: C 9957, C 10591. Between the kiln, the red, the light brown, and the lower dark brown strata: **54**. Between the kiln, the red, the light brown, and the lower dark brown strata, and the LM IA fill east of Building T: C 10490. Between this LM IA fill, and the red and the lower dark brown strata: **48**, C 10562. Between this LM IA fill, and the red, the light brown, and the lower dark brown strata: C 10595. See also above, note 53.

TABLE 4. ESTIMATED NUMBER OF VASES IN THE KILN AND THE DUMP[67]

Vessel Shape	Kiln	Dump	Total
Conical cups			
type C	50	260	310
type D	—	7	7
type E	—	70	70
type F	—	80	80
type P	80	45	125
type Q	20	20	40
type V	—	25	25
Teacups	—	8	8
Straight-sided cups,			
narrow	—	15	15
wide	—	5	5
Bell cups	9	11	20
Side-spouted cups	8	15	23
Convex-sided bowls	—	7	7
Conical bowls	1	4	5
Kalathoi,			
fine	2	15	17
medium-coarse	4	66	70
Bridge-spouted jars,			
fine	16	67	83
medium-coarse	1	32	33
Collar-necked jugs,			
fine	6	24	30
medium-coarse	—	25	25
Ewers,			
fine	2	21	23
medium-coarse	2	10	12
Rhyta,			
globular	—	20	20
piriform	—	3	3
Oval-mouthed amphoras	4	66	70
Basins	2	10	12
Large jars	—	5	5
Pithoi	2	8	10
Fine pedestaled vases	—	5	5
Total	209	949	1,158
Wasters	3	312	315
Coarse slabs	3	62	65
Sherds (count)	1,467	24,564	26,031
Sherds (kg)	20.995	435.138	456.133
Sherds (avg. wt.)	0.014	0.018	0.018

Sherd totals include wasters and slabs.

67. See note 41.

CATALOGUE

This catalogue presents an overview of the vase shapes, and accompanying decorative motifs, that are thought to have been produced in the kiln. Representative examples of each shape or variety have been selected (**1–59**). In addition, there are examples of coarse slabs that may have been used in pottery production (**60–61**). Finally, the catalogue includes all closely datable, lustrous dark-on-light patterned vase fragments that have been found in association with the kiln dump pottery but are not considered to have been fired in this kiln (**62–70**) (see above, p. 27).

Within each group, the vases have been organized roughly according to size. Smaller shapes are discussed first because they are more informative with regard to dating and changes in production than are larger shapes. Each shape or variety is briefly introduced, and more detailed discussion is reserved for the pottery analysis section. References to comparanda from Kommos and elsewhere will also be listed in the analysis.

In each entry the Kommos inventory number is given in parentheses next to the catalogue number. Since all the listed vases are illustrated (Figs. 32–38), verbal descriptions are short, focusing on details that are not obvious from the drawings. Each entry records the extent of preservation of the vessel as well as basic dimensions, which are expressed in meters. All rim diameters are taken from the rim exteriors. Fabrics of kiln pottery show little variation and are discussed in an introductory paragraph below. For each catalogued vase, the color of the clay matrix and the inclusion density are listed. Color notations are specified for the vessel surfaces as well as for the wall in cross-section (fracture). On vases covered with a dark or light slip, the surface color of the fabric has been measured either in places where the slip had flaked off or in the fracture just below the slipped surface.[68] The color terminology is that of the Munsell Soil Color Charts. The corresponding Munsell codes have been summarized in Tables 5 and 6. Percentages of inclusions have been estimated through the use of standardized charts.[69] For more detailed description and discussion of fabrics, see below (Chapter 3).

Few aspects of manufacture are mentioned in the catalogue; they will be discussed in more detail below (pp. 103–110). Unusual features are noted in the catalogue, such as whether a vessel has a warped body or is coil-built. In addition, the quality of the attachment of appendages is noted: appendages are considered to be "well-integrated" if they are so well attached to the body that there is no noticeable seam. Decoration is described briefly, and paint colors are noted in the same manner as are the fabric colors (see also Tables 5 and 6). Vessels are in a fresh condition unless otherwise specified. Findspots in the dump are described by their soil stratum and their position with regard to the kiln. Trench and pail numbers are given for each entry. If fragments of a single vase were located in more than one pail, the number of sherds found in each pail is added in brackets. Vessels sampled for fabric analysis by Day and Kilikoglou have their sample numbers and fabric groups indicated. Fabric samples are also listed in Table 12 (pp. 112–113).

68. A vessel may be slipped with a layer of fine, pale-colored clay or with a coat of levigated clay firing to a red, brown, or black color. Pale-colored coatings are also more narrowly referred to as "slips," and dark-colored ones as "paints."

69. The charts were developed by the Russian sedimentologist M. S. Shvetsov, and are reproduced in Terry and Chilingar 1955, figs. 1–4. I thank Sarah J. Vaughan of Bristol University for bringing these charts to my attention.

TABLE 5. MUNSELL SOIL COLOR NOTATIONS FOR CATALOGUE ENTRIES 1–61

Inventory No.	Fracture		Surfaces		Slip		Pattern	
	Core	Near Surfaces	Int.	Ext.	Int.	Ext.	Int.	Ext.
1 C 10216	7.5YR 7/6	7.5YR 7/6	10YR 8/3–8/4	10YR 8/3–8/4				
2 C 10161	7.5YR 7/6	7.5YR 7/6	10YR 8/3–8/4	10YR 8/3–8/4				
3 C 10308	7.5YR 7/6	7.5YR 7/6	10YR 8/3–8/4	10YR 8/3–8/4				
4 C 9968	7.5YR 7/6	7.5YR 7/6	10YR 8/4	10YR 8/4				
5 C 9951	7.5YR 8/4	7.5YR 8/4	10YR 8/3	10YR 8/3				
6 C 9987	7.5YR 7/6	7.5YR 7/6	10YR 8/3	10YR 8/3				
7 C 10110	7.5YR 7/6	7.5YR 7/6	7.5YR 7/6	7.5YR 7/6				
8 C 9944	2.5YR 6/6	2.5YR 6/6	10YR 8/2	10YR 8/2				
9 C 9945	5YR 7/6	5YR 7/6	7.5YR 7/6	10YR 8/2				
10 C 10271	5YR 7/6	5YR 7/6	10YR 8/3	10YR 8/3				
11 C 9916	5YR 6/6	5YR 6/6	7.5YR 7/6	7.5YR 7/6	7.5YR 4/2	7.5YR 4/2		
12 C 10166	7.5YR 8/6	7.5YR 8/6	7.5YR 8/4	7.5YR 8/4	7.5YR 5/3	7.5YR 5/3		
13 C 9917	5YR 7/8	5YR 7/8	5YR 7/8	5YR 7/8	2.5–5YR 6/8	2.5–5YR 6/8		
14 C 10164	5YR 7/6	5YR 7/6	5YR 8/4	5YR 8/4	2.5YR 5/8	5YR 6/8		
15 C 9915	5YR 7/8	5YR 7/8	7.5YR 8/6	7.5YR 8/6	2.5–5YR 6/8	2.5–5YR 6/8		
16 C 10395	7.5YR 7/6	7.5YR 7/6	7.5YR 7/6	7.5YR 7/6			2.5YR 5/8	2.5YR 5/8
17 C 9932	5YR 7/8	5YR 7/8	5YR 7/8	5YR 7/8	2.5YR 6/8	2.5YR 6/8	10YR 8/2	
18 C 10488	10YR 8/6	10YR 8/6	10YR 8/6	10YR 8/4	2.5YR 6/8	2.5YR 6/8		Fugitive
19 C 8929	10YR 8/6	10YR 8/6	10YR 8/4	10YR 8/4	10YR 4/1	10YR 4/1		Fugitive
20 C 8937	5YR 7/6	5YR 7/6	5YR 7/8	5YR 7/8	2.5YR 5/8–5/6 to 5YR 7/8	2.5YR 5/8–5/6 to 5YR 7/8		
21 C 9984	7.5YR 7/6	7.5YR 7/6	7.5YR 8/6	7.5YR 8/6	2.5YR 6/8	2.5YR 6/8		
22 C 10299	7.5YR 7/6	7.5YR 7/6	7.5YR 7/6	7.5YR 7/6	10YR 8/4	10YR 8/4		
23 C 9947	10YR 8/4	10YR 8/4	10YR 8/4	10YR 8/4	2.5Y 8/3	2.5Y 8/3		
24 C 9992	5YR 7/6	5YR 7/6	7.5YR 8/6	7.5YR 8/6			2.5YR 5/8 to 5YR 6/8	2.5YR 5/8 to 5YR 6/8
25 C 10167	5YR 6/6	5YR 6/6	10YR 8/4	10YR 8/4				
26 C 9985	7.5YR 7/6	7.5YR 7/6	10YR 8/4	10YR 8/4	10YR 4/1	10YR 4/1		Fugitive
27 C 10564	7.5YR 7/3–7/4	7.5YR 7/3–7/4	7.5YR 8/4	7.5YR 8/4	7.5YR 4/3–6/6 to 2.5YR 6/8	7.5YR 4/3–6/6 to 2.5YR 6/8	Fugitive	Fugitive
28 C 10533	5YR 7/8	7.5YR 7/6	2.5Y 8/3	2.5Y 8/3				
29 C 10510	7.5YR 7/4	7.5YR 7/4	7.5YR 8/6	7.5YR 8/6	5YR 3/2–6/8 to 2.5YR 5/8	5YR 3/2–6/8 to 2.5YR 5/8	10YR 8/2	10YR 8/2
30 C 10286	5YR 7/6	5YR 7/6	5YR 7/4	5YR 7/4	2.5Y 8/3	2.5Y 8/3		
31 C 9931	5YR 7/6	5YR 7/6	10YR 8/4	10YR 8/4	10YR 4/3–4/2	10YR 4/3–4/2		
32 C 9930	2.5YR 6/6–6/8	2.5YR 6/6–6/8	10YR 8/6	10YR 8/4	7.5YR 3/0–3/2	7.5YR 3/0–3/2 to 5YR 4/6	10YR 8/2	
33 C 10337	5YR 7/6	5YR 7/6	7.5YR 7/6	7.5YR 8/4	7.5YR 2/0 to 10R 5/6	2.5Y 8/3	5Y 8/2	10YR 4/2
34 C 10580	7.5YR 7/6	7.5YR 7/6	7.5YR 7/4	7.5YR 7/4				
35 C 10550	5YR 7/6	5YR 7/6	7.5YR 8/4	7.5YR 8/6	2.5YR 5/6–5/8	2.5YR 5/6–5/8		10YR 8/4
36 C 10282	7.5YR 7/4 to 5YR 7/8	7.5YR 7/4 to 5YR 7/8	7.5YR 8/6 to 10YR 8/3	7.5–10YR 8/6	7.5YR 2/0 to 5YR 5/4	7.5YR 2/0 to 5YR 5/4		
37 C 8959	5YR 6/4–7/6	5YR 6/4–7/6	7.5YR 8/4	10YR 8/4	10YR 3/2 to 7.5YR 5/6	10YR 3/2 to 7.5YR 5/6		
38 C 10535	5YR 7/6	5YR 7/6	7.5YR 8/4	7.5YR 8/4	7.5YR 4/3–6/6	7.5YR 4/3–6/6		
39 C 10508	5YR 6/8–7/8	5YR 6/8–7/8	7.5YR 7/6	7.5YR 7/6				
40 C 9935	2.5YR 6/8	7.5YR 7/3	5YR 6/8	5YR 6/8	2.5YR 5/8	2.5YR 5/8		10YR 8/4–8/2
41 C 10501	5YR 7/8	5YR 7/8	7.5YR 8/4	7.5YR 8/4	5YR 5/6–3/4	5YR 5/6–3/4		
42 C 10504	5YR 7/6	5YR 7/6	7.5YR 8/6	7.5YR 8/6	10R 5/8 to 2.5YR 5/8	10R 5/8 to 2.5YR 5/8		

TABLE 5, CONT'D

Inventory No.	Fracture		Surfaces		Slip		Pattern	
	Core	Near Surfaces	Int.	Ext.	Int.	Ext.	Int.	Ext.
43 C 10500	5YR 7/6	5YR 7/6	10YR 8/4	10YR 8/6	2.5YR 5/8–6/8 to 5YR 5/3–6/8	2.5YR 5/8–6/8 to 5YR 5/3–6/8		10YR 8/2
44 C 10502	5YR 7/6	5YR 7/6	7.5YR 8/6	7.5YR 8/6	2.5–5YR 6/8	2.5–5YR 6/8		10YR 8/4
45 C 10499	5YR 7/6	5YR 7/6	5YR 7/4	7.5YR 8/6	2.5YR 6/8–5/8	2.5YR 6/8–5/8		
46 C 9934	5YR 7/6	5YR 7/6	7.5YR 7/6	7.5YR 7/6		10YR 8/4–8/6		
47 C 10568	10YR 8/4	10YR 8/4	10YR 8/4	10YR 8/4	10YR 6/6	10YR 6/6		
48 C 10554	2.5YR 6/4–4/2	10YR 8/4	10YR 8/3	10YR 8/3	10YR 3/1	10YR 3/1		
49 C 8973	5YR 7/6	5YR 7/6	10YR 8/6	10YR 8/6	10YR 3/1	10YR 3/1		
50 C 10404	5YR 7/4	5YR 7/4	5YR 7/6	5YR 7/6		7.5YR 4/2 to 5YR 5/8		10YR 8/2
51 C 10511	7.5YR 6/3	7.5YR 6/3	7.5YR 7/4	7.5YR 7/4	7.5YR 5/3	7.5YR 2/0		5Y 8/2
52 C 8971	5YR 7/8	5YR 7/8	5YR 7/6	7.5YR 8/6				7.5YR 4/3–5/6
53 C 10597	5YR 7/6	5YR 7/6	7.5YR 7/4	5YR 7/6	10YR 8/3	10YR 8/3		2.5YR 6/8–5/8
54 C 10577	2.5YR 6/8	5YR 7/6	2.5Y 8/3	2.5Y 8/3				
55 C 10534	7.5YR 6/3	7.5YR 7/6	10YR 8/4	10YR 8/4				
56 C 10593	5YR 7/6	5YR 7/6	10YR 8/3	10YR 8/3				10R 4/8
57 C 10168	5YR 7/6	5YR 7/6	7.5YR 8/6	7.5YR 8/6	2.5Y 8/3	2.5Y 8/3		
58 C 10613	2.5YR 5/6	7.5YR 7/6	7.5YR 7/4	7.5YR 7/4		7.5YR 2/0		10YR 8/2 to 5Y 8/3
59 C 8947	5YR 7/6	5YR 7/6	5YR 7/6	5YR 7/4				
60 C 8935	5YR 6/8	5YR 6/8	5YR 5/6 (top)	2.5YR 5/6 (bottom)	10YR 8/2	10YR 8/2		
61 C 10599	10YR 4/2	10YR 4/2	2.5YR 6/8 (top)	2.5YR 5/8 (bottom)	10YR 7/4 (top)	10YR 8/2 (bottom)		

Fabric colors on slipped vase surfaces were read in those areas where the slip had flaked off, or in the fracture just below the coated surface.

TABLE 6. MUNSELL SOIL COLOR NOTATIONS FOR CATALOGUE ENTRIES 62–70

Inventory No.	Fracture		Surfaces		Slip	Pattern		Added White
	Core	Near Surfaces	Int.	Ext.	Ext.	Int.	Ext.	Ext.
62 C 9908	7.5YR 8/4	7.5YR 8/4	10YR 8/4	10YR 8/6–8/4		10YR 3/2 to 7.5YR 6/8	10YR 3/2 to 7.5YR 6/8	
63 C 9983	7.5YR 8/6	7.5YR 8/6	7.5YR 8/4	10YR 8/4			7.5YR 3/2 to 7.5YR 7/6–6/6	10YR 8/2
64 C 10290	5YR 7/6	5YR 7/6	7.5YR 7/6	7.5YR 8/4			5YR 6/8	
65 C 9437	7.5YR 7/4	7.5YR 7/4	10YR 8/4	10YR 8/4			10YR 4/2 to 7.5–5YR 6/8	Fugitive
66 C 9982	5YR 7/3	7.5YR 8/4	7.5YR 8/6	7.5YR 8/6	10YR 8/4		2.5YR 5/8–6/8	
67 C 9993	7.5YR 7/2–7/3	7.5YR 7/2–7/3	7.5YR 7/2–7/3	10YR 8/6	2.5Y 8/2		2.5Y 4/2–6/4	
68 C 10320	7.5YR 7/4	7.5YR 7/4	7.5YR 7/4	7.5YR 7/4	10YR 8/3		10YR 3/2	
69 C 10137	10YR 8/3–7/3	10YR 8/3–7/3	10YR 8/3–7/3	10YR 8/3–7/3			10YR 6/6–3/2	
70 C 9444	5YR 7/8	5YR 7/8	5YR 7/8	7.5YR 7/8	7.5YR 8/4		2.5YR 5/8–6/8	Fugitive

Dark-patterned on a lustrous pale ground. Fabric colors on slipped vase surfaces were read in those areas where the slip had flaked off, or in the fracture just below the coated surface.

TABLE 7. FABRIC TEXTURE CLASSIFICATION

Fabric Texture	Usual Grit Size in mm	Grit Density in %
Fine	<0.1–2	1–3
Medium-coarse	<0.1–4	5–15
Coarse	<0.1–7	20–30

KILN FABRICS

Kiln vases typically have been fired to a reddish yellow color in the fracture, shading to paler reddish yellow or very pale brown at vessel surfaces. Inclusions are angular to subangular in shape. White grits (10YR 8/1) are always present. They are accompanied by various combinations of pale brown (10YR 6/3) to light yellowish brown (10YR 6/4), brown (7.5YR 5/2), dark brown (7.5YR 3/2), reddish yellow (5YR 6/8, 7.5YR 7/6, 7.5YR 7/8), yellowish red (5YR 5/8), and red (7.5R 5/6) inclusions. Grits range in size from less than 0.1 mm to 7 mm, that is, from silt to pebble size on the Wentworth scale.[70] They typically occur in a wide range of sizes within the fabric of an individual vessel, the majority consisting of smaller particles. Kiln fabrics have been defined as fine, medium-coarse, and coarse on the basis of the size and the density of their inclusions (Table 7).[71] Grits in fine fabrics usually do not exceed 2 mm in size, and those of medium-coarse fabrics seldom surpass 4 mm, while coarse fabrics often have larger inclusions.

CONICAL CUPS[72]

TYPE C

1 (C 10216). Conical cup   Fig. 32

80% preserved, mended from 3 sherds. Complete profile. H. 0.030–0.036, Diam. rim 0.070–0.076, Diam. base 0.032.

Fine fabric with reddish yellow fracture and very pale brown surfaces.

2% inclusions. Warped body. Unpainted.

Kiln, channel 3 (trench 95A, pail 174).

2 (C 10161). Conical cup   Fig. 32

95% preserved, mended from 2 sherds. Complete profile. H. 0.036–

---

70. Shepard 1956, p. 118.

71. These categories largely correspond to the fine buff, tempered buff, and coarse red fabric groups established by Hancock and Betancourt (1987), whose tempered buff group, however, encompasses medium-coarse as well as coarse buff fabrics, as defined in the present classification. The criteria for distinguishing fine, medium-coarse, and coarse fabrics used in this pottery catalogue differ slightly from those applied in the ceramic analysis by Day and Kilikoglou (see below), and are based on the entire vessel or vessel part rather than on thin-sections, resulting

sometimes in different identifications: cf. results for **15, 23, 40, 46, 55**.

72. The term "conical cup" is employed here in the same conventional sense as has been used by many authors (cf. Caskey 1972, p. 393; Coldstream and Huxley 1972, pp. 279–280, 285, 294; Catling, Catling, and Smyth 1979, pp. 23, 27, 32, 39, 40, 44, 50; Wiener 1984; Betancourt 1985, figs. 66, 78, 113:A–C; *Kommos* II, fig. 59: nos. 1600, 1614, 1615, etc.; Gillis 1990, p. 5; Warren 1991, pp. 330–331; *Kommos* III, pp. 111, 113, etc.). It designates a class of cups that are more or less conical in shape, lack offset rims or appendages,

and are either plain or minimally decorated. The term "conical" is a misnomer, because it also includes cups that are ovoid or semiglobular. An alternative name, used by Popham (1984, p. 156), Cummer and Schofield (1984, pp. 47–48), Davis and Lewis (1985, p. 84), and J. L. Davis (1986, p. 86), is "handleless cup." The term "conical cup" is preferred here, however, because it is the most widely used, and because I want to reserve the term "handleless cup" for handleless examples of straight-sided cups, bell cups, and teacups.

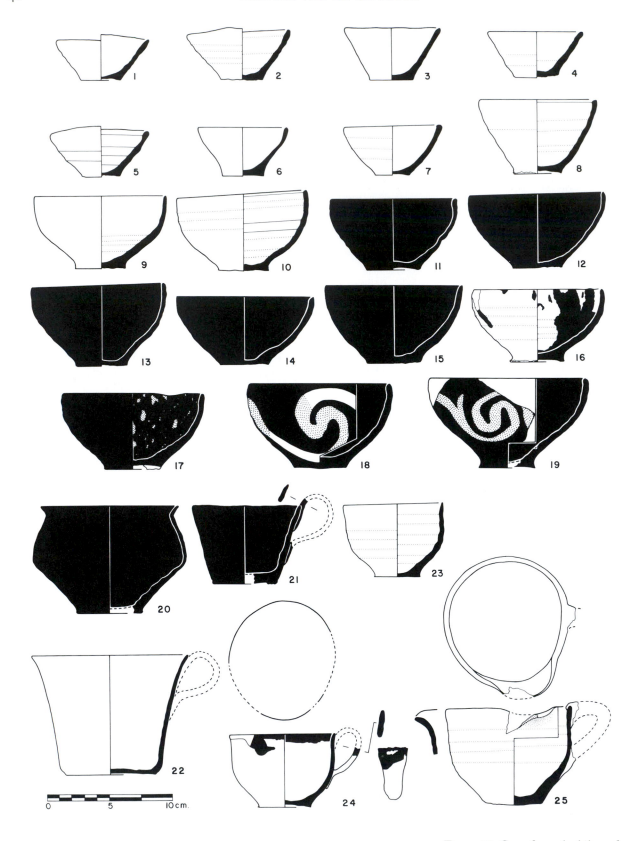

Figure 32. Cups from the kiln and dump

0.042, Diam. rim 0.075–0.082, Diam. base 0.034.

Fine fabric with reddish yellow fracture and very pale brown surfaces. 2% inclusions. Warped body and rim.[73] Unpainted.

Kiln, channel 2 (trench 95A, pails 142, 172).

3 (C 10308). Conical cup   Fig. 32

25% preserved, single sherd. Complete profile. H. 0.042, Diam. rim 0.075, Diam. base 0.034.

Fine fabric with reddish yellow fracture and very pale brown surfaces. 2% inclusions. Slightly warped. Unpainted.

Kiln, channel 4 (trench 95A, pail 133).

4 (C 9968). Conical cup   Fig. 32

50% preserved, mended from 3 sherds. Complete profile. H. 0.037, Diam. rim 0.076, Diam. base 0.034.

Medium-coarse fabric with reddish yellow fracture and very pale brown surfaces. 5% inclusions. Slightly warped. Unpainted. Calcite encrustations and limonite stains.[74]

Dump, dark brown soil stratum northeast of kiln (trench 87B, pail 111).

5 (C 9951). Conical cup   Fig. 32

75% preserved, mended from 4 sherds. Complete profile. H. 0.036–0.041, Diam. rim ca. 0.068–0.08, Diam. base 0.030.

Fine fabric with pink fracture and very pale brown surfaces. 1% inclusions. Warped. Unpainted.

Dump, red soil stratum northeast of kiln (trench 87B, pail 105A).

---

73. The rim shape conforms to what Gillis calls a "pouring ovoid" (Gillis 1990, pp. 83–84, pl. 9:b). It is unclear whether the rim outline of **2** was deliberately distorted to facilitate pouring.

74. For limonite, see above, note 38.

6 (C 9987). Conical cup   Fig. 32

30% preserved, mended from 3 sherds. Complete profile. H. 0.040, Diam. rim 0.072, Diam. base 0.033.

Fine fabric with reddish yellow fracture and very pale brown surfaces. 1% inclusions. Unpainted.

Dump, red soil stratum east of kiln (trench 87B, pail 107).

7 (C 10110). Conical cup   Fig. 32

Intact. H. 0.040, Diam. rim 0.077, Diam. base 0.028.

Fine fabric with reddish yellow fracture and surfaces. 1% inclusions. Unpainted.

Dump, red soil stratum northwest of kiln (trench 95A, pail 152).

TYPE D

8 (C 9944). Conical cup   Fig. 32

70% preserved, single sherd. Complete profile. H. 0.059–0.062, Diam. rim 0.093, Diam. base 0.038.

Fine fabric with light red fracture and white surfaces. 2% inclusions. Unpainted. Surfaces and breaks coated with limonite.

Dump, red soil stratum east of kiln (trench 87B, pail 107C).

TYPE E

9 (C 9945). Conical cup   Fig. 32

50% preserved, mended from 5 sherds. Complete profile. H. 0.057–0.059, Diam. rim 0.093–0.105, Diam. base 0.040–0.042.

Fine fabric with reddish yellow fracture and interior surface, and white exterior surface. 1% inclusions. Slightly warped. Unpainted. Surfaces and breaks coated with limonite.

Dump, red soil stratum east of kiln (trench 87B, pail 107C).

Fabric sample 95/12; fabric group 1b.

TYPE F

10 (C 10271). Conical cup   Fig. 32

65% preserved, single sherd. Complete profile. H. 0.058–0.065, Diam. rim 0.090–0.114, Diam. base 0.039–0.040.

Fine fabric with reddish yellow fracture and partially very pale brown surfaces. 1% inclusions. Warped. Unpainted.

Dump, dark brown soil stratum west of kiln (trench 95A, pail 216).

TYPE P

11 (C 9916). Conical cup   Fig. 32

40% preserved, mended from 6 sherds. Complete profile. H. 0.057, Diam. rim 0.101, Diam. base 0.042.

Fine fabric with reddish yellow fracture and paler reddish yellow surfaces. 1% inclusions. Warped. Thick dark brown monochrome in and out.

Kiln, channel 1 (trench 87B, pail 90).

12 (C 10166). Conical cup   Fig. 32

90% preserved, mended from 4 sherds. Complete profile. H. 0.060–0.061, Diam. rim 0.106, Diam. base 0.040–0.042.

Fine fabric with reddish yellow fracture and pink surfaces. 1% inclusions. Brown monochrome in and out. Calcite deposits on interior and exterior.

Kiln, channel 2 (trench 95A, pail 172).

13 (C 9917). Conical cup   Fig. 32

70% preserved, mended from 11 sherds. Complete profile. H. 0.064, Diam. rim 0.104–ca. 0.118, Diam. base 0.041.

Fine fabric with reddish yellow fracture and surfaces. 2% inclusions. Dilute light red to reddish yellow monochrome in and out.

Kiln, channel 1 (trench 87B, pail 90).

Fabric sample 95/11; fabric group 1b.

TYPE Q

14 (C 10164). Conical cup   Fig. 32

30% preserved, single sherd. Complete profile. H. 0.053–0.054, Diam. rim 0.108, Diam. base 0.039–0.043.

Fine fabric with reddish yellow fracture and pink surfaces. 2% inclusions. Warped body, indented base. Exterior dilute reddish yellow monochrome, interior red. Interior lightly coated with calcite.

Kiln, channel 2 (trench 95A, pail 172).

15 (C 9915). Conical cup   Fig. 32

50% preserved, mended from 5 sherds. Complete profile. H. 0.061–0.063, Diam. rim 0.110, Diam. base 0.045–0.046.

Fine fabric with reddish yellow fracture and paler reddish yellow surfaces. 2% inclusions. Slightly warped. Light red to reddish yellow monochrome in and out.

Kiln, channel 1 (trench 87B, pail 90A).

Fabric sample 95/15; fabric group 2a.[75]

TYPE V[76]

16 (C 10395). Conical cup   Fig. 32

60% preserved, 11 sherds mended into 2 nonjoining pieces. Complete profile. H. 0.056–0.058, Diam. rim 0.100–0.110, Diam. base 0.039–0.043.

Fine fabric with reddish yellow fracture and surfaces. 1% inclusions. Warped. Dilute red-colored splashes in and out.

Dump, red soil stratum west of kiln (trench 95A, pail 191).

17 (C 9932). Conical cup   Fig. 32

60% preserved, mended from 13 sherds. Complete profile. H. 0.060–

TEACUPS[77]

20 (C 8937). Teacup   Fig. 32

20% preserved of rim, body, and base; 3 sherds mended into 2 nonjoining pieces. Composite profile. H. 0.084, Diam. rim 0.110, max. Diam. 0.122, Diam. base 0.051.

Fine fabric with reddish yellow fracture and surfaces. 1% inclusions.

0.061, Diam. rim 0.112–0.115, Diam. base 0.043–0.044.

Fine fabric with reddish yellow fracture and surfaces. 1% inclusions. Slightly warped. Dilute light red coating in and out, white splashes on interior. Limonite stains.

Dump, red (trench 87B, pail 107C [5]) and light brown (trench 90C, pail 94 [8]) soil strata east of kiln.

18 (C 10488). Conical cup   Fig. 32

30% preserved, mended from 4 sherds. Complete profile. H. 0.066–0.069, Diam. rim 0.11, Diam. base 0.040–0.042.

Fine fabric with yellow fracture and interior surface, and very pale brown exterior surface. 1% inclusions. Dilute light red coating in and out, white retorted spirals on the exterior.

Dump, dark brown soil stratum northeast of kiln (trench 87B, pails 109 [1], 111 [2]), and LM IA fill east of Building T (trench 88A, pail 37 [1]).

19 (C 8929). Conical cup   Fig. 32

55% preserved, 9 sherds mended into 8 nonjoining pieces. Composite profile. H. 0.0715, Diam. rim 0.124, Diam. base 0.045.

Fine fabric with yellow fracture and very pale brown surfaces. 3% inclusions. Dilute dark gray coating in and out, white retorted spirals on the exterior, including at least one hooked.

Dump, dark brown soil stratum north of kiln (trench 87B, pail 112D [7]), and mixed context on court north of stoa (trench 91B, pails 50 [1], 51 [1]).

Dilute red to reddish yellow monochrome in and out.

Dump, red soil stratum east (trench 87B, pail 108 [1]) and dark brown stratum north (trench 87B, pail 112B [2]) of kiln.

Fabric sample 95/35; fabric group 1b.

75. For the difference between my fabric texture identification and that of Day and Kilikoglou (below), see above, note 71.

76. Some cups of this type are irregular in shape, with profiles varying between ovoid and semiglobular (e.g., **16** and **18**). Rather than being assigned to a semiglobular type W, they have been lumped here with the ovoid cups of type V.

77. The term "teacup" is employed here in the same sense as it is used by Warren (1991, p. 330; *contra* Popham 1984, p. 155). It refers to a rounded cup, either semiglobular or ovoid in shape, with an offset rim lending the cup an S-shaped profile. The other class of S-profile cups is bell cups (called teacups by Popham [1984, p. 155]). Teacups, as defined here, differ from bell cups by their larger size, wider proportions, and, at least at Kommos, smoother surfaces and either monochrome coating or intricate patterned decoration. Bell cups at Kommos are either unpainted or dark-dipped, unlike Knossian bell cups, which may carry complex patterns (e.g., Warren 1991, fig. 9:M–N). Betancourt (1985, fig. 93; 1990) prefers the terms "semiglobular" or "hemispherical" cups for teacups.

STRAIGHT-SIDED CUPS

21 (C 9984). Straight-sided cup
Fig. 32

35% preserved, mended from 3 sherds. 40% rim and body, 20% base. Complete profile except for most of handle. H. 0.062, Diam. rim 0.075–0.085, Diam. base 0.05.

Fine fabric with reddish yellow fracture and paler reddish yellow surfaces. 1% inclusions. Warped rim. Dilute light red monochrome in and out.

Dump, dark brown soil stratum northeast of kiln (trench 87B, pail 115).

22 (C 10299). Straight-sided cup
Fig. 32

55% preserved, 7 sherds mended into 3 nonjoining pieces. 60% rim and upper body, 30% lower body, 60% base. Composite profile minus handle. H. 0.095, Diam. rim 0.124–0.130, Diam. base 0.072.

Fine fabric with reddish yellow fracture and surfaces. 1% inclusions. Very pale brown slip in and out.

Dump, dark brown (trench 95A, pails 164 [1], 193 [1]) and red (trench 95A, pail 189 [5]) soil strata west of kiln.

BELL CUPS

23 (C 9947). Bell cup, handleless
Figs. 25, 32

85% preserved, mended from 7 sherds. 50% rim, 90% body, complete base. Complete profile. H. 0.057–0.061, Diam. rim 0.080–0.090, Diam. base 0.036.

Fine fabric with very pale brown fracture and surfaces. 3% inclusions. Pale yellow slip in and out.

Dump, red soil stratum east (trench 87B, pails 106B, 107) and dark brown stratum north (trench 87B, pail 116B) of kiln.

Fabric sample 95/19; fabric group 3.[78]

24 (C 9992). Bell cup
Fig. 32

95% preserved, single sherd. Almost complete, with 20% rim and upper part handle missing. Complete profile minus upper part handle. H. 0.057–0.058, Diam. rim 0.084–0.094, Diam. base 0.042.

Fine fabric with reddish yellow fracture and paler reddish yellow surfaces. 1% inclusions. Dark-dipped rim fired to dilute red and reddish yellow.

Dump, dark brown soil stratum northeast of kiln (trench 87B, pail 116D).

SIDE-SPOUTED CUPS

25 (C 10167). Side-spouted cup
Fig. 32

95% preserved, single sherd. Body almost complete, handle stubs. Complete profile minus handle. H. 0.074–0.078, Diam. rim 0.099 (at handle), Diam. base 0.042–0.045.

Medium-coarse fabric with reddish yellow fracture and very pale brown surfaces. 10% inclusions. Unpainted. Largely coated with calcite.

Kiln, channel 2 (trench 95A, pail 172).

Fabric sample 95/4; fabric group 2a.

78. For the difference between my fabric texture identification and that of Day and Kilikoglou (below), see above, note 71.

CONVEX-SIDED BOWLS

26 (C 9985). Convex-sided bowl

Fig. 33

33% preserved, 7 sherds mended into 3 nonjoining pieces. 33% rim and upper body, 10% lower body, 95% base. Composite profile. H. 0.152, Diam. rim 0.200, Diam. base 0.095.

Medium-coarse fabric with reddish yellow fracture and very pale brown surfaces. 10% inclusions. Dilute dark gray coated in and out. Exterior white-painted, thick retorted, hooked spirals covering most of body, and bands on top and below.

Dump, red soil stratum east of kiln (trench 87B, pail 107 [3]); dark brown soil stratum east (trench 87B, pail 111B [1]), northeast (trench 87B, pail 111 [2]) and north (trench 87B, pail 112B [1]) of kiln.

Fabric sample 95/37; fabric group 3.

27 (C 10564). Convex-sided bowl

Fig. 33

25% preserved, 17 sherds mended into 10 nonjoining pieces. 90% rim, 25% body, no base, stubs of 1 horizontal handle with circular section, other handle missing. Composite profile, except for base. Pres. H. 0.210, Diam. rim 0.271.

Medium-coarse fabric with pink fracture and paler pink surfaces. 10% inclusions. Exterior upper body: white bands on a dark brown to reddish yellow to light red ground. Interior: dark-dipped rim with thick white bars.

Dump, red soil stratum east of kiln (trench 87B, pails 96 [4], 106C [1]); dark brown soil stratum east (trench 87B, pail 111B [1]), northeast (trench 87B, pails 116 [6], 116C [2]), and north (trench 87B, pails 116A [2], 116B [1]) of kiln.

CONICAL BOWLS

28 (C 10533). Conical bowl   Fig. 33

20% preserved, mended from 6 sherds. 45% rim, 25% body, 1 lug, no base. Profile preserved except for base. Pres. H. 0.105, Diam. rim 0.210–0.230.

Medium-coarse fabric with reddish yellow fracture and pale

yellow surfaces. 10% inclusions. Unpainted.

Kiln, channels 2 (trench 95A, pails 142 [1], 172 [4]) and 3 (trench 97F, pail 72 [1]).

Fabric sample 95/3; fabric group 2a.

KALATHOI OR FLARING BOWLS

FINE

29 (C 10510). Kalathos   Fig. 33

50% preserved, 18 sherds mended into 10 nonjoining pieces. 45% rim, 50% body, 50% base. Composite profile. H. 0.125–0.126, Diam. rim 0.170–0.190, Diam. base 0.060.

Fine fabric with pink fracture and reddish yellow surfaces. Fewer than 1% inclusions. Interior and exterior: fine white-painted reeds on a reddish brown to reddish yellow to red ground.

Dump, dark brown soil stratum north of kiln (trench 87B, pails 116A [2], 116B [2]; trench 95A, pails 148 [7], 205 [7]).

MEDIUM-COARSE

30 (C 10286). Kalathos   Fig. 33

30% preserved, 4 sherds mended into 2 nonjoining pieces. 25% rim and upper body, 40% lower body, 70% base. Complete profile. H. 0.104–0.106, Diam. rim 0.170–0.186, Diam. base 0.090.

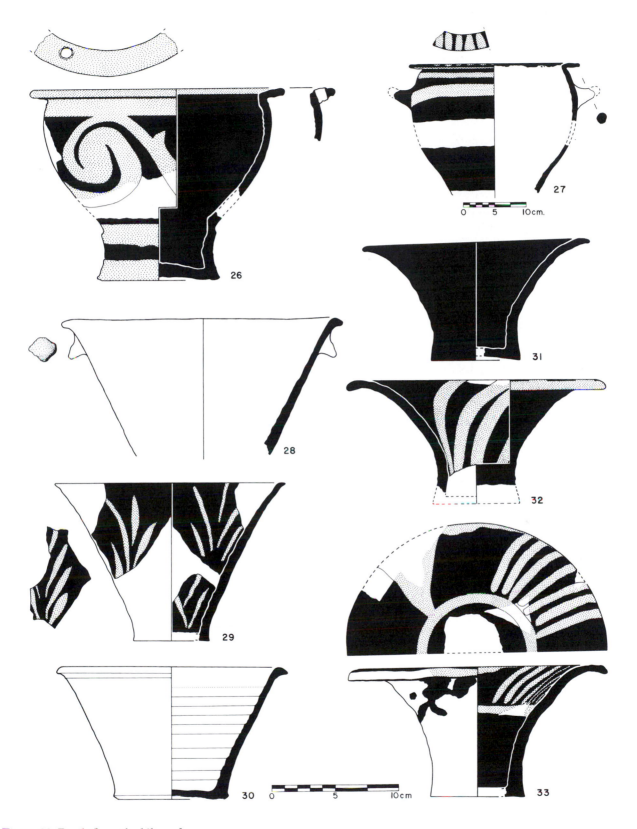

Figure 33. Bowls from the kiln and dump

Medium-coarse fabric with reddish yellow fracture and pink surfaces. 15% inclusions. Fine pale yellow slip on interior and exterior.

Dump, dark brown soil stratum north of kiln (trench 95A, pail 148).

31 (C 9931). Kalathos   Fig. 33

25% preserved, mended from 9 sherds. 20% rim, 30% body, 15% base. Complete profile. H. 0.092–0.095, Diam. rim 0.180, Diam. base 0.070.

Medium-coarse fabric with reddish yellow fracture and very pale brown surfaces. 5% inclusions. Interior and exterior monochrome dark brown to dark grayish brown.

Dump, light brown soil stratum east (trench 90C, pail 94 [8]) and dark brown soil stratum west (trench 95A, pail 181 [1]) of kiln.

BRIDGE-SPOUTED JARS

FINE

34 (C 10580). Bridge-spouted jar
                                        Fig. 34

33% preserved, 16 sherds mended into 10 nonjoining pieces. 10% rim, 25% upper body, 50% lower body, 60% base, 33% spout, one handle. Composite profile. H. 0.151, Diam. rim 0.106, max. Diam. 0.157, Diam. base 0.064–0.066.

Fine fabric with reddish yellow fracture and pink surfaces. 1% inclusions. Handle attachment not well-integrated. Unpainted.

Dump, red (trench 87B, pails 96 [2], 106A [1], 106B [5], 106C [1], 107 [3], 107B [1]) and dark brown (trench 87B, pails 111C [1], 111D [2]) soil strata east of kiln.

35 (C 10550). Bridge-spouted jar
                                        Fig. 34

20% preserved, 16 sherds mended into 5 nonjoining fragments. 40% rim, 33% upper body, 20% lower body, spout, parts of two handles. About three-quarters of profile preserved, missing base and part of lower body. Pres. H. 0.132, Diam. rim 0.087, max. Diam. 0.156.

32 (C 9930). Kalathos   Fig. 33

30% preserved, mended from 13 sherds. 33% rim and body. Composite profile minus base. Pres. H. 0.089, Diam. rim 0.205, Diam. base 0.069.

Medium-coarse fabric with light red fracture, yellow interior surface, and very pale brown exterior surface. 10% inclusions. Coated dark brown to very dark gray, with some yellowish red on exterior. Groups of white arcs covering entire interior surface. White interior rim band.

Dump, light brown soil stratum east (trench 90C, pail 94 [11]), red soil stratum northwest (trench 95A, pail 152 [1]), and dark brown soil stratum west (trench 95A, pail 164 [1]) of kiln.

Fabric sample 95/29; fabric group 2a.

36 (C 10282). Bridge-spouted jar
                                        Fig. 34

4 joining sherds preserving 35% rim and upper body, spout, one handle. Pres. H. 0.045, Diam. rim 0.098, max. Diam. 0.130.

Fine fabric with pink to reddish yellow fracture, reddish yellow to yellow exterior surface, and reddish yellow to very pale brown interior

Fine fabric with reddish yellow fracture, paler reddish yellow exterior surface, and pink interior surface. 2% inclusions. Irregular contours. Handle and spout attachments not well-integrated. Thick retorted spirals covering most of exterior body; partial rim band in white continuing on spout; barred handles. Patterns painted in very pale brown on a vivid red ground. Interior red-dipped rim.

Dump, light brown soil stratum east of kiln (trench 90C, pail 94 [1]); red soil stratum east (trench 87B, pails 106D [10], 106E [1]), northwest (trench 95A, pails 152 [1], 188 [1]), and west (trench 95A, pail 156 [2]) of kiln.

Fabric sample 95/38; fabric group 2a.

33 (C 10337). Kalathos   Fig. 33

80% preserved, single sherd. 75% rim, 90% body, 25% base. Complete profile. H. 0.101–0.102, Diam. rim 0.205, Diam. base 0.075.

Medium-coarse fabric with reddish yellow fracture, paler reddish yellow interior surface, and pink exterior surface. 10% inclusions. Interior upper body decorated with white arcs on a black to red ground, arranged in irregular groups bordered above and below by a white band. Exterior body covered with fine pale yellow slip, rim dipped in dark grayish brown paint dripping over body.

Dump, red soil stratum northwest of kiln (trench 95A, pail 152).

Fabric sample 95/25; fabric group 2a.

surface. 1% inclusions. Spout and handle attachments quite well-integrated. Exterior dilute black to reddish brown monochrome. Interior dark-dipped rim.

Kiln, channel 4 (trench 95A, pail 131).

MEDIUM-COARSE

37 (C 8959). Bridge-spouted jar
                                        Fig. 34

25% preserved, 40 sherds with few joins. 15% rim, 25% body, 33% base, complete spout, handle scar. Worn surfaces. Composite profile. H. 0.245, Diam. rim 0.166, max. Diam. 0.236, Diam. base 0.108.

Medium-coarse fabric with light reddish brown to reddish yellow fracture, very pale brown exterior surface, and pink interior surface. 10% inclusions. Handle attachment well-integrated, but not spout attachment. Exterior very dark grayish brown to dilute strong brown monochrome. Interior dark-dipped rim.

Dump, dark brown soil stratum northeast of kiln (trench 87B, pails 116 [4], 116C [2], 116D [2], 118 [9], 118A [6], 120 [17]).

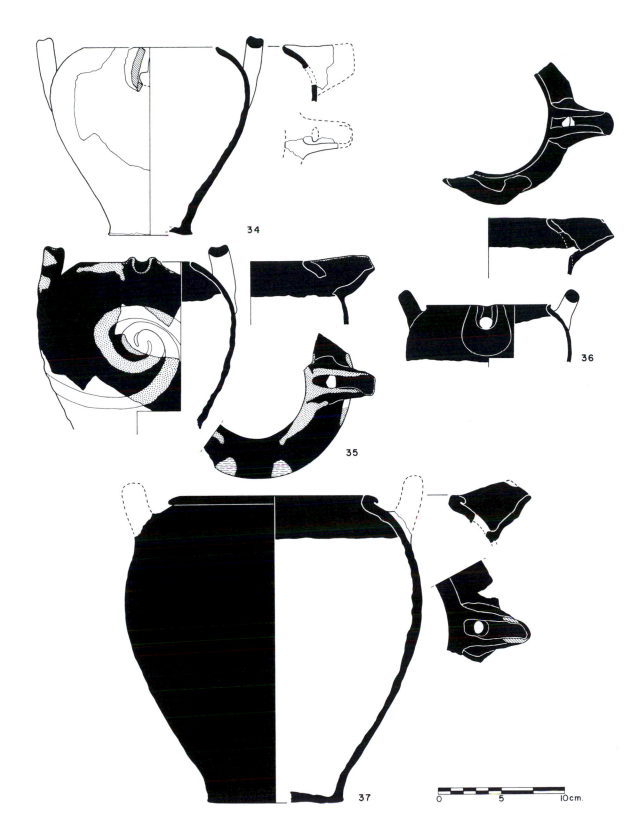

Figure 34. Bridge-spouted jars from
the kiln and dump

COLLAR-NECKED JUGS

FINE

38 (C 10535). Collar-necked jug
　　　　　　　　　　　　　Fig. 35

Single sherd preserving 25% rim and neck, beginning of shoulder, lug, most of spout. Pres. H. 0.03, Diam. rim 0.096.

Fine fabric with reddish yellow fracture and pink surfaces. 1% inclusions. Exterior monochrome dark brown to dilute light brown. Interior dark-dipped neck.

Shape variant: relatively tall, insloping neck, straight rim, spout pulled from rim.

Kiln, channel 3 (trench 97F, pail 72).

39 (C 10508). Collar-necked jug
　　　　　　　　　　　　　Fig. 35

Single sherd preserving 10% rim and neck with complete lug, 25% shoulder. Pres. H. 0.08, Diam. rim 0.144.

Fine fabric with reddish yellow fracture and paler reddish yellow surfaces. Fewer than 1% inclusions. Unpainted.

Shape variant: sloping shoulder, short, in-sloping neck, tapering rim.

Dump, red soil stratum west of kiln (trench 95A, pail 157).

MEDIUM-COARSE

40 (C 9935). Collar-necked jug
　　　　　　　　　　　　　Fig. 35

70% preserved, mended from 41 sherds. 50% rim, neck, and upper body, 80% lower body, complete base, spout, lug, 66% strap handle. Complete profile. H. 0.185–0.188, Diam. rim perpendicular to spout 0.112, max. Diam. 0.154, Diam. base 0.074–0.078.

Medium-coarse fabric with light red to pink fracture and reddish yellow surfaces. 7% inclusions. Exterior: 3 thick, retorted spirals painted in very pale brown to white on a dilute red ground. Interior dark-dipped neck.

Shape variant: piriform body, short neck, thickened rim, spout pulled from rim.

Dump, dark brown (trench 87B, pail 110 [9]), light brown (trench 90C, pail 94 [14]), and red (trench 87B,

pails 108 [12], 113 [5]) soil strata east and red soil stratum west (trench 95A, pail 156 [1]) of kiln.

Fabric sample 95/53; fabric group 1b.[79]

41 (C 10501). Collar-necked jug
　　　　　　　　　　　　　Fig. 35

Single sherd preserving 5% rim and neck, entire strap handle. Pres. H. 0.092, Diam. rim ca. 0.14, max. Diam. ca. 0.173.

Medium-coarse fabric with reddish yellow fracture and pink surfaces. 5% inclusions. Exterior dilute yellowish red to dark reddish brown monochrome. Interior dark-dipped neck.

Shape variant: relatively tall, vertical neck, everted and thickened rim.

Dump, red soil stratum east of kiln (trench 87B, pail 106D).

42 (C 10504). Collar-necked jug
　　　　　　　　　　　　　Fig. 35

3 sherds mended into 2 non-joining pieces, preserving 50% rim and neck, beginning of shoulder, beginning of spout. Pres. H. 0.040, Diam. rim 0.122.

Medium-coarse fabric with reddish yellow fracture and paler reddish yellow surfaces. 5% inclusions. Exterior dilute red monochrome. Interior dark-dipped neck and shoulder.

Shape variant: relatively tall, insloping neck with convex profile, thickened rim, spout pulled from rim.

Dump, light brown (trench 87B, pail 83 [2]) and red (trench 87B, pail 107B [1]) soil strata east of kiln.

43 (C 10500). Collar-necked jug
　　　　　　　　　　　　　Fig. 35

3 nonjoining sherds preserving 25% rim, neck, and shoulder, lug, beginning of spout. Pres. H. 0.068, Diam. rim 0.10, max. Diam. 0.153.

Medium-coarse fabric with reddish yellow fracture, yellow exterior surface, and very pale brown interior surface. 5% inclusions. Thick, retorted spirals, painted in white on a dilute red to light red exterior ground including reddish brown and reddish yellow streaks. Interior neck dipped

reddish yellow.

Shape variant: short, insloping neck, everted rim, spout pulled from rim.

Dump, dark brown soil stratum west of kiln (trench 95A, pail 179).

44 (C 10502). Collar-necked jug
　　　　　　　　　　　　　Fig. 35

2 joining sherds preserving spout and adjacent part of neck. Pres. H. 0.035.

Medium-coarse and coarse fabrics with reddish yellow fracture and paler reddish yellow surfaces. Body 5% inclusions (medium-coarse), spout 20% (coarse). Spout surface not smoothed; attachment to neck not well-integrated. Two very pale brown neck bands on dilute light red to reddish yellow exterior ground; bands continue onto spout. Interior dark-dipped neck.

Shape variant: short, vertical neck, everted rim, attached spout of a coarser fabric.

Dump, red soil stratum east of kiln (trench 87B, pail 107).

45 (C 10499). Collar-necked jug
　　　　　　　　　　　　　Fig. 35

7 sherds mended into 2 non-joining pieces, preserving 50% neck, rim, and shoulder, but all of spout. Pres. H. 0.065, Diam. rim 0.120.

Medium-coarse fabric with reddish yellow fracture, paler reddish yellow exterior surface, and pink interior surface. 5% inclusions. Spout attachment to neck not well-integrated. Exterior dilute light red to red monochrome. Interior dark-dipped neck and shoulder.

Shape variant: sloping shoulder, short, everted neck, straight rim, attached spout of similar fabric.

Dump, red (trench 87B, pails 106A [1], 106D [4]) and dark brown (trench 87B, pail 111C [2]) soil strata east of kiln.

Fabric sample 95/30; fabric group 2a.

---

79. For the difference between my fabric texture identification and that of Day and Kilikoglou (below), see above, note 71.

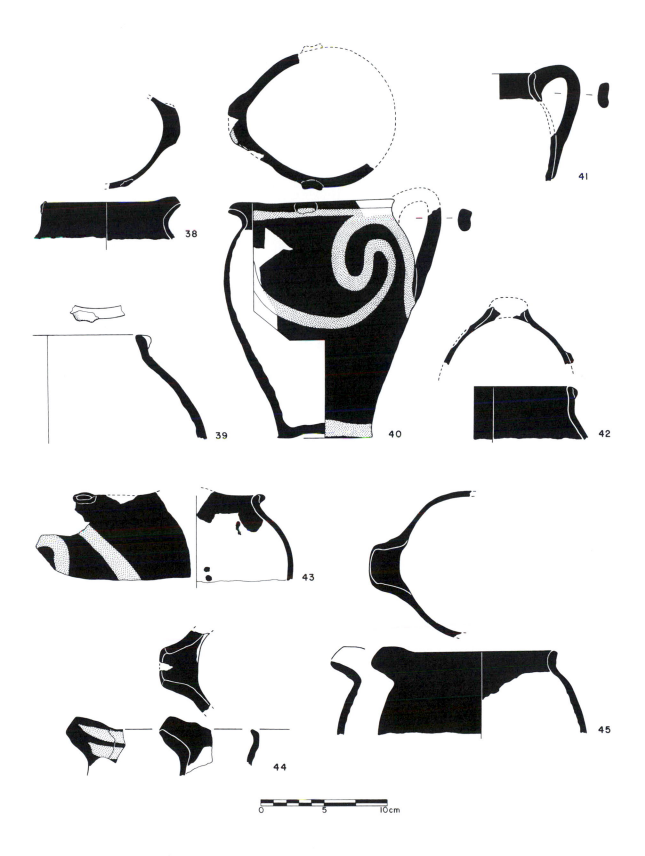

Figure 35. Collar-necked jugs from
the kiln and dump

EWERS

46 (C 9934). Ewer?   Fig. 36

66% preserved, 16 sherds mended into 3 nonjoining pieces. 30% neck and shoulder, 85% mid and lower body, complete base. Handle fragment possibly belongs. Most of profile, lacking upper neck and rim. Pres. H. 0.185, Diam. neck 0.043, max. Diam. 0.111, Diam. base 0.057–0.060.

Medium-coarse fabric with reddish yellow fracture and paler reddish yellow surfaces. 10% inclusions. Exterior fine, very pale brown slip turning yellow in places.

Dump, light brown (trench 90C, pail 94 [14]), red (trench 87B, pail 106D [1]), and dark brown (trench 87B, pail 111D [1]) soil strata east of kiln.

Fabric sample 95/41; fabric group 1b.[80]

47 (C 10568). Ewer   Fig. 36

33% preserved, 23 sherds mended into 6 nonjoining pieces. 75% rim and neck, 25% upper body, 10% base, handle attachments. Composite profile, lacking most of lower body. Restored H. 0.243, Diam. rim 0.085, max. Diam. 0.171, Diam. base 0.105.

Very pale brown fracture and surfaces. Body 10% inclusions (medium-coarse), neck 1% (fine), handle 20% (coarse). Join of neck to shoulder as well as handle attachments well-integrated. Exterior brownish yellow monochrome. Interior dark-dipped neck.

Dump, light brown (trench 87B, pail 93 [11]; trench 90C, pail 94 [1]) and red soil (trench 87B, pails 93A [6], 106D [2]) strata east of kiln; dark brown soil stratum northeast of kiln (trench 87B, pails 111 [1], 115 [1]) and court north of stoa (trench 95A, pail 165 [1]).

Fabric sample 95/39; fabric group 3.

48 (C 10554). Ewer   Fig. 36

25% preserved, 16 sherds mended into 4 nonjoining pieces. Almost complete rim and neck, 33% upper body, 25% base, nearly intact handle. Pres. H. 0.140, Diam. rim 0.101–0.105, pres. max. Diam. 0.223, Diam. base 0.116.

Medium-coarse fabric with light reddish brown to weak red fracture and very pale brown surfaces. 10% inclusions. Join of neck to shoulder and handle attachments well-integrated. Overfired. Exterior

very dark gray monochrome. Interior dark-dipped neck.

Dump, red (trench 87B, pail 106E [2]) and dark brown (trench 87B, pails 111D [11], 115 [1], 118 [2]) soil strata east of kiln.

Fabric sample 95/46; fabric group 2b.

49 (C 8973). Ewer   Fig. 36

5 sherds mended into 2 nonjoining pieces, preserving 30% rim, 80% neck, tiny portion of shoulder (nonjoining), upper handle attachment. Worn surfaces. Pres. H. 0.115, Diam. rim 0.155.

Reddish yellow fracture and yellow surfaces. Body 10% inclusions (medium-coarse), neck ring 25% (coarse). Interior neck narrowed by coarse clay reinforcement coil (30% inclusions). Exterior very dark gray monochrome. Interior dark-dipped neck.

Dump, dark brown soil stratum east of kiln (trench 87B, pails 115 [1], 116E [4]).

Fabric sample 95/40 taken from body; fabric group 2a.

RHYTA

50 (C 10404). Globular rhyton
     Fig. 36

50% preserved, 19 sherds mended into 5 nonjoining pieces. 10% upper body, 50% lower body, 75% base, complete nipple, no rim. Pres. H. 0.13, max. Diam. 0.165.

Fine fabric with pink fracture and reddish yellow surfaces. 2% inclusions. Nipple attachment well-integrated. White-painted thick retorted spirals on dilute dark brown to yellowish red exterior ground; 3 bands below. Nipple plugged.

Dump, light brown (trench 87B, pail 93 [3]; trench 90C, pail 86 [1]) and red (trench 87B, pails 93A [1],

106B [1], 106C [1]) soil strata east of kiln; dark brown soil stratum north of kiln (trench 87B, pails 116 [4], 116A [1], 116B [4]; trench 91B, pail 46 [1]; trench 95A, pail 148 [2]).

Fabric sample 95/31; fabric group 1a.

51 (C 10511). Piriform rhyton
     Fig. 36

7 sherds mended into 2 nonjoining pieces, preserving 16% midbody, 60% lower body with beginning of spout. Upper body, including neck and rim, as well as lower spout lacking. Pres. H. 0.13, pres. max. Diam. 0.125.

Fine fabric with light brown fracture and pink surfaces. 1% inclusions. Overfired. Thick retorted spirals painted in greenish white on black exterior ground. Interior dark-dipped spout, dilute brown.

Dump, red soil stratum east of kiln (trench 87B, pails 93A [1], 96 [1], 106A [2], 106B [2]); mostly LM III2/B unit north of kiln (trench 91B, pail 48 [1]).

---

80. For the difference between my fabric texture identification and that of Day and Kilikoglou (below), see above, note 71.

Figure 36. Ewers (46–49) and rhyta
(50–51) from the dump

OVAL-MOUTHED AMPHORAS

52 (C 8971). Oval-mouthed
amphora   Fig. 37

50% preserved, 42 sherds with
many joins. Complete rim and neck,
both handles, 60% upper body, 10%
mid body, 30% lower body, 60% base.
Complete profile. H. 0.420, Diam.
rim 0.066–0.113, max. Diam. 0.261,
Diam. base 0.176.

Medium-coarse fabric with
reddish yellow fracture and interior
surface, and paler reddish yellow
exterior surface. 10% inclusions.
Coil-built. Attachments of neck and
handles well-integrated. Paint
splatters, colored dilute dark brown
to strong brown, over entire exterior
clay surface, including rim and
handles. Interior unpainted.

Dump, dark brown soil stratum
northeast (trench 87B, pails 112 [2],
112C [1], 114 [1], 115 [4], 116 [9],
116D [12]) and east (trench 87B, pail
116E [10]) of kiln. Also in mixed
MM II–LM IA debris just west of
Gallery 6 of Building P (trench 90A,
pail 46 [3]), providing a *terminus post
quem* for the date of this disturbance.

Fabric sample 95/57; fabric
group 2a.

53 (C 10597). Oval-mouthed
amphora   Fig. 37

25% preserved, 50 sherds
mended into 32 nonjoining pieces.
33% rim, 50% neck and shoulder,
25% body, 33% base, handle scar, no
lower body. Pres. H. 0.355, Diam.
rim 0.075–0.144, max. Diam. 0.261,
Diam. base 0.131.

Medium-coarse fabric with
reddish yellow fracture and exterior
surface, and pink interior surface. 7%
inclusions. Coil-built. Body apparently much more piriform than that
of **52**. Large simplified plant motif
covering either side of exterior body,
painted in dilute light red to red on a
very pale brown slip. Traces of paint
on rim. Interior coated with very pale
brown slip.

Dump, light brown soil stratum
east of kiln (trench 87B, pails 82 [14],
83 [6]); dark brown soil stratum
northeast (trench 87B, pails 109 [8],
111 [19], 112 [1]) and north (trench
87B, pail 112B [2]) of kiln.

Fabric sample 95/52; fabric
group 2a.

BASINS

54 (C 10577). Basin   Fig. 37

10 sherds mended into 3 nonjoining pieces, preserving 33% rim
and upper body, part of base. Composite profile. Rest. H. 0.266, Diam.
rim 0.392, Diam. base 0.114.

Coarse fabric with light red
to reddish yellow fracture and pale
yellow surfaces. 20% inclusions.
Slightly overfired. Unpainted.

Kiln, channels 1 (trench 87B,
pails 90 [2], 90A [1]), 2 (trench
95A, pails 142 [1], 172 [1]), and 3
(trench 97F, pail 73 [1]). Dump,
light brown soil stratum east of kiln
(trench 90C, pail 90 [1]); dark
brown (trench 87B, pail 105 [2]) and
red (trench 87B, pail 105A [1]) soil
strata north of kiln.

Fabric sample 95/1; fabric group
4.

55 (C 10534). Basin   Fig. 37

16% preserved, 11 sherds
mended into 5 nonjoining pieces. 20%
rim, 25% upper body, 5% lower body,
no base, 2 handle fragments. Pres. H.
0.265, Diam. rim 0.430.

Coarse fabric with light brown
and reddish yellow fracture and very
pale brown surfaces. 25% inclusions.
Coil-built. Handle attachment well-
integrated. Unpainted. Plastic and
impressed rope band below the rim.

Kiln, channel 3 (trench 97F, pail
72 [6]) and firing pit (trench 95A, pail
111 [1]). Dump, light brown (trench
87B, pail 97 [1]) and red (trench 87B,
pail 96 [2]) soil strata east of kiln; red
soil stratum northwest of kiln (trench
95A, pail 150 [1]).

Fabric sample 95/2; fabric group
2a.[81]

81. For the difference between my
fabric texture identification and that
of Day and Kilikoglou (below), see
above, note 71.

Figure 37. Large shapes from the kiln and dump (52–58); coarse slab fragment (61)

LARGE CLOSED JARS

56 (C 10593). Jar   Fig. 37

6 sherds mended into 3 non-joining pieces, preserving 40% rim, 30% neck, 25% upper shoulder with handle scar, 15% lower body. Pres. H. 0.114 (upper part) and 0.080 (lower part), Diam. rim 0.22, est. Diam. base ca. 0.170.

PITHOI

57 (C 10168). Pithos   Fig. 37

7 joining base fragments preserving 75% base and small part of lower body. Pres. H. 0.068, Diam. base 0.297.

Coarse fabric with reddish yellow fracture and paler reddish yellow surfaces. 25% inclusions. Coil-built. Slightly overfired. Exterior and interior pale yellow slip. Coated with calcite.

Kiln, channels 2 (trench 95A, pail 172 [6]) and 3 (trench 97F, pail 72 [1]).

Fabric sample 95/6; fabric group 4.

FINE PEDESTALED VASES

59 (C 8947). Pedestaled vase
                         Figs. 38, 41

75% preserved, mended from 4 sherds. 20% stem, 97% foot. Complete profile of base. Pres. H. 0.083, Diam. base 0.094.

COARSE SLABS

60 (C 8935). Slab   Figs. 38, 43

25% body, 20% rim, mended from 6 sherds. Diam. 0.65, Th. 0.021–0.023.

Medium-coarse fabric with reddish yellow fracture, yellowish red top surface, and red lower surface. 10% angular inclusions: white, brown, pale brown to light yellowish brown, light reddish brown (2.5YR 6/4); max. size 0.005, avg. size 0.0015. Coated entirely with a fine white slip, polished. Thin layer of dull yellow, flaky substance, perhaps unbaked clay, covering slipped surface

Medium-coarse fabric with reddish yellow fracture and very pale brown surfaces. 10% inclusions. Neck and handle attachments well-integrated. Exterior dark splashes on neck and shoulder, executed in dilute red on the clay ground. Plastic and impressed rope band at bottom of neck

58 (C 10613). Pithos   Fig. 37

36 sherds with few joins, preserving 15% rim, 20% body, 4 horizontal handles. No base. Diam. rim 0.40.

Coarse fabric with red and reddish yellow fracture and pink surfaces. 30% inclusions. Coil-built. Rim and handle attachments well-integrated. Slightly overfired. Thick retorted spirals executed in white to pale yellow on a black exterior ground. Interior dark-dipped rim.

Dump, light brown (trench 87B, pail 93 [2]; trench 90C, pail 94 [1])

Fine fabric with reddish yellow fracture and interior surface, and pink exterior surface. 1% inclusions. Unpainted.

Dump, red soil stratum east of kiln (trench 87B, pails 106A [1], 107

(indicated by crosshatching in Fig. 38).

Dump, dark brown soil stratum north (trench 87B, pails 112A [1], 112B [3], 116A [1]) and northwest (trench 95A, pail 146 [1]) of kiln.

61 (C 10599). Slab   Fig. 37

33% body and rim, mended from 7 sherds. Straight edge L. 0.18, curved edge Diam. 0.65, Th. 0.027–0.031.

Medium-coarse fabric with dark grayish brown fracture, light red top surface, and red bottom surface. 20%

and two rope bands above the base. Interior unpainted. 11 incised vertical lines on neck, and 5 surviving, irregularly spaced diagonal (rope?) impressions on rim, all made before firing.

Dump, dark brown soil stratum northeast of kiln (trench 87B, pails 111A [2], 112 [4]).

and red soil strata east of kiln (trench 87B, pails 96 [1], 106B [1], 106D [1], 106E [2], 107 [1], 107B [1]); dark brown soil stratum east (trench 87B, pail 111D [3]), north (trench 87B, pails 105 [2], 116A [1]; trench 91B, pails 45 [16], 48 [1]; trench 95A, pails 146 [1], 148 [1]), and west (trench 95A, pail 179 [1]) of kiln.

[1]), and dark brown soil stratum northeast (trench 87B, pail 111A [1]) and north (trench 87B, pail 116B [1]) of kiln.

angular inclusions: white, brown, pale brown to light yellowish brown, yellowish red, light reddish brown (2.5YR 6/4); max. size 0.007, avg. size 0.002. Top coated with fine, very pale brown slip, bottom possibly with white slip. No trace of polish.

Dump, light brown soil stratum east of kiln (trench 87B, pails 82 [2], 83 [5]).

Figure 38. Fine pedestal base (59) and coarse slab fragment (60) from the dump; lustrous dark-on-light patterned fragmentary vases from kiln mound (62) and dump (63–69); waster (C 10279)

DARK-ON-LIGHT PATTERNED VASES

62 (C 9908). Bowl   Fig. 38

50% preserved, 23 sherds mended into 2 nonjoining pieces. 25% rim and upper body, 70% lower body and base. No handles. Complete profile. H. 0.095, Diam. rim 0.18–0.29, Diam. base 0.12.

Fine fabric with pink fracture, yellow to very pale brown exterior surface, and very pale brown interior surface. 1% angular inclusions: white, brown, pale brown to light yellowish brown, dark brown, yellowish red, and olive gray (5Y 4/2); max. size 0.0025, avg. size 0.001. Resembles kiln pottery fabric. Warped. Exterior rim band (sloppy), fine tortoise-shell ripple (multiple brush) on upper body, bands on lower body. Interior rim band, running spirals on upper body, foliate band of short stubby leaves on lower body, large and irregular spiral on base. Sloppily painted in very dark grayish brown to dilute reddish yellow. Exterior and interior polished after decoration, causing dark paint to smear.

Kiln mound, just east of kiln (trench 87B, pails 91 [11], 112 [6], 115 [6]).

63 (C 9983). Teacup   Fig. 38

2 joining sherds preserving 25% rim and 10% upper body. Pres. H. 0.041, Diam. rim 0.135.

Fine fabric with reddish yellow fracture, very pale brown exterior surface, and pink interior surface. 1% angular inclusions: white, brown, dark brown, reddish yellow, yellowish red, and red; max. size 0.0015, avg. size 0.0007. Resembles kiln pottery fabric. Exterior fine tortoise-shell ripple (multiple brush) and rim band executed in dark brown to dilute reddish yellow. White wavy line with filler arcs on rim band. Interior dark-painted rim band, showing brush strokes. Polished lightly and carefully on both interior and exterior.

Dump, dark brown soil stratum north of kiln (trench 87B, pail 112D).

64 (C 10290). Teacup   Fig. 38

6 sherds mended into 4 nonjoining pieces, preserving 35% upper and mid body. Rim and most of lower body lacking. Interior surface worn. Pres. H. 0.055, max. Diam. 0.160.

Fine fabric with reddish yellow fracture, paler reddish yellow interior surface, and pink exterior surface. 1% angular inclusions: white, pale brown to light yellowish brown, dark brown, yellowish red; max. size 0.0003, avg. size 0.0002. Resembles kiln pottery fabric. Exterior rim band above two patterned body zones separated by a band. Upper: retorted spirals. Lower: fine tortoise-shell ripple. Executed in dilute reddish yellow. Interior decoration and surface treatment not preserved. Exterior polished carefully after decoration.

Dump, red (trench 95A, pail 136 [3]) and dark brown (trench 95A, pail 205 [3]) soil stratum north of kiln.

65 (C 9437). Bridge-spouted jar   Fig. 38

13 sherds mended into 7 nonjoining pieces, preserving 30% rim, 15% upper body, one handle with circular section. Handle worn (not polished). Pres. H. 0.12, Diam. mouth 0.120, max. Diam. 0.227.

Pink fracture and very pale brown surfaces. Fine body: fewer than 1% angular inclusions: white, brown, dark brown, reddish yellow, and yellowish red; max. size 0.002, avg. size 0.0007. Coarse handle: 30% inclusions. Resembles kiln pottery fabric. Handle attachment well-smoothed. Exterior two registers of fine tortoise-shell ripple (multiple brush) on upper body, separated by sloppy bands of different widths. Executed in dark grayish brown to dilute reddish yellow. White diagonal bars on dark-painted rim and handle. Interior dark-dipped rim. Exterior polished after decoration,

causing tortoise-shell ripple lines to smear.

Dump, dark brown soil stratum east (trench 87B, pails 111C [1], 115 [1], 115A [4], 116D [1], 118 [4]) and north (trench 87B, pail 118A [2]) of kiln.

66 (C 9982). Bridge-spouted jar?   Fig. 38

7 sherds mended into 4 nonjoining pieces, preserving 10% upper body. No rim or lower body. Polish worn, some pitting. Pres. H. 0.085.

Fine fabric with pink fracture and reddish yellow surfaces. 1% angular inclusions: white, brown, pale brown to light yellowish brown, dark brown, reddish yellow, and yellowish red; max. size 0.001, avg. size 0.0005. Resembles kiln pottery fabric. Abruptly inturning shoulder, resembling that of bridge-spouted jar. Exterior crocus clusters painted red to dilute light red on very pale brown slip. Polished after decoration.

Dump, dark brown soil stratum northeast of kiln (trench 87B, pail 115).

67 (C 9993). Closed vessel   Fig. 38

Single sherd preserving small part of lower body. Paint worn. Pres. H. 0.048.

Fine fabric with pinkish gray to pink fracture and interior surface, and yellow exterior surface. 2% angular inclusions: white, brown, pale brown to light yellowish brown, and dark brown; max. size 0.0015, avg. size 0.0007. Does not resemble kiln pottery fabric. Exterior greenish white slip, polished hard before decoration. Fine crisscross marks visible in polish. Fine tortoise-shell ripple pattern above wide band, painted dark grayish brown to dilute light yellowish brown.

Dump, dark brown soil stratum north of kiln (trench 87B, pail 116).

68 (C 10320). Closed vessel   Fig. 38

Single sherd preserving part of upper and mid body. Surfaces worn, paint mostly gone. Pres. H. 0.06, max. Diam. 0.118.

Fine fabric with pink fracture and surfaces. 1% angular inclusions: white, dark brown, and reddish yellow; max. size 0.004, avg. size 0.001. Does not resemble kiln pottery fabric. Exterior very pale brown slip, polished rather hard before decoration. Register of linked, blob-centered spirals with thickened outer loops, painted very dark grayish brown.

Dump, dark brown soil stratum northeast of kiln (trench 87B, pail 105).

69 (C 10137). Closed vessel   Fig. 38

Single sherd preserving part of upper body. Partially burned to a light gray color. Pres. H. 0.025.

Fine fabric with very pale brown fracture and surfaces. 1% angular inclusions: brown, dark brown, dark bluish gray (5B 4/1); max. size 0.001, avg. size 0.0005. Does not resemble kiln pottery fabric. Exterior reed pattern painted very dark grayish brown to dilute brownish yellow. Surface carefully polished after decoration.

Dump, dark brown soil stratum west of kiln (trench 95A, pail 161).

70 (C 9444). Stirrup jar?   Fig. 38

38 sherds mended into 12 nonjoining pieces, preserving 25% mid and lower body, including base. Exterior surface lightly worn, interior surface eroded away. Composite profile, lacking shoulder, rim, spout, and handles. Pres. H. 0.261, max. Diam. 0.311, Diam. base 0.160.

Medium-coarse fabric with reddish yellow fracture and interior surface, and paler reddish yellow exterior surface. Fabric has bright orange hue on surfaces and fracture. 10% angular inclusions: brown, reddish yellow, bluish gray (5B 6/1), white, weak red (10R 5/4), light reddish brown (2.5YR 6/4), and very dark gray to dark gray (2.5YR 3.5/0); max. size 0.004, avg. size 0.0015. Perhaps East Cretan. Exterior coated with pink slip. Decoration in three registers separated by bands. Groups of tortoise-shell ripple (multiple brush) on mid body, traces of curvilinear design on shoulder, no decoration preserved on lower body. Painted red to dilute light red. Added white horizontal bands on red base band (omitted in drawing). Surface carefully polished after decoration, causing tortoise-shell ripple lines to smear.

Dump, light brown soil stratum northeast of kiln (trench 87B, pail 97 [1]); red soil stratum west of kiln (trench 95A, pails 189 [3], 191 [4]); dark brown soil stratum northeast (trench 87B, pails 105 [1], 112 [1], 114 [1], 115 [2]) and north (trench 87B, pails 112C [6], 116 [1]; trench 91B, pails 45 [3], 46 [4], 47 [4], 48 [4]; trench 95A, pails 134 [1], 145 [1]) of kiln; and mixed MM II–LM IIIA2/B unit north of kiln (trench 91B, pail 50 [1]).

ANALYSIS OF VASE SHAPES AND DECORATION

CONICAL CUPS (1–19; Fig. 32)

Conical cups[82] outnumber by far any other vessel shape present in either the kiln or the dump. More than 650 conical cups have been recovered among a total of 1,158 vases (Table 4; Fig. 39). Of these conical cups, 183 have so far been restored and studied (Table 8). They conform to a Protopalatial and Neopalatial conical cup typology that has been developed over the last few years on the basis of stratified finds from Kommos.[83] This Kommian typology is based on criteria of shape and decoration.

Represented in the dump are conical cup types C, D, E, F, P, Q, and V, and inside the kiln types C, P, and Q. To type C (1–7) belong relatively small unpainted cups with slightly convex or straight-flaring walls, and low-proportioned bodies (maximum height to rim diameter ratio = 0.61). Rims are either rounded or tapering. Type D (8) cups resemble type C examples in profile and rim shape, but they are taller, with height : rim diameter proportions greater than 0.61. Type D cups differ quite widely in shape and dimensions, but they always are taller and more slender than type C cups. The remainder are large ovoid and semiglobular cups that either are unpainted (types E and F, respectively), are dark monochrome coated (types P and Q, respectively), or carry linear decoration (ovoid type V).

Table 8 and Figure 40 show the relative frequencies of conical cup types. By far the most common are type C examples. Cups of types E, F, P, and Q are quite frequent, but types D and V are rare. In the dump, type C cups are more numerous than all other conical cup types combined, but in the kiln they are outnumbered by type P examples.

The type C cups produced in this kiln are compact in shape, resembling in this respect LM IA conical cups from other central Cretan sites as well as from Akrotiri.[84] It is remarkable that in LM IA, in spite of local differences, all those sites adopted a light, compact cup with similar conical to slightly convex shape as their most common conical cup variety. It replaces the wider, heavier cups common in MM III and early in LM IA, which differed much more widely among Knossos, Mallia, and the Mesara sites. The type C cups from the kiln area at Kommos include two varieties, which were distributed over the dump and the kiln in a nonrandom manner. Most type C specimens found in the dump had convex sides and either straight or rolled-in rims (5–7). All type C cups from within the

TABLE 8. RELATIVE FREQUENCIES OF CONICAL CUP TYPES IN KILN AND DUMP

	No. Estimated	No. Restored
KILN		
type C	50	30
type P	80	20
type Q	20	4
Totals	150	54
DUMP		
type C	260	89
type D	7	5
type E	70	6
type F	80	8
type P	45	9
type Q	20	3
type V	25	9
Totals	507	129

Estimates include restored vessels.

82. For the use of the term "conical cup," see above, note 72.

83. Van de Moortel 1997, pp. 32–81, figs. 5–10. The Kommian conical cup typology seems to be applicable to published cups from Phaistos and Aghia Triada, but works less well outside the Mesara (see below).

84. Cf. LM IA conical cups from Phaistos (Levi 1976, fig. 630:f), Aghia Triada (La Rosa 1986, figs. 28:a–d,

36:a, b, 76:f–h, 80:m–n, 84:b), Seli (Cucuzza 1993, pls. 5: V-1, XXV-5, XXV-6, XXVII-17; 14a: all except XXVI-1; 15a: V-1, XVIII-3; 15c: XX-1), Knossos (Catling, Catling, and Smyth 1979, fig. 36: V.241–248; Popham 1984, pls. 129:a.1–4, b.1–3, 144:9), Mallia (Pelon 1970, pls. XVI:1, a–c, XXXVII:10), and Akrotiri (*Thera VI*, pl. 34). The degree of similarity of the cups from Phaistos, Aghia Triada,

and Akrotiri cannot be ascertained without closer study. The examples from Seli, Knossos, and Mallia show only superficial similarities with the Kommos cups. The cups from the Minoan Unexplored Mansion have been dated by Popham to the MM IIIB/LM IA transition, which—it will be argued here—may overlap with the lifetime of the Kommos kiln.

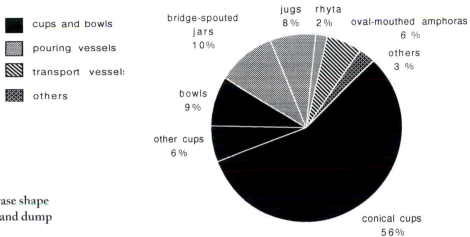

Figure 39. Estimated vase shape frequencies in the kiln and dump (N = 1,158)

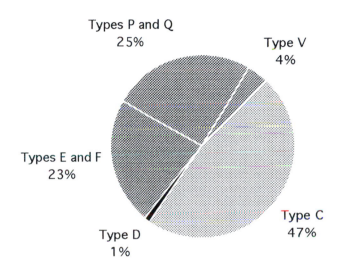

Figure 40. Estimated frequencies of conical cup types in the kiln and dump (N = 657)

kiln, however, had straight-flaring walls and straight rims (**1–4**); few examples of this variety were found in the dump. The two varieties have been encountered elsewhere at Kommos, such as, among other places, in a stratigraphical sequence of floors within Building T that shows that the cups with flaring walls belong to the final stage of LM IA currently identified at Kommos, whereas those with convex sides appear in the advanced stage just preceding it.[85] It will be argued below that the lifetime of the kiln straddled the advanced and final stages of LM IA (pp. 89–102).

85. For a brief ceramic overview of the new LM IA chronology of Kommos, see below (pp. 89–94). A more detailed presentation is being prepared for publication. Many examples of the two type C varieties have been found in unpublished LM IA floor deposits of House X and Building T. Some occurred in stratified sequences in Building T,

Room 16 (trench 62D, pail 80: C 8281), Room 22, west end (trench 52A, pail 43; trench 56A1, pail 96: C 6499, C 6503), Room 20/22, west end (trench 52A, pails 45, 40; trench 53A1, pails 67, 68, 70, 73; trench 56A1, pails 96, 96A: C 6905, C 6931, C 6933), and Room 42 (trench 62D, pails 79, 81, 82: C 8246). They were abundant in a fill in Room 1

(trench 73A, pails 118, 120, 122; trench 86B, pails 8, 9, 10) and in a floor deposit and overlying fill in Room 2 (trench 80A, pails 49, 61, 62, 63, 64, 65, 66, 66A, 66C, 67, 67A, 68, 69) of House X. A LM IA conical cup from the Kommos Hillside published by Watrous belongs to the variety with flaring walls (*Kommos* III, fig. 12: no. 2).

Type C cups differ from the large ovoid and semiglobular cups of types E, F, P, Q, and V not only in body shape, but also in wall thickness and surface treatment. The larger types have relatively thinner walls, their rims are better finished, and their surfaces are better smoothed. While type C cups are undecorated, more than half of the large ovoid and semi-globular conical cups are dark-slipped or have painted decoration. In all these respects, the large decorated conical cup types resemble contemporary teacups, and body sherds of the two shapes often are indistinguishable. Because of the many differences between type C cups and the large conical cup types, one may be justified in assigning them to two different categories, type C representing a class of simple, quickly produced cups, and types E, F, P, Q, and V a class that was somewhat more time-consuming to make. These two classes seem to be sufficiently pronounced in shape, wall thickness, and surface treatment to have been distinguished also by the Minoans.

The conical cup types other than type C from the kiln and dump are also paralleled at Kommos and elsewhere.[86] The range of patterned decoration found on type V cups from the kiln dump is illustrated in Figure 32 (16–19). A unique characteristic of most spiral-decorated examples is the opposing curl or hook embellishing the spirals (19). Hooked spirals of this kind have not yet been attested at other Minoan sites and seem to be characteristic of Kommos, where they are restricted to the LM IA phase.[87] They also occur on a medium-coarse convex-sided bowl from the dump (26).

OTHER CUPS (20–25; Fig. 32)

Teacups and straight-sided cups are rare in the dump, and are altogether absent from the kiln.[88] The remains of only 8 teacups in a relatively fresh condition have been identified in the dump, of which 6 are monochrome painted and 2 are decorated with light-on-dark patterned, thick retorted spirals. Only one (20) has a restorable profile. No teacups have been found inside the kiln. Teacups typically are squat and have their point of maximum diameter at mid-body, their profiles turning sharply toward the base.

86. Type D at Kommos (*Kommos* III, fig. 12: nos. 22, 24), Aghia Triada (La Rosa 1986, fig. 36:c), and Seli (Cucuzza 1993, pl. 14a: XXVI-1). Types E/F at Aghia Triada (La Rosa 1986, fig. 84:a) and Seli (Cucuzza 1993, pls. 14d; 15a: XVIII-1, XXV-3). Types P and Q at Aghia Triada (La Rosa 1986, figs. 28:h, 92:d–f, 96:b–c) and Seli (Cucuzza 1993, pls. 5: XXVII-3, XXVII-16, XXX-1; 15a: XXVII-8; 15c: XII-2, XXI-1, XXVII-3, XXX-1). Type V at Kommos (*Kommos* III, p. 111; see also note 87) and Aghia Triada (La Rosa 1986, fig. 28:f). All these types have also been found in recently excavated and still unpublished LM IA contexts from Kommos.

87. Outside the dump, hooked spirals have thus far been attested on four mendable conical cups from stratified floor deposits: an early LM IA example from Building T (trench 93A, pail 5: C 9431), two early LM IA cups from a pebble floor in the east part of the South Stoa, east of the dump (trench 84C, pails 51, 52: C 9646, C 9647), and one from an advanced LM IA floor deposit in Room 2 of House X (trench 80A, pail 66: C 9696). For illustrations, see Van de Moortel 1997, figs. 7, 8.

88. For the use of the term "teacup," see above, note 77.

In shape and decoration they resemble most closely advanced LM IA tea-cups found elsewhere at Kommos, but they are also comparable to early LM IA examples from the site as well as some MM IIIB/LM IA transitional teacups from Knossos.[89]

Straight-sided cups occur more frequently in the dump than teacups. They come in two size groups. Cups of normal size (**21**) are coated monochrome in and out. About 15 examples are present in the dump, but none in the kiln. These range in body proportions from squat to slender, and do not differ substantially in shape from MM III or early LM IA examples found at Kommos or elsewhere.[90] Most kiln dump examples have been fired to a red color. In addition, 5 cups of considerably larger dimensions (**22**) have been found in the dump. They are unpainted. They resemble in shape and size some extraordinarily large straight-sided cups, decorated with light-on-dark spirals, which were found in a phase III context at

89. The closest comparanda are unpublished teacups (C 9695, C 9724) from a recently excavated advanced LM IA floor deposit in Room 2 of House X at Kommos. Teacups with sharply turning profiles also appear in early LM IA at Kommos (e.g., *Kommos* II, pl. 100: no. 1987), but these have taller proportions than those of the kiln dump and of House X. LM IA teacups from Kommos published by Watrous (*Kommos* III, pl. 2: nos. 9–11) are too fragmentary to reveal much of their body profiles. They are dark-on-light patterned, unlike the kiln dump teacups. Dark-on-light as well as light-on-dark patterned teacup fragments have been published from the House of the Alabaster Threshold at Aghia Triada, dated to the MM IIIB/LM IA transition, but they, too, lack identifiable profiles (D'Agata 1989, pls. XXI:e, XXII:b). Other dark-on-light teacups of LM IA date from Aghia Triada have more rounded profiles than the kiln dump examples from Kommos (La Rosa 1986, figs. 36:e, 92:b). Some transitional MM IIIB/LM IA teacups from Knossos also have sharply turning body profiles (Warren 1991, fig. 10:A, B, D, E; Popham 1984, pl. 141:5, 6). Popham's designation "MM IIIB/LM IA" (i.e., either MM IIIB or LM IA) is here preferred over Warren's "MM IIIB–LM IA" (i.e., MM IIIB *and* LM IA). Other transitional examples (Warren 1991, fig. 10:F–I; Popham 1984, pl. 141:1–4, 7–11) and all mature LM IA teacups from Knossos have softer curves (Popham 1967, pl. 62:h; 1977, pl. 30:e, f; 1984, pl. 143:1, 4;

Catling, Catling, and Smyth 1979, fig. 31: V.226; *PM* II, fig. 349:q). MM III teacups from Kommos and Phaistos are semiglobular, ovoid, or baggy, and are distinct from the teacups from the dump (Van de Moortel 1997, pp. 85, 352, fig. 12; *Kommos* II, fig. 25: no. 494, fig. 60: nos. 1708, 1710, 1715, 1721, pl. 86: nos. 1714, 1719, pl. 100: no. 1984; Levi and Carinci 1988, pp. 191–192, pl. 85:g–l; Pernier 1935, figs. 221:b, 223:a–c, 224:a; Pernier and Banti 1951, fig. 226:a–b). LM IB teacups from the Mesara are larger in size than are LM IA cups, and have tauter shapes with a higher point of maximum diameter than before. For Kommos, see *Kommos* III, fig. 17: nos. 257–260, pl. 6: nos. 261, 262; and unpublished teacups C 7917, C 8046, C 9041, C 9296, C 9297, C 9365, C 9366, C 9375, C 9376, C 9377, C 9381, C 9600, C 9605, C 9606 from House X; for Aghia Triada, see La Rosa 1986, fig. 52:b; for Seli, see Cucuzza 1993, pls. 4a–f, 14b–c; for Chalara, see Levi 1967–1968, figs. 79:a, c, 80:b. LM IB teacups from the Mesara are mostly dark-on-light patterned, and have single instead of multiple patterned zones. Preferred motifs are foliate bands with paired, elongated leaves, friezes of blob-tailed running spirals, and multiple wavy lines (cf. Cucuzza 1993, p. 79; Pernier and Banti 1951, pp. 363, 491–492).

90. For squat MM III cups from Kommos, see, e.g., *Kommos* II, figs. 25: nos. 489, 491, 493; 30: nos. 635, 638. For more slender MM III examples, see, e.g., *Kommos* II, fig. 25: no. 490;

pls. 29: no. 577, 36: no. 639, 84: no. 1661. Published examples from early LM IA contexts at Kommos are too fragmentary to show body proportions (*Kommos* II, fig. 41: nos. 875–878). For squat and slender straight-sided cups from a mixed MM III–LM IA context, see *Kommos* II, fig. 67: nos. 1971–1974, 1976–1979. Comparable examples come from LM IA contexts at Aghia Triada (D'Agata 1989, pls. XXI:a, XXII:a; La Rosa 1986, fig. 99:b). A similar range of profiles is found also among early LM IA straight-sided cups from Knossos (Warren 1991, fig. 9:A–L; Popham 1977, fig. 1:B; 1984, pl. 142). Mature LM IA examples from Knossos are quite squat, however (Popham 1967, pl. 62:a, b; 1984, pl. 143:2; *PM* II, fig. 349:f–h, o, s, x), except for ribbed Vapheio cups, a variety that does not occur in the Kommos kiln dump (Popham 1967, pl. 62:d, e; 1984, pl. 143:5). In LM IB contexts at Kommos, straight-sided cups, now dark-on-light patterned, are extremely rare. An unpublished fragment (C 3535) comes from a LM II context in Room 5 of Building T (from a part of the building formerly called Building J). This cup shape has not been reported from LM IB contexts elsewhere in the Mesara (Pernier and Banti 1951, p. 491; Halbherr, Stefani, and Banti 1977; La Rosa 1985, 1986, 1989; Cucuzza 1993). A fragment of a Knossian example with reed pattern (C 7679) comes from a LM IB–IIIA1 dumped fill under room N4 and court N6.

Phaistos, and in a MM III or early LM IA context at Kommos.[91] This is the first documented appearance of unpainted straight-sided cups, of whatever size, in the western Mesara.

Bell cups (**23, 24**) and medium-coarse side-spouted cups (**25**) belong to a modest class of handled cups. Bell cups are either undecorated or sloppily dark-dipped. They occur somewhat more frequently in the kiln and the dump than do straight-sided cups, and their fresh condition leaves no doubt that they are kiln products. Approximately 11 bell cups are represented in the dump, and another 9 inside the kiln, including a restorable example (C 10522).[92] About half of the cups are unpainted (**23**), and the others have dark-dipped rims fired red or brown (**24**). One cup is known to have been made without handles (**23**); it is likely that there were several more, because few bell cup handles have been identified. Bell cups have strap handles that are distinct from teacup and normal-sized straight-sided cup handles because of their unpainted or dark-dipped surfaces. They are smaller in size than handles of the outsized unpainted straight-sided cups from the dump. Handleless bell cups are unparalleled in other contexts at Kommos. In all other respects the bell cups from the kiln and dump are similar to MM III and LM IA examples found previously at the site and elsewhere.[93] This cup shape does not continue in LM IB at Kommos, and also seems to disappear elsewhere in the Mesara at that time.[94]

Medium-coarse side-spouted cups from the kiln and dump appear for the first time as a homogeneous cup type at Kommos (**25**). With at least 15 examples found in the dump and 8 inside the kiln, they occur about as frequently as bell cups. They are rather large cups with bell-shaped bodies, straight rims, open spouts formed by pulling at the rim, and vertical handles with circular section attached to the interior as well as the exterior of the rim. Spouts are located at ca. 90° clockwise from the handles. Surfaces are

91. Oversized straight-sided cups were found in Room 104 at Phaistos (Levi and Carinci 1988, p. 206, pl. 89:n–o; Levi 1976, pl. 212:t; Pernier 1935, p. 372, fig. 224:d–e; Pernier and Banti 1951, fig. 268). For a MM III or early LM IA example from the hillside at Kommos, see *Kommos* II, p. 187, no. 1982.

92. Fabric sample 95/18.

93. Bell cups are never common at Kommos, and occur exclusively in MM III and LM IA. For MM III examples, see *Kommos* II, p. 39, figs. 5, 60: no. 1723; pls. 29: no. 578, 100: no. 1988. For early LM IA, see Betancourt 1986, fig. 3:9. Similar bell cups have been found in as yet unpublished, later LM IA contexts in House X and Building T. Transitional MM IIIB/LM IA examples from the House of the Alabaster Threshold at Aghia Triada resemble those from Kommos (D'Agata 1989, p. 95,

pl. XXII:i). Bell cups also occur in MM III and LM IA at Knossos. Transitional MM IIIB/LM IA and mature LM IA examples from that site may be undecorated or carry a variety of decorative patterns, and include handleless (Catling, Catling, and Smyth 1979, fig. 35: V.240) as well as handled varieties (Warren 1991, fig. 9:M–O; Popham 1977, pl. 31:a–c; 1984, pl. 141:14–16).

94. No bell cups have been reported from LM IB contexts at Chalara (Levi 1967–1968), Seli (Cucuzza 1993), Aghia Triada (Halbherr, Stefani, and Banti 1977; La Rosa 1985, 1986, 1989), Phaistos (Pernier and Banti 1951), or Kannia (Levi 1959). The single local example from Kommos, dated to LM IB by Watrous (*Kommos* III, p. 113) comes from a mixed LM IA–B fill (*Kommos* III, p. 5, no. 80). There is no compelling reason for dating it to LM IB rather than to LM IA.

roughly finished. Most examples are unpainted, but one or two have dark paint blobs on the interior and the exterior. Several are overfired to a greenish hue. Medium-coarse side-spouted cups are consistent in fabric, shape, quality of manufacture, and surface finish. They resemble in fabric, and to some extent shape, MM IIB and MM III milk jugs from Phaistos and large semiglobular cups from Kommos.[95] However, they are smaller in size and have squatter and generally more open bodies. They also share similarities with a few odd side-spouted cups from phase III Phaistos and from a mixed MM III–LM IA context at Kommos.[96] However, these earlier examples are extremely rare and vary considerably in shape and dimensions, unlike the ones from the kiln and dump.

Bowls   (26–33; Fig. 33)

The kiln pottery includes convex-sided, conical, and flaring bowls or kalathoi. Convex-sided and conical bowls are rare. Since there is no reason to believe that these bowl types would have been especially liable to break during firing, it appears that this bias in shape reflects the preference for types produced in the Kommos kiln, or at least in its last period of use (cf. below, pp. 98–100).

Conspicuously absent from the kiln and the dump are restorable examples of convex-sided bowls in fine fabrics. This suggests that such bowls were not produced in this kiln, or at least not in its last stage of use. A new shape is a rare convex-sided bowl variety with medium-coarse fabric, a wide, everted rim, and a constricted, offset, splaying base. An estimated 7 examples have been assigned to it. They were made in two parts joined at the waist. No convincing parallels for this variety have been found elsewhere at Kommos, nor have they been published from other Cretan sites.[97] One restored example (26) is decorated with hooked retorted spirals similar to those found on type V conical cups (19). Such hooked spirals appear to be unique to Kommos as well (see above, p. 68). Some distinctions can be made between 27 and the other six convex-sided bowls. Whereas those six bowls are comparable in size and decoration, three being dark monochrome coated in and out, and three carrying white-painted, thick retorted

95. For the development of milk jugs at Phaistos until phase III, see Levi and Carinci 1988, pp. 217–220; Levi 1976, pl. 214:a–i. They are closely paralleled at Kommos by some MM IIB and MM III examples identified as "large semiglobular cups" by Betancourt (*Kommos* II, p. 108, no. 596; p. 157, nos. 1245, 1246; and p. 184, no. 1879).

96. For examples from Phaistos, see Levi and Carinci 1988, p. 215, pl. 91:d–f. For a Kommos example, see *Kommos* II, p. 114, no. 681. A second example (C 10082) comes from a MM III or early LM IA context in Room 23 of Building T. Fragments of a milk jug also have been found in a LM IA

deposit at Aghia Triada (La Rosa 1986, fig. 92:h). Even though it is roughly contemporary with the Kommian side-spouted cups, its shape is more closed, resembling that of MM IIB–III milk jugs. A mature LM IA coarse side-spouted cup from Acropolis Deposit F at Knossos is quite different in shape and fabric (Catling, Catling, and Smyth 1979, p. 51, fig. 36: V.253). A LM IB cup from Kannia (Levi 1959, fig. 28:b) resembles the kiln dump examples more closely.

97. A medium-coarse, light-on-dark patterned basin fragment with a wide, everted rim has been found in a MM III context on the Central Hillside at Kommos (*Kommos* II,

pl. 106, fig. 26: no. 547). However, its rim diameter (ca. 0.35–0.40 m) is much larger than that of the largest globular bowl (27) of the kiln dump, and the rim projects on the interior of the body, unlike the rims of the kiln dump bowls 26 and 27. Its lower body is lost. The splaying base profiles of the kiln dump bowls are paralleled on a bridge-spouted jar base from Kommos, dated by Betancourt to MM III (*Kommos* II, p. 177, pl. 87: no. 1736), and by some phase III pitharakia and a four-handled jar from Phaistos (Levi and Carinci 1988, pls. 73:b, c, 74:i), but the examples from the dump have significantly wider diameters.

spirals on the exterior, bowl **27** stands out by its exceptionally large size, its
body decoration of broad white bands, and its barred rim. Since it is lacking its body immediately below the point of maximum diameter, we do
not know whether it had decoration in addition to the bands on its upper
body. Furthermore, **27** is the only example of this type that is certain to
have had handles. Unusual are the circular perforations in the rim of **26**,
and in the upper body of an uninventoried monochrome bowl. Their purpose is uncertain. It is possible that they served for the insertion of thong
handles, but they also may have facilitated the tying of a lid.[98]

Only 5 examples of medium-coarse conical bowls have been found in
the kiln and dump. They form a homogeneous variety with similar body
shapes, sloping rims, and unpainted surfaces. Since these bowls include a
quite fresh example from within the kiln (**28**), they may be considered as
kiln products, in spite of their low numbers. They resemble unpainted
kalathoi (**30**) but surpass them in size, and in addition are furnished with
lugs. Conical bowls or basins of comparable size have been found at other
sites, but none are particularly close comparanda to the kiln dump examples.[99]

With at least 87 examples, kalathoi represent the most abundant shape
in the dump after conical cups and bridge-spouted jars (Table 4). Those
with medium-coarse fabrics outnumber by far the fine examples. An estimated 17 kalathoi have fine fabrics (**29**). They tend to have rather straight
to slightly concave profiles and slender proportions. Their rims are either
rounded, flattened, or sloping. Seven are unpainted, including two found
inside the kiln. Two are monochrome coated, and one has a monochrome
interior and an exterior rim band. The other kalathoi are decorated in and
out with a light-on-dark painted reed pattern (**29**). Dark coats usually
have been fired brown or red, rarely black. Reed patterns do not occur on
any other shape from the kiln or dump, and may have been chosen to
emphasize the steep contours of the fine kalathoi.[100] The leaves are arranged in pairs without centerline, an arrangement that will be the rule
among dark-on-light patterned foliate sprays and bands on LM IA–II

98. The possibility of thong handles
was suggested to me by Rutter. The
practice of tying lids is discussed by
Miriam Tadmor for Chalcolithic and
Early Bronze Age storage and transport vessels from Israel (Tadmor 1992,
p. 149). Bowls from these periods had
single holes, indicating that their lids
were attached on only one side, allowing them to be lifted during eating or
drinking. I thank G. A. London for
bringing this reference to my attention.

99. Cf. a phase II example from
Phaistos (Levi and Carinci 1988,
pl. 13:n), a MM IIIB/LM IA example
from the Minoan Unexplored Mansion
(Popham 1984, pls. 128:i, 145:3), and a
small, fragmentary basin from the

House of the Alabaster Threshold at
Aghia Triada (D'Agata 1989, p. 94,
pl. XXII:d). The latter closely resembles the conical bowls from the dump
in body and rim shape, but it has
handles instead of lugs, and it is light-
on-dark pattern-decorated instead of
being unpainted.

100. Similar reed patterns are
characteristic of the lower bodies
of dark-on-light piriform jugs and
occasionally a dark-on-light kalathos
in LM IB at Kommos, e.g., C 207,
C 2752, C 3321 (*Kommos* III, nos. 43,
265, 325; the last example is identified
by Watrous as a cup, but is rather a
kalathos).

vases from Kommos, and on LM IA and LM IB vases from other Mesara sites.[101] The fine kalathoi from the kiln dump show that this decorative tradition goes back in Kommos at least to the light-on-dark patterned tradition of LM IA.[102]

The large majority of kalathoi from the kiln and dump have medium-coarse fabrics. At least 70 are represented, of which 4 come from within the kiln and 2 are wasters. Like the conical bowls they are highly standardized in shape. Unpainted kalathoi have body profiles and rims similar to those of the fine kalathoi. Decorated examples, however, have splaying bases, waisted lower bodies, markedly flaring upper bodies, and broadly spreading, often overhanging rims.[103] Somewhat more than half of the kalathoi are unpainted (**30**), including two from inside the kiln. Sixteen are coated dark monochrome, as a rule on both surfaces (**31**). The remaining sixteen are pattern-decorated, usually with white-painted motifs on the interior and with either a monochrome or dark-dipped exterior (**32**, **33**); a few are merely dark-dipped or splattered in and out.

The most common white-painted motifs are groups of vertical arcs that either are restricted to the upper body (**33**) or extend over the entire interior surface (**32**). Such arc patterns are not found on any other vessel shape from the kiln or dump. The groups of short arcs follow in the tradition of MM III basins and fruitstands from Kommos and Phaistos.[104] Both the short and the long arc motifs (**32**) curve clockwise, emphasizing the torsional stresses exerted on the body as it was thrown on the counter-clockwise-turning wheel (see below). The orientation of the painted arcs closely resembles that of the diagonal compression ridges found on the lower bodies of kalathoi **31**, **32**, and **33**. Compression ridges occur when

101. Cf. dark-on-light patterned bowl **62**, dating to LM IA (below, p. 96); a LM IA teacup from Phaistos (Levi 1976, p. 375, fig. 584); a LM IA kalathos and globular rhyton from Aghia Triada (La Rosa 1984, fig. 284; 1986, fig. 36:d, f); LM IA closed vases and a teacup from Seli (Cucuzza 1993, pls. 23, 40b); LM IB and LM II teacups, bowls, and jugs from Kommos (*Kommos* III, pp. 5–6, 15, 21, 23, 103, nos. 83, 86, 264, 265, 266, 267, 325, 352, 392, 1780, 1783); a LM IB cup-rhyton and sherds from Phaistos (Pernier and Banti 1951, figs. 174, 229:f–i, 262–263); LM IB amphoroid jars, amphora, table, lid, and teacup from Chalara (Levi 1967–1968, figs. 70:b, 71:d–g, i, 74:a, 77:c, d, 79:a); a LM IB footed pyxis, clay disc, and pithos from Aghia Triada (Halbherr, Stefani, and Banti 1977, figs. 11, 13:b, 93); a LM IB bridge-spouted jar and pithoid jars from Kannia (Levi 1959, fig. 30:a–c); and LM IB teacups from

Seli (Cucuzza 1993, pls. 4, 14). For a discussion of foliate motifs without central stalks in LM IA–B Aghia Triada and Phaistos, see Pernier and Banti 1951, pp. 501–503, 528, fig. 287:3.

102. A similarly decorated kalathos from Kommos, published by Betancourt (*Kommos* II, p. 168, pl. 99: no. 1968), and dated by him to early LM IA, comes from a mixed MM III–LM IA context on the Southern Hilltop. A tall tumbler from Phaistos is decorated with similar reed motifs painted white on a dilute, red-brown ground (Pernier 1935, p. 379, fig. 227:b). It was found out of context.

103. A kalathos with pronounced concave walls and an overhanging rim similar to that of **31** already occurs in phase III at Phaistos (Levi and Carinci 1988, pl. 111:a). A similar example comes from a final LM IA context at Seli (Cucuzza 1993, pls. 7 and 19: XX-2). The rims of kalathoi **32** and

33 of the kiln dump have an even wider overhang. At Knossos, concave-flaring bowls exhibiting similarities to the Mesara examples have been found in the Stratigraphical Museum Extension site (Warren 1991, p. 323, pl. 78:D), dated to the MM IIIB/LM IA transition, as well as in the Magazine of the Lily Vases (*PM* I, fig. 421:8) and in the East–West Stairs deposit, dating to mature LM IA (Warren and Hankey 1989: p. 73; Popham 1977, pp. 194–195, pl. 31:j). The kalathos from the East–West Stairs deposit is perforated (*PM* III, fig. 186:A). The plain kalathos **30** is paralleled in overall shape, but not in rim profile, by an unpainted early LM IA vessel from Kommos (*Kommos* II, fig. 65: no. 1874).

104. For phase III examples from Phaistos, see Levi and Carinci 1988, pp. 22–23; Levi 1976, p. 376, fig. 586:i, pl. 185:d, f, i. Cf. a MM III rim fragment from Kommos illustrated by Betancourt (*Kommos* II, fig. 35: no. 747).

strong stresses are exerted on the clay body as it is being thrown on the wheel.[105] They are found on many vases from the kiln and dump, but are especially pronounced where the body makes a tight curve, such as on the lower bodies of concave-flaring kalathoi, at the shoulders and necks of narrow-necked jugs (**46, 47**), inside the spouts of piriform rhyta (**51**), and inside the hollow stems of fine pedestaled vases (**59**: Fig. 41). Compression ridges are more pronounced on interior than on exterior surfaces. It is possible that curving arc patterns were preferred over other designs for medium-coarse kalathoi because they emphasize the torsion of the body. The fact that out of all the vessel shapes prone to having compression ridges on their interior surfaces, only kalathoi carry interior decoration, may also explain why such patterns do not appear on any other shapes.[106]

BRIDGE-SPOUTED JARS   (34–37; Fig. 34)

With approximately 116 examples, this pouring vessel is after the conical cup the most popular vase shape in the kiln and the dump. Bridge-spouted jars occur somewhat more frequently than do jugs, representing 10% of the estimated number of vases, as opposed to 8% for the jugs (Fig. 39). A preponderance of bridge-spouted jars over jugs also has been noticed by Watrous among LM IA pottery from the Kommos hillside houses.[107]

Most bridge-spouted jars are small and have fine fabrics (**34–36**). An estimated 83 examples have been found, including 16 inside the kiln. Of these, 24 are unpainted (**34**), 39 are dark monochrome coated (**36**), and 20 are decorated with light-on-dark patterned, thick retorted spirals (**35**). With some exceptions, the fine bridge-spouted jars from the kiln and dump resemble in shape MM III and LM IA examples found at Kommos and elsewhere in the Mesara. Their bodies are either ovoid or piriform, having as a rule more slender proportions than in MM III.[108] Squat globular or ovoid jars, as do sometimes occur in MM III, are absent in the kiln and

Figure 41. Pedestal base C 8947 (**59**) with stretch marks on its interior.
T. Dabney

105. Rye 1981, p. 75; Glock 1987, p. 100, fig. 1:3. Cf. Rice 1987, pp. 358–360; Blackman, Stein, and Vandiver 1993, p. 64, fig. 4; Courty and Roux 1995, p. 30, figs. 6:b, 16:a. For further discussion about what causes these compression ridges, see below (p. 106).

106. I thank Rutter for this last suggestion.

107. *Kommos* III, p. 112.

108. For fine MM III bridge-spouted jars from Kommos, see *Kommos* II, figs. 25: no. 498, 30: nos. 644, 645, 38: no. 791, 39: no. 822, 60: nos. 1736, 1742, 64: no. 1854; pls. 27: no. 523, 36: no. 642, 37: no. 643, 73: no. 1392. For early LM IA examples from Kommos, see *Kommos* II, figs. 42: no. 890, 68: nos. 1993, 1996; pls. 52: no. 884, 101: no. 1994, 102: nos. 2001, 2002. Only one rim fragment has been published from a late LM IA context at Kommos (*Kommos* III, p. 2, pl. 18:

no. 14). It is light-on-dark patterned, and its profile is not illustrated. For phase III examples from Phaistos, see Levi and Carinci 1988, pp. 131–134; Levi 1976, pls. 198:a, c, e, 199, 200:a–i, l, 201:a–f, h. For MM III Aghia Triada, see La Rosa 1977, fig. 11:a, b; 1986, fig. 31. For LM IA Seli, see Cucuzza 1993, pls. 6: XXIII-1, 16c, e. Jar XXIII-1 carries polychrome decoration on a black ground. Several dark-on-light patterned examples from the postdestruction fill in the Edificio Ciclopico at Aghia Triada, dated to mature LM IA, have piriform bodies with highly constricted lower bodies and disc bases, unlike the bridge-spouted jars fired in the Kommos kiln (La Rosa 1986, figs. 76:d, 80:a, 92:a). Knossos has yielded many fewer MM III and LM IA bridge-spouted jars than has the Mesara, and they show a number of morphological differences.

Fine examples come from the North-West Lustral Basin (*PM* I, fig. 298:b), Hogarth's House Yard (*PM* I, fig. 298:c), and Acropolis Deposits B and E (Catling, Catling, and Smyth 1979, figs. 19: V.112; 20: V.126). The illustrated fragment from Hogarth's House Yard has a stepped ledge rim unknown in the Mesara, and Catling's second example is much smaller than any of its Mesara counterparts. For transitional MM IIIB/LM IA examples from Knossos, see Warren 1991, fig. 5:F, pl. 77:A–C. One of these (fig. 5:F) has an offset, insloping rim not found among bridge-spouted jars of the Mesara. A LM IA bridge-spouted jar illustrated by Popham (1967, pl. 77:b) is quite different in shape from the jars produced in the Kommos kiln. More comparanda from Seli and Knossos are listed below, notes 192, 195.

dump.[109] It is not certain whether bridge-spouted jars with pedestal bases similar to those reported from phase III Phaistos were produced in the Kommos kiln.[110] As in MM III and early LM IA at Kommos and in phase III at Phaistos, the fine bridge-spouted jars of the kiln and dump either are hole-mouthed or have upturned rims—that is, none has a ledge rim.

There are some differences between the bridge-spouted jars from the dump and those found within the kiln. Most examples from the dump are similar in size to **34** and **35**, and as a rule they have thin grooved strap handles. In contrast, bridge-spouted jars found inside the kiln (**36**) and some from the dump tend to be smaller, and they no longer have thin grooved strap handles but handles with circular section or thickened strap handles. Handles with circular section on fine bridge-spouted jars begin in the MM IIIB/LM IA transitional stage at Knossos, but in the Mesara the practice is not attested before late LM IA; it is common in LM IB.[111] The fact that some of the fine bridge-spouted jars found in the kiln and dump (**34**) are unpainted also may have been a relatively late LM IA phenomenon at Kommos, since it has not been attested earlier. The chronological implications of these differences will be discussed in more detail below (p. 98).

Medium-sized bridge-spouted jars (**37**) have medium-coarse fabrics. Approximately 33 examples have been identified, including a possible one inside the kiln. They closely resemble in shape MM III and early LM IA examples from Kommos as well as phase III jars from Phaistos.[112] They have elongated globular or rather plump ovoid bodies, folded-back ledge rims, and almost vertically rising handles with circular section. Five are unpainted, 18 are dark monochrome coated (**37**), and 9 carry light-on-dark thick retorted spirals. Absent from the kiln and dump, however, are

109. For Kommos, see *Kommos* II, figs. 30: nos. 644, 645, 39: no. 822, 64: no. 1854; pl. 73: no. 1392. For Phaistos, see Levi and Carinci 1988, pl. 57:i–m. For Aghia Triada, see La Rosa 1986, fig. 31. A squat ovoid bridge-spouted jar also was found in a LM IA context at Seli (Cucuzza 1993, pls. 16a, b).

110. Levi and Carinci 1988, pp. 133–134, pl. 58:a–g; Levi 1976, pls. 202, 203; Pernier and Banti 1951, figs. 264:b, 267:b. Five fragmentary pedestal bases perhaps belonging to bridge-spouted jars have been found in the dump, but thus far it has not been possible to connect such bases definitely with a particular shape. These painted base fragments are quite different in shape from the fine unpainted base **59**.

111. In LM IA, round-sectioned handles appear both on fine bridge-spouted jars with light-on-dark decoration and on lustrous dark-on-light patterned examples with ledge rims. The earliest examples come from MM

IIIB/LM IA transitional contexts in Knossos (Warren 1991, fig. 5:F; Popham 1984, pl. 145:1). See note 89 for our use of Popham's designation "MM IIIB/LM IA." An unpainted specimen from the South-West Basement (*PM* II, fig. 403:E) is dated by Warren to MM IIIB or the transitional stage (Warren 1991, p. 334), but may be later in date; see Macdonald 1990, p. 19. For a mature LM IA example from Knossos, see *PM* II, fig. 253:D. Handles with circular section are rare on fine bridge-spouted jars from LM IA contexts in the Mesara. For Kommos, see also **65** (which may not be a Kommos product), and perhaps *Kommos* III, pl. 3: no. 125; for Seli, see Cucuzza 1993, pls. 6: XXI-3, 16d. They are much more common in LM IB in the Mesara, occurring on fine bridge-spouted jars of either decorative scheme (*Kommos* III, fig. 14: no. 124; Halbherr, Stefani, and Banti 1977, figs. 75–78; La Rosa 1986, fig. 46:b; Pernier and Banti 1951, fig. 107:b; Levi 1959, figs. 25:e, g,

h, 30:c; 1967–1968, figs. 64, 72:a–c).

112. For Kommos, see *Kommos* II, figs. 27: no. 599; 40: no. 826; 41: no. 861. For Phaistos, see Levi and Carinci 1988, pp. 115–116, pls. 50:e, f, 52:a, b; Levi 1976, pls. 198:b, d, f, 200:k, m, 201:g, i. Levi and Carinci point out that the near-vertical orientation of the handles of medium-sized and large bridge-spouted jars in phase III represents a change from the more slanted orientation of earlier bridge-spouted jar handles. A dark-on-light patterned example from Kommos is dated by Watrous to LM I (*Kommos* III, pl. 4: no. 203). It has a ledge rim but its profile is not illustrated. Also at Knossos, large MM III and LM IA bridge-spouted jars with coarse fabrics have round-sectioned handles in near-vertical positions. Examples come from Acropolis Deposits B and E (Catling, Catling, and Smyth 1979, figs. 20: V.128; 29: V.208, V.215). Jars V.128 and V.208 have upturned rims unlike their Mesara counterparts.

the small, crudely made bridge-spouted jars produced in medium-coarse fabrics that were common during MM III and early LM IA at Kommos.[113] Their absence will be one of the arguments for dating the kiln pottery later than early LM IA (see below).

JUGS (38–49; Figs. 35–36)

Jugs occur somewhat less frequently in the kiln and dump than do bridge-spouted jars (see above, p. 74). Only collar-necked jugs and ewers are sufficiently numerous to be accepted as part of the kiln output. Juglets and narrow-necked spouted jugs cannot be shown to have been produced in this kiln, even though these are common LM IA varieties. Thus far there is no evidence that beak-spouted narrow-necked jugs with fine fabrics were produced or consumed at Kommos in this period.[114] The dump debris did include a single, almost intact juglet (C 10045) as well as some fragments of two large medium-coarse jugs with narrow necks provided with conical knobs (e.g., C 10594). The juglet is slipped a very pale brown, but is otherwise unpainted and lacks a handle. The two medium-coarse narrow-necked jugs were splattered with dark paint fired bright red and brown. In spite of the freshness of their surfaces, the juglet and narrow-necked jugs are too rare to be accepted as products of this kiln, but the possibility should be kept in mind, especially since part of the kiln dump is likely to have been carried off in Minoan times (see above). Juglets (with handles) are found, along with collar-necked jugs and ewers, in LM IA consumer contexts at Kommos.[115]

COLLAR-NECKED JUGS

An estimated 30 examples from the kiln and dump have fine fabrics and the other 25 collar-necked jugs have medium-coarse fabrics that are quite

113. *Kommos* II, figs. 27: no. 600; 36: no. 752; 63: no. 1842; pls. 32: no. 601; 75: no. 1501; 76: no. 1502; 95: no. 1880; 96: no. 1881.

114. Beak-spouted narrow-necked jugs with fine fabrics are likewise absent from LM IA contexts at Aghia Triada, and only one example has been published from a final LM IA context at Seli (Cucuzza 1993, pl. 21d). However, because of the relative scarcity of published pottery, it is too early to draw firm conclusions regarding the scarcity of this jug variety in the other Mesara sites during the LM IA period. Beaked jugs with fine fabrics occur more frequently in the area, including at Kommos, in LM IB (*Kommos* III, fig. 14: no. 112; Pernier and Banti 1951, figs. 64, 106, 224; Halbherr, Stefani, and Banti 1977, figs. 21, 37, 81, 165, 175; Levi 1967–1968, figs. 73:c, 75; Cucuzza 1993, pl. 21c). From LM IB

Kannia comes a tall beaked jug with medium-coarse fabric, provided with pointed knobs at the neck (Levi 1959, fig. 26:b). Beaked jugs occur in LM IA at Knossos (Catling, Catling, and Smyth 1979, fig. 31: V.223) and elsewhere (cf. Niemeier 1980, pp. 49–50; Catling, Catling, and Smyth 1979, p. 46).

115. For early LM IA jugs, see *Kommos* II, p. 125, nos. 828, 829. To these may be added an unpublished collar-necked jug (C 6684), two ewers (C 6652, C 9419), and a juglet (C 7511) from LM IA contexts in Building T. The earliest well-dated collar-necked jug from Kommos is an unpublished example (C 9641) from an advanced LM IA fill in Room 2 of House X (trench 80A, pail 61). The jug fragments of a LM IA deposit on the Hillside listed by Watrous (*Kommos* III, p. 2, nos. 15–19) are too small to reveal to which jug type they belong.

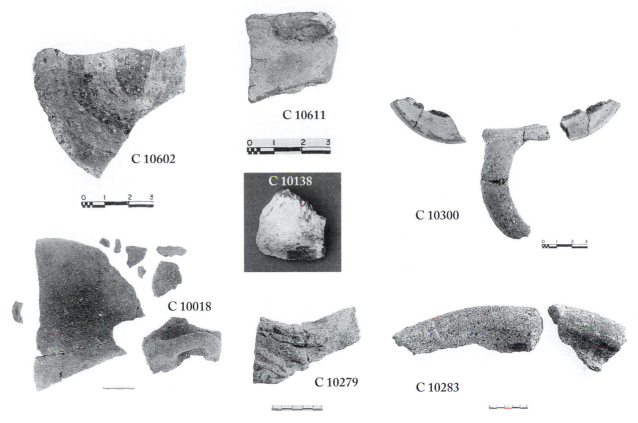

Figure 42. Wasters of collar-necked jugs (C 10602, C 10611), ewer (C 10300), oval-mouthed amphoras (C 10018, C 10138, C 10279), pithos (C 10283). T. Dabney

finely textured (5–7% inclusions). Six fine fragmentary specimens come from the kiln (38). Three or four jug fragments, including one with a fine fabric, are wasters (e.g., Fig. 42). Painted decoration usually is minimal. It is estimated that roughly 15 examples are unpainted (39), 25 are dark monochrome coated (38, 41, 42, 45), 10 carry light-on-dark patterned, thick retorted spirals (40, 43), and 5 are splattered with dark paint.

All collar-necked jugs have a troughed spout at the rim, a thick vertical strap handle opposite the spout, and a pair of small, horizontal ledge lugs placed opposite each other, and spaced roughly equidistant from the handle and the spout. There is a tremendous variety in morphological detail, however. Shoulders may be pronounced (40, 43) or gently sloping (39, 45). Necks may be very short (39, 40, 43, 44, 45) or somewhat taller (38, 41, 42). They either are vertical (41, 44), slightly everted (40, 45), or insloping (38, 39, 42, 43), and may be convex (42). Rims may be straight (38, 39, 45), everted (41, 43, 44), or thickened (40, 42). The largest amount of variation occurs among spouts. Some jugs have small spouts that simply have been pinched out from the rim (38, 40, 42), while others have more substantial ones, modeled separately and attached to the rim in a sloppy manner (44, 45). Sometimes the spout is of a coarser fabric than the body (44).

Collar-necked jugs make their first appearance at Kommos in the advanced stage of LM IA (see above, note 115). It is clear that those produced in the kiln are less standardized than are other common shapes, such as kalathoi, bridge-spouted jars, or oval-mouthed amphoras. They also are far less standardized than LM IB collar-necked jugs from the Mesara and mature LM IA and LM IB examples from northern Crete and elsewhere, which all have tall, straight necks and added spouts.[116] Since the various states of the different attributes of kiln jugs cannot be clustered so as to define distinct varieties of the basic form, but instead crosscut one another, it is unlikely that they result from production by multiple potters. Rather, since this jug type had only recently appeared in Kommos, the lack of morphological standardization seems to reflect an experimental stage in the production history of the collar-necked jug.

Several collar-necked jugs show morphological affinities with MM III and early LM IA pitharakia from Kommos as well as with phase III pitharakia and spouted jars from Phaistos and Kamilari.[117] Jug **40** shares with pitharakia and spouted jars a piriform body of comparable size and abruptly incurving shoulder. A similar shoulder is found on fragment **43**. In addition, jugs **40**, **43**, **44**, and **45** have short, slightly everted necks that may be topped by rolled rims (**40**, **43**, **44**), much like those of pitharakia and tubular-spouted jars. These similarities suggest that collar-necked jugs at Kommos developed out of pitharakia and tubular-spouted jars, vase shapes that do not occur among the kiln output. Pitharakia are actually in marked decline during LM IA at Kommos.[118] Thus, rather than imitating a Knossian shape, as has been suggested by Watrous, the collar-necked jug may represent a purely local development at Kommos.[119]

Some collar-necked jugs produced by the kiln already show characteristics that will be standard on later examples at Kommos and elsewhere.

116. For an unstratified LM I collar-necked jug and a LM IB example from Kommos, see *Kommos* III, p. 104, fig. 65: no. 1801 and p. 15, fig. 17: no. 264, respectively. LM IB examples also have been reported from Aghia Triada (Halbherr, Stefani, and Banti 1977, figs. 73, 74; La Rosa 1986, fig. 51:a; 1989, p. 89, pl. XVIII:d), Chalara (Levi 1967–1968, fig. 73:a, b, d, e), Kannia (Levi 1959, fig. 25:f), and Mallia (Pelon 1966, fig. 23:1). Collar-necked jugs dating to mature LM IA and LM IB have been published from Knossos (*PM* II, figs. 253:B, 349:i; Popham 1967, pls. 76:c, 80:a), Akrotiri (*Thera* II, fig. 27; *Thera* VI, pl. 78:b; Marthari 1990, p. 62, fig. 5:a; Niemeier 1980, figs. 27, 37), Kythera (Coldstream and Huxley 1972, p. 287, pl. 79: E55, E62, F61), and elsewhere (see Niemeier 1980, p. 51; cf. Betancourt 1985, fig. 94:D, pl. 18:G).

117. For examples of MM III pitharakia from Kommos, see *Kommos* II, figs. 29: no. 609, 60: no. 1750, 66: no. 1885, 69: no. 2007; *Kommos* III, p. 12, fig. 16: no. 214. For pitharakia from Phaistos and Kamilari, see Levi and

Carinci 1988, pp. 167–170, pls. 72–73; Levi 1976, pls. 204–206. For a spouted jar that closely resembles **40**, see Levi and Carinci 1988, pl. 46:f; Levi 1976, pl. 197:d, f. A few tubular-spouted jars from Phaistos, dating to phase Ib, bear resemblances to LM IA collar-necked jugs as well; one even has lugs at the rim (Levi and Carinci 1988, pl. 45:f–i).

118. From good MM III contexts at Kommos come 12 pitharakia (*Kommos* II, nos. 472, 496, 497, 609, 647, 648, 724, 792, 1747, 1751, 1752, 1855). In contrast, only one comes from an early LM IA floor (*Kommos* II, no. 885), and one is mentioned from a later LM IA fill (*Kommos* III, p. 112). No pitharakia or spouted jars occur among the unpublished LM IA floor deposits from House X and Building T, except for a nonlocal, handmade example (C 6913) from the west end of Rooms 20/22 in Building T. Tubular-spouted jars are rare at Kommos in all periods. For a MM III example, see *Kommos* II, no. 646. Two unpublished lustrous dark-on-light patterned examples (C 6911, C 8337) come from late LM IA contexts in Building T.

I thank J. B. Rutter for drawing my attention to these as well as to the handmade jar from Building T. Two tubular-spouted jars datable to LM IB have been found in House X (*Kommos* III, pl. 7: no. 300; C 9315).

119. Lacking LM IA collar-necked jugs from Kommos, Watrous (*Kommos* III, p. 114) suggested that the LM IB examples from the Mesara had been inspired by LM I jugs from Knossos, which in turn would have imitated a bronze jug type (cf. Coldstream and Huxley 1972, p. 287, note 2). However, the new evidence from the kiln as well as from House X and Building T at Kommos shows that collar-necked jugs developed at Kommos quite early in LM IA, before they became popular in northern Crete and Thera in the mature stage of LM IA (Niemeier 1980, p. 51; see below, p. 101, note 196). A possible MM IIIB/LM IA transitional example from Knossos would be roughly contemporary with the earliest Kommian examples, but its identification is uncertain because its spout is not preserved (Warren 1991, pp. 322–323, fig. 6:A, pl. 77:E).

These are the relatively tall collar necks of some jugs (**38, 41, 42**) and the well-developed spouts attached to the rims of a few others (**44, 45**). The different fabric texture of one of the attached spouts appears to be experimental, because it is not found on later collar-necked jugs.[120]

EWERS

Remains of 35 different ewers have been identified, including 4 inside the kiln. Among the ewers are 4 wasters (e.g., Fig. 42: C 10300). Bodies are ovoid or piriform in shape, necks are concave-flaring, and rims are sloping. A single handle with circular section rises vertically from the shoulder and encompasses the rim—that is, it is attached to the rim on both its interior and exterior faces (**47, 48**). Encompassing handles also occur on early LM IA ewers. This jug type is extremely rare earlier at Kommos, however, and encompassing handles already occur on several phase IB and phase III ewers at Phaistos, so this style of handle attachment cannot be taken as diagnostic for LM IA ewers throughout the Mesara.[121] An estimated one-half of the ewers from the kiln and dump are solidly coated with dark monochrome paint (**47, 48, 49**), one-fourth are unpainted (**46**), and the rest either carry light-on-dark thick retorted spirals or are dark-dipped.

The ewers from the kiln and dump include medium-sized (**46, 47**) and large (**48, 49**) examples, ranging in height from an estimated 0.20 to 0.40 m. Medium-sized ewers make up about two-thirds of the total. They may be rather squat (**47**) or more elongated in shape (**46**). Ewers of this size also occurred in early LM IA at Kommos, but have not yet been attested earlier at the site.[122] Many Kommian LM IA examples combine two types of fabric: their bodies and handles are medium-coarse, while necks and rims are fine.[123] The practice of combining fine and medium-coarse fabrics has a long tradition in the Mesara, going back to the

120. The spout of **44** may have been of a coarser fabric than the rest of the jug in order to prevent cracking, which could have occurred because of the different moisture contents of the newly made spout and the leather-hard rim and neck to which it was attached (cf. van As and Jacobs 1987, pp. 42, 51). I thank G. A. London for drawing my attention to this point. Possibly for the same reason, the practice of attaching medium-coarse handles to fine vessels had been quite widespread in the Minoan Mesara since at least the Prepalatial period (see note 124 below).

121. The phase Ib ewers from Phaistos are large in size, and the phase III ewers are medium-sized (Levi and Carinci 1988, pl. 37:a–c; Levi 1976, pls. 84:d, 85:c–d, 194:c–e, g). Not all have encompassing round-sectioned handles. Such handles occur occasionally at Knossos from MM III onward (Catling, Catling, and Smyth 1979, fig. 24:

V.155; *PM* I, pl. VII:c; possibly Warren 1991, fig. 5:C) as well as in mature LM IA at Akrotiri (*Thera* III, pl. 50:2) and in LM IB (Betancourt 1985, fig. 101, pl. 21:F, G). Knossian ewers usually have handles that end below the rim, sometimes even halfway up the neck, features not found in the Mesara (Catling, Catling, and Smyth 1979, figs. 16: V.7, 24: V.152, 25: V.152bis; *PM* I, figs. 404:f, 415:B). Such handles also are found in LM IB at Aghia Triada (Halbherr, Stefani, and Banti 1977, figs. 79, 163).

122. For medium-sized early LM IA examples, see *Kommos* II, p. 125, fig. 40: no. 829, and unpublished ewer C 9419 from an early LM IA context in trench 84A, just south of Building T's south facade. I thank J. B. Rutter for bringing the latter example to my attention. A MM III ewer from Kommos is large (*Kommos* II, no. 614).

123. Cf. early LM IA ewer C 9419 (see note 122).

Prepalatial period.[124] Large ewers from the kiln and dump, 5 in all, have rims with considerable overhang. They are medium-coarse in fabric, except for their heavy, square-sectioned neck rings made of a coarse fabric (**49**). Such neck rings are paralleled at Kommos and elsewhere.[125]

Rhyta (50–51; Fig. 36)

This shape is relatively rare in the dump, being represented by about 20 globular specimens (**50**) and 3 piriform ones (**51**). During this preliminary study no complete profile was restored. However, the mended parts are quite large and many are in a fresh condition, so that it seems likely that they are kiln products. It is possible that occasionally conical rhyta also were fired in this kiln.[126] Rhyta shaped like animals, animal heads, cups, or alabastra have not been identified among the kiln or dump debris.[127] All

124. No comprehensive study has yet been done on the combination of different fabric textures in Mesara vases, but various instances of this practice have been noted, such as the presence of coarser handles on fine EM IIA jugs from Aghia Kyriaki (Wilson and Day 1994, p. 36) and of coarser appliqué features on EM and MM pottery from the Mesara (Day and Wilson 1998, p. 355). In the Protopalatial period, fine clay was used for barbotine plastic ornaments on medium-coarse vases (Betancourt 1985, pp. 83–85; cf. Levi and Carinci 1988, pp. 17–20; *PM* IV, pp. 120–130, pl. XXIX), and large medium-coarse bowls covered with a thick, fine buff slip on the interior are fairly common at Kommos. One such bowl has been published by Betancourt (*Kommos* II, no. 177), and many occur in newly excavated, unpublished Protopalatial fills at the site. In the Neopalatial period the handles of fine and medium-coarse closed vases occasionally are coarser than their bodies. This practice has been observed by the present author on two MM III bridge-spouted jars (*Kommos* II, nos. 599, 644) as well as on MM III oval-mouthed amphoras from Kommos; it also has been noted occasionally on LM IA and LM IB vases from Kommos (*Kommos* II, no. 829; unpublished jugs C 9641 and C 9329 from House X as well as jug C 3358 from Building T). A most striking example is the dark-on-light patterned bridge-spouted jar **65** associated with the kiln dump, which has a fine body and a coarse handle. Levi and Carinci mention coarser

handles on small bridge-spouted jars from phase III at Phaistos (Levi and Carinci 1988, pp. 131–134), and Banti reports that a coarser handle texture is common in LM IB at that site (Pernier and Banti 1951, p. 495). Collar-necked jugs in the kiln dump sometimes have spouts made of fabrics coarser than the body (**44**).

125. Large ewers with neck rings are rare in Kommos. For a MM III example, see *Kommos* II, fig. 29: no. 614. An early LM IA example from Building T (C 6652) and a ewer from the terrace north of Building P (C 7053) are unpublished. The latter example also has an interior coil; it was brought to my attention by Rutter. None of the large phase Ib ewers from Phaistos or of the medium-sized phase III ewers from Phaistos and Kamilari has a neck ring (Levi and Carinci 1988, pl. 37:a–e; Levi 1976, pls. 85:d, 194:b–e, g). Neck rings do occur on large ewers from MM III and LM IA deposits at Knossos (Catling, Catling, and Smyth 1979, fig. 24: V.152; *PM* I, figs. 404:f, 415:B, pl. VII:c; Warren 1991, fig. 5:C), in mature LM IA at Akrotiri (*Thera* III, pl. 50: 1–2), and in LM IB at Aghia Triada (Halbherr, Stefani, and Banti 1977, figs. 79, 163).

126. A possible conical rhyton in a fine fabric decorated with the white-painted, thick retorted spirals on a washy red ground typical of the kiln pottery has been found in the fill of an early LM IIIA2 terrace north of Building P. It is likely to have been produced in the kiln. This example was brought to my attention by Rutter.

127. For the development of various

types of Minoan rhyta, see Koehl 1981, fig. 1. Globular, piriform, conical, and alabastron-shaped rhyta have been found in MM III and early LM IA contexts at Kommos (*Kommos* II, figs. 31: nos. 652–655, 32: no. 656, 61: no. 1772, 69: nos. 2011–2015; pls. 88: no. 1765, 89: no. 1779, 103: no. 2012), and globular rhyta occur in later LM IA and LM IB (see below, note 128). Globular, conical, alabastron-shaped, bull's head, and animal rhyta come from phase III contexts at Phaistos (Levi and Carinci 1988, pp. 141–146, fig. 257, pls. 63:b, c, e, f, 64:b, c, g; Pernier 1935, fig. 213; Pernier and Banti 1951, fig. 257). The only LM IA rhyton reported from elsewhere in the Mesara is a globular example from Aghia Triada (La Rosa 1984, fig. 284; 1986, fig. 36:f). A mature LM IA conical rhyton has been found at Seli di Kamilari, but Cucuzza convincingly argues that it was manufactured outside the Mesara, more specifically at Gournia (Cucuzza 1993, pp. 71–72, pls. 11a, 19d). Even though cup-rhyta occur in mature LM IA deposits at Knossos, in Acropolis Deposit F and in the palace (Catling, Catling, and Smith 1979, fig. 31: V.250, V.251; Popham 1977, fig. 1:E, F; *contra* Macdonald 1990, p. 87), the earliest examples reported from the Mesara date to LM IB (Pernier and Banti 1951, figs. 171, 174; Halbherr, Stefani, and Banti 1977, fig. 14). Apart from the globular and cup-rhyta listed above, piriform and conical examples also have been found in LM IB contexts in the Mesara (Pernier and Banti 1951, figs. 103:a, 104, 105; Halbherr, Stefani, and Banti 1977, figs. 19, 190).

piriform rhyta and nearly all globular ones have fine fabrics, two being medium-coarse. Light-on-dark patterned, thick retorted spirals occur on almost all examples (**50, 51**), except on 3 globular ones that are coated dark monochrome.

Some of the globular rhyta (**50**) presumably had narrow mouth openings with ledge rims, whereas others were wide-mouthed with short, everted rims. They resemble in shape MM III and LM IA examples found at the site, sharing their flattish bottom.[128] It is peculiar that the spout opening of the restored globular rhyton from the dump (**50**) was nearly entirely blocked by a small lump of baked clay, which had been fired in place (Fig. 36). It is possible that the plugging was accidental. The fragmentary piriform rhyta from the dump have narrower proportions than their predecessors.[129] No rims have yet been attributed to these.

OVAL-MOUTHED AMPHORAS (52–53; Fig. 37)

A prominent shape in the kiln and dump is the oval-mouthed amphora. An estimated 70 examples are represented, including fragments of 3 or 4 inside the kiln and about 5 that have become wasters (e.g., Fig. 42). As many as one-half of the amphoras may be unpainted. About one-fourth carry large, simple plant motifs on either side of the body, executed in dark colors on a very pale slip (**53**). Another 10 have dark-painted splattered decoration (**52**), and 5 may simply be dark monochrome coated.

These amphoras closely resemble LM IA examples found in House X at Kommos (C 9463, C 9471), and also share similarities with Neopalatial examples from the Mesara, Knossos, and Akrotiri.[130] The plant design of **53** is closely paralleled on amphoras from Aghia Triada, Akrotiri, and the

128. For MM III and early LM IA examples, see *Kommos* II, figs. 32: no. 656; 69: nos. 2014, 2015. A later LM IA globular rhyton (C 9046) was found in House X and is unpublished. Watrous published a fragmentary globular rhyton dating to LM IB, but did not illustrate its profile (*Kommos* III, p. 20, pl. 8: no. 332). The two phase III examples from Phaistos are more baggy in shape (Levi and Carinci 1988, p. 145, pl. 63:b, c).

129. Cf. *Kommos* II, figs. 31: no. 654; 69: no. 2013.

130. MM III examples from Kommos are highly fragmentary (*Kommos* II, fig. 26: no. 756; pls. 44: no. 755, 73: no. 1383, 78: no. 1536). For LM I, only one amphora has been published, by Watrous, coming from a mixed LM I context (*Kommos* III, p. 9, pl. 4: no. 147). A second amphora from the same context is not local (*Kommos* III, p. 9, pl. 3: no. 148). For phase III amphoras from Phaistos, see Levi and Carinci 1988, pl. 21:d–g; Levi 1976, pls. 188:h,

k, 189:a, c, 190:a, c. A dark-banded, possible amphoriskos fragment from Aghia Triada (La Rosa 1986, fig. 76:a) and two polychrome-on-dark patterned fragments from Seli (Cucuzza 1993, pls. 9: XXV-13, 38a: F-12) are dated to LM IA. An amphora with a dark-painted plant motif similar to that of **53** comes from the lowest level of the Complesso della Mazza di Breccia at Aghia Triada, dated to LM I (*AR* 1991, p. 67, fig. 58). A few dark-on-light patterned examples come from LM IB destruction contexts at Aghia Triada (Halbherr, Stefani, and Banti 1977, figs. 27, 166, 167), Chalara (Levi 1967–1968, fig. 74), and Kannia (Levi 1959, fig. 12). Securely dated MM III amphoras from Knossos are comparable in shape to those from the Kommos kiln and dump, but they do not include dark-on-light patterned examples (Catling, Catling, and Smyth 1979, figs. 20: V.58; 25: V.159; 26: V.153, V.158). Amphoras from a transitional MM IIIB/LM IA context at Knossos are either light-on-

dark patterned or ripple-decorated (Warren 1991, pp. 321–322, fig. 5:A, B, pl. 76). Two examples from the Temple Repositories, downdated by Warren to LM IA (Warren and Hankey 1989, pp. 73–74), also are light-on-dark patterned (*PM* I, p. 605, figs. 404:b, 446). In contrast, an amphora from the South-West Basement has a simple dark-painted plant motif similar to that of **53** (*PM* I, fig. 403:A). It has been dated by Warren to MM IIIB or early LM IA (Warren 1991, p. 334), but an amphora with a similar motif comes from a mature LM IA context in Akrotiri (*Thera* I, pl. B8:1). Macdonald recently has downdated the South-West Basement deposit to mature LM IA, correctly in my opinion (Macdonald 1996, p. 19). Also, a mature LM IA amphoriskos from the House of the Frescoes is dark-on-light patterned (*PM* II, fig. 253:A). A trickle-painted example of comparable date has a disc base unknown at Kommos (Catling, Catling, and Smyth 1979, fig. 35: V.232).

South-West Basement at Knossos. The two restored examples show some degree of morphological variation. Even though both have the same maximum diameter, **53** has a taller body with slenderer proportions than **52**, and a smaller base diameter. On the front and the back side its neck has been pulled out more than the neck of **52**. Further study of the kiln amphoras is needed in order to determine whether morphological variations correlate with differences in decoration and perhaps manufacturing techniques, in which case it would be likely that more than one potter was using this kiln to fire amphoras.

BASINS   (54–55; Fig. 37)

This shape is rare in the dump, 10 examples being a generous estimate. Nevertheless, the presence of two fresh-looking fragmentary basins inside the kiln (**54, 55**) suggests that they are kiln products. Moreover, three wasters may represent parts of this vessel type. All basins are unpainted. Even though most of the estimated 10 basins represented in the dump resemble **54**, this variety has few parallels at Kommos or elsewhere in the Mesara, and none at Knossos. Comparanda range in date from early Protopalatial to LM II, and include some examples from a mixed LM I context at Kommos.[131] Basins with horizontal handles and a molded rope band below the rim such as **55** have been found in MM III through LM II contexts at Kommos, and in LM IB contexts elsewhere in the Mesara and Mallia; they also resemble a LM I bucket jar from Knossos.[132] There is a large variation in rim shapes, however, and such basins usually are cylindrical in shape, unlike **55**, which has a conical body.

LARGE CLOSED JARS   (56; Fig. 37)

This shape is also rare in the dump, but the preserved fragments are in extremely fresh condition and thus likely to have been fired in the kiln. Only 5 examples have been identified, 1 being unpainted, 1 brown monochrome coated, and 2 dark-splattered (**56**). Also 3 or 4 waster fragments are of this shape.

This jar type does not have close comparanda in contemporary contexts at Kommos or elsewhere in the Mesara, nor at Knossos. In shape and

131. LM I comparanda are smaller, however, and have dark-painted decoration (*Kommos* III, p. 8, fig. 15: nos. 128–130). For an unpainted LM II example with horizontal handle, see *Kommos* III, fig. 21: no. 417. A few deep basins or vats from Phaistos, dated to phase I, are comparable to **54** in profile and size, but carry elaborate polychrome decoration (Levi and Carinci 1988, pl. 12:a; Levi 1976, pl. 56:b: XXVIIIa).

132. For two miniature basins from the Kamilari tomb, which closely resemble **55**, see Levi 1961–1962, fig. 83:a–d. For a MM III rim fragment from Kommos, see *Kommos* II, fig. 24: no. 466. Other Kommian comparanda come from a mixed MM III–LM IA context (*Kommos* II, fig. 65: no. 1877) and from a mixed LM I context (*Kommos* III, p. 9, fig. 16: nos. 149, 150); all are fragmentary as well. A LM I bucket jar from the South House at Knossos is comparable in details of shape and in its rope moldings, but it is taller and dark-on-light patterned (*PM* II, fig. 213). Evans dated it to LM IA, but Popham prefers to downdate it to LM IB (Popham

1967, p. 341, note 14; 1970, p. 59). His change of date is not followed by everyone (Macdonald 1996, p. 24, note 55). A probable LM IB example from Seli (Cucuzza 1993, pls. 10, 29a: XXXI-3) has an incised net pattern on its interior, as does a LM II basin from Kommos (*Kommos* III, fig. 22: no. 439). For a LM IB basin from Mallia, see Pelon 1966, pp. 572–574, fig. 17. For a bucket jar from Phaistos comparable to the basin from the kiln dump, see Levi 1976, p. 303, fig. 469.

decoration it resembles a number of so-called stamnoid jars found in late phase Ib and phase II contexts at Phaistos, as well as a LM IB jar from Chalara.[133] In spite of the absence of MM III or early LM IA examples, the kiln dump jars may be successors to the Protopalatial "stamnoid" jars. The various marks found on the rim and neck of **56** do not occur on any of the other examples of this shape in the dump and have no known parallels elsewhere at Kommos or in the Mesara.[134] The marks on the rim appear to be rope impressions.

PITHOI   (57–58; Fig. 37)

Fragments of this shape occurred throughout the dump as well as inside the kiln, and include a few wasters (e.g., Fig. 42: C 10283). The fragments from within the kiln probably served as fire supports (**57**; see below, p. 84). In all, the pithos fragments from the dump and kiln do not represent more than 10 examples, and some of these are quite worn. We were able to gather large parts of 2 pithoi, but have not yet mended these, and hence only a few representative fragments are illustrated.

Since no pithoi have yet been mended, little can be said about their body shapes, and only rim shapes and decorative schemes will be reviewed here. Some pithoi have round-sectioned rims, and others have thickened rims with squared sections (**58**). It seems that light-on-dark patterned decoration is associated with pithoi with square-sectioned rims. Two fragments with similar rims from the dump are light-on-dark patterned, two may be dark-coated, and one is unpainted. In contrast, none of the rounded-rim pithoi carry white-painted motifs on a dark ground, but one example carries dark-patterned decoration, and four are unpainted. The fact that light-on-dark patterning is associated with square-rimmed pithoi is significant, because it continues a tradition of Protopalatial and phase III pithoi from Phaistos.[135] The retorted spiral motif of **58** is paralleled on a few of these Phaistian examples.

133. For phase IB and II "stamnoid" jars, see Levi and Carinci 1988, p. 13, pls. 7, 8; Levi 1976, figs. 324, 1077, pls. 52:b, 53:a, c, d, 168:c, 169:a, c–g, 170:a–c, e, g: LXXVa. All are decorated with dark-painted motifs, often with added white, and they usually carry rope moldings as well. For the LM IB example from Chalara, see Levi 1967–1968, fig. 83:b.

134. Groups of vertically incised lines bearing some resemblance to those of **56** have been found on imported and locally made vases from Kea belonging to periods V, VI, and VII, corresponding in date to MM III, LM IA, and LM IB (Bikaki 1984, pls. 4, 18: IV-45, IV-46, 11, VI-14, VI-15, 12, VII-12, VII-15, VII-16, VII-40; Warren and Hankey 1989, pp. 67, 77, 79). No pattern can be detected with regard to the number of strokes, their location on the vessel, or the vase shape on which they occur, however, and the resemblances need not be significant. None of the vases from Kea has rope impressions resembling those found on the rim of **56**.

135. Cf. Levi 1976, pls. 49:b, 50:a–c, 168:a, d, 183:c: XXVIa, LXXIb, and fig. 611, pls. 47, 48:a, c, 49:a, c, 50:d, 51:a, 52:a, 166:a–c, 167:a–d, 183:a, b, d: XXVa; Pernier 1935, pls. XXXVI–XXXIX. No pithoi with thickened, square-sectioned rims have been found in Protopalatial or Neopalatial deposits at Kommos other than in the dump. Too few Protopalatial and Neopalatial examples have been published from Knossos to enable us to establish whether rim shape and decorative scheme correlate. Several square-rimmed pithoi from this site, ranging in date from MM II to LM IA, carry light-on-dark patterned decoration (*PM* II, pl. IX:f; *PM* I, figs. 409, 427:a; Hood 1958, fig. 28), but this decorative scheme is found also on a round-rimmed example, dating to MM III or LM IA (*PM* I, fig. 420). For a discussion of the dates, see Warren and Hankey 1989, pp. 52, 62, 73–74. On the other hand, late LM IA and LM IB pithoi from the Mesara, including those with square rims, are either dark-on-light patterned or unpainted (Cucuzza 1993, pls. 8, 24, 25a, 28, 29b; Halbherr, Stefani, and Banti 1977, pp. 56–57, 140–141, 166, 249, 288, figs. 26, 92; La Rosa 1986, fig. 46l:m; 1989, pl. XVIII:a; Pernier and Banti 1951, pp. 396, 505–506; Levi 1967–1968, figs. 68–69).

Plastic decoration is found among the pithoi from the dump. Rope moldings appear only on unpainted fragments, just below the rim and above the base as well as elsewhere on the body. All rope designs are of the thin, molded variety that is also typical of Protopalatial and MM III pithoi. None is in the form of raised, incised bands such as occur in mature LM IA and LM IB in the Mesara and elsewhere.[136]

The pithos fragments found inside the kiln are few and do not join with any fragments from the dump. Rather than belonging to the kiln load, they may have been used as fire supports bridging the channels (see above, p. 22) or as spacers preventing the pots from touching each other or the kiln during firing.[137]

Fine Pedestaled Vases (59; Figs. 38, 41)

Fragments of 5 fine pedestal bases have been found, mostly east and occasionally north and northwest of the kiln. The bases have wide, hollow stems and splaying, molded feet (59). They show little variation in size. All are unpainted and are made of fine fabrics, fired either yellowish red or pale yellow. The best preserved example (59) has a stem that tapers in thickness near the top. The interior surface of this upper part is rough, most likely because it had been attached to the now missing upper portion of the vessel.

Since only base fragments of this shape have been found in the dump, and these do not closely resemble any known vase shape from Kommos or any other western Mesara site, it is as yet impossible to reconstruct with certainty the upper parts of these vases. It is possible that they are parts of so-called fruitstands. A Kommian example dating to MM III has a similarly molded base, but is larger in size and has a medium-coarse instead of a fine fabric.[138] A poorly preserved LM IB example reportedly has a fine fabric, but its base is lost.[139] Because of their modest sizes and fine fabrics it is more likely that the pedestal bases from the kiln dump carried some sort of large cups. A small, monochrome coated, one-handled cup from Anemospilia, dating to MM III, has a pedestal base resembling those from

136. For MM II and MM III pithoi with rope moldings from Kommos, see *Kommos* II, figs. 20: no. 320, 37: no. 760; pls. 12: no. 236, 45: nos. 761, 762, 67: no. 1258, 76: nos. 1517, 1518, 1523–1526. For Phaistian examples, see Levi and Carinci 1988, pls. 1:a, b, e, 2:b, 3:d, e; Levi 1976, pls. 47:a, b, 48, 52:b, 167:d, 183:b. For Knossos, see *PM* I, figs. 174, 175; *PM* III, fig. 179. Some examples come from the LM IB destruction level at Chalara (Levi 1967–1968, figs. 68:a, b, 69:b). Pithoi decorated with flat, incised rope bands have been found in a late LM IA context at Seli (Cucuzza 1993, pl. 25a) and in LM IB contexts at Aghia Triada (Halbherr, Stefani, and Banti 1977, fig.

92), Phaistos (Pernier and Banti 1951, figs. 43, 46, 47, 151), Chalara (Levi 1967–1968, fig. 68:c, d), Kannia (Levi 1959, fig. 29:b–f), and Mallia (Pelon 1966, figs. 24, 25; 1970, pl. XXII:3). Flat, incised rope bands do not seem to appear in the Mesara before late LM IA. A pithos from Kouses decorated with such bands is dated by Marinatos to MM IIIB (Marinatos 1927, fig. 8). However, a LM IA date as proposed by Lembesi (1976b, p. 38) is more likely because the small vessels found in the same house are said by Marinatos to be almost all of LM I date (Marinatos 1927, p. 61), and an amphora from the house is closely paralleled by an amphora from the

Temple Repositories, downdated by Warren to LM IA (Marinatos 1927, fig. 5:a, b; Warren and Hankey 1989, pp. 73–74).

137. Hampe and Winter (1962, p. 36, pl. 10:6) have recorded the use of bat, pithos, and roof tile fragments as spacers in traditional Cretan kilns. Other pottery fragments could also be used: see pp. 26–27 and note 6 above.

138. *Kommos* II, fig. 58: no. 1586. A MM IIB fruitstand with a simpler base also has a medium-coarse fabric and is larger than the pedestal bases from the kiln dump (*Kommos* II, fig. 51: no. 1262).

139. *Kommos* III, pl. 8: no. 334.

the kiln dump.[140] Also MM III/LM I chalices from Kato Syme have hollow, pedestaled bases; most of the illustrated examples are plain, but one has molded decoration resembling those of the Kommian pedestal bases.[141] However, no remains of cup bowls with roughened lower exterior bodies that could have belonged with these bases have yet been identified in the kiln dump.

COARSE SLABS   (60–61; Figs. 37–38, 43)

Sixty-five fragments, representing at least 18 large slabs, were encountered throughout the dump and inside the kiln.[142] In the dump, 62 fragments were widely distributed throughout the three soil strata, occurring in 37 out of 138 pails, or in more than one out of every four pails.[143] In the kiln channels and firing pit an additional 3 fragments were encountered. Only 3 of those 65 slabs were restorable to some extent (**60, 61**, C 10073; Fig. 43). This is a remarkably poor recovery rate in view of the fact that the slab fragments were easily identifiable among the dump material by their shape, fabric, and surface finish. Perhaps their fragmentary condition is a result of many fragments having been reused. Similar coarse slab fragments, many with curved edges, have been found elsewhere at Kommos, but they have not yet been studied.[144] An unusually large concentration of 10 slab fragments was found in the light brown stratum east of the kiln.[145] It is possible that these had been reused as blocking material for the presumed eastern entrance to the firing chamber (see above, p. 33).

One of the slabs is sufficiently preserved for us to recognize its semicircular shape (**61**). Since other fragments have finished edges we know that they were square or rectangular. The remaining specimens, an estimated 10 or so, have curving edges, and may have been either semicircular or circular in shape (**60**).[146] All are made of a coarse red fabric, which differs from the kiln fabrics described above and resembles that of cooking pots. Their top and sometimes also bottom surfaces are covered with a fine pale buff slip, which was polished to a luster at least on two curved, fragmentary slabs (**60**, C 10073). Fine concentric or spiral striations are visible on the top surface of **60**. Remnants of fine clay adhere to the top of **60**, and to the top and bottom surfaces of C 10073. There is no evidence that these slabs were fired in this kiln.

140. Sakellarakis and Sapouna-Sakellaraki 1991, p. 144, fig. 121.

141. No comprehensive study of the Kato Syme chalices has appeared, but a few have been illustrated in preliminary reports. In particular the base of the chalice shown by Lembesi (1976a, fig. 9) is very close in its overall shape and molded decoration to **59**. For other examples, see Lembesi 1976a, fig. 8; 1979, pl. 224:a; 1990, pl. 134:b; 1991a, fig. 6; 1991b, pl. 173:c, f, g; 1994, pl. 206:c.

142. Most of these have been in-ventoried: **60** (C 8935), C 10011, C 10052, C 10073, C 10136, C 10147, C 10213, C 10214, C 10284, C 10285, C 10303, C 10407, **61** (C 10599).

143. Slab fragments have been found in the following units of the dump: trench 87B, pails 82, 83, 105B, 106, 108, 111, 112A, 112B, 116, 116A, 116B, 116C; trench 90C, pails 86, 94; trench 91B, pail 46; trench 95A, pails 76, 94, 110, 136, 139, 140, 146, 147, 148, 150, 156, 157, 160, 165, 166, 178, 188, 189, 198; trench 95B, pail 175; trench 95C, pail 203; trench

97C, pail 40. In the kiln: trench 95A, pails 100, 111, 114.

144. Blitzer 1995, p. 521.

145. Trench 87B, pails 82, 83.

146. Square or rectangular: C 10136, C 10284, C 10285, C 10303. Semicircular or circular: **60**, C 10011, C 10073, C 10213, C 10214. The remaining inventoried slabs do not have preserved edges, and their original shape cannot be determined. Other examples with straight or curving edges have not been inventoried.

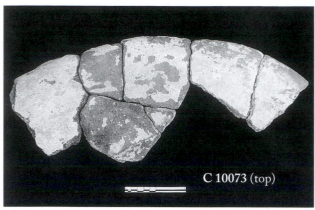
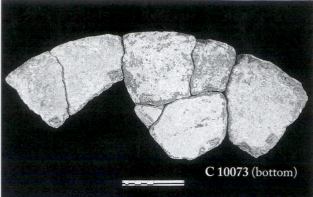

C 10073 (top)

C 10073 (bottom)

The primary function of these slabs is a matter of conjecture, and it may not have been the same for all morphological varieties. It seems unlikely that they served as lids or baking trays.[147] Because of their large size, flat shape, and fine buff slip, it is more likely that they were originally produced as slabs for wedging clay. While wedging of large quantities of clay probably was done by foot on the floor, the slabs may have served for the final wedging of small quantities of clay for the manufacture of small or medium-sized serving vessels or even for the formation of coils or vessel appendages.[148] It seems unlikely that the potter would have gone through all this effort just to prepare a flat, smooth surface for wedging. However, for lack of a better explanation, this is proposed as a possible function for the semicircular slabs.

An alternative interpretation is that they served as bats placed on top of the wooden or clay heads of potters' wheels. Square bats are still used on turntables by some traditional potters on Cyprus.[149] Circular bats have been found in the archaeological record, and also in present-day traditional pottery workshops in Greece, where they are used on turntables as well as on potters' wheels.[150] Since square bats exist there is no reason why semicircular slabs could not have been used for this purpose as well.

C 8935 (60)

Figure 43. Slabs C 10073 (top and bottom views) and C 8935 (60).
T. Dabney

147. Blitzer has suggested for similar slabs found elsewhere at Kommos that they had served as lids for large basins (Blitzer 1995, p. 521). However, no trace of a handle has been found on any example from the dump, not even on **60**, which has its center preserved. Also, the fine buff slip would not have been necessary for lids. Having been made of a coarse red fabric, the slabs might have been used as baking trays. However, the lack of any indication of secondary burning (e.g., blackened or mottled surface) on any of the fragments goes against this interpretation.

148. Traditional methods of wedging large quantities of clay by foot movements on the floor are described in ethnographic studies (Hampe and Winter 1962, pp. 27–28, pl. 1:5; Voyatzoglou 1984, pp. 133–134; Blitzer 1984, p. 148; Blitzer 1990, p. 681, pl. 100:d; Rice 1987, p. 119, fig. 5.2).

149. London 1989a, p. 72, fig. 1; 1989b, pp. 223–224. Square bats are used on square turntables. Elsewhere on Cyprus, traditional potters have round turntables with round bats.

150. The first scholar to relate clay discs from Minoan contexts to the bats used by modern Cretan potters was Xanthoudides (1927). However, his twelve clay and stone discs from Gournia, Tylissos, Knossos, Phaistos, and Aghia Triada have since been reinterpreted by Evely (1988) as wheelheads, because they have central depressions, ridges, grooves, or raised rims. Evely (1988, pp. 89, 97–100) himself identifies only three or four clay discs from Phaistos and Mallia as bats. Being Protopalatial in date, they are older than the slabs from Kommos. Also their fabric is different, being a coarse "pithos" fabric, while the Kommos slabs have a coarse red fabric resembling that of cooking pots. For present-day examples from Greece, see Betancourt 1985, pl. 6:B; Voyatzoglou 1984, p. 135; Fiandra and Pelagatti 1962, pp. 15–16, 18, figs. 1, 3, pls. II:1, V:1; Hampe and Winter 1962, p. 17, figs. 12–14, pls. 4, 5, 43:1–2, and passim.

Figure 44. Modern bat (Diam. ca. 0.65 m) supporting unfired basin *(center)* in workshop at Thrapsano, 1994. A. Van de Moortel

Only a few Minoan clay discs identifiable as bats have been published to date. Minoan bats are circular in shape, and, like the Kommos slabs, they have a smooth, slipped top surface and a rougher bottom surface. Modern examples are fixed to the wheelhead by means of wet clay. Bats provide a smooth and level surface on which the potter can throw his vessel. After a pot is finished, it can be lifted from the wheel, complete with the bat on which it has been shaped, so that no strain needs to be applied to the still wet vessel walls. Bats may be made of clay, wood, or stone. Clay bats are especially appreciated by present-day traditional potters, because their porous clay surface allows the base of the pot standing on it to dry more quickly, and more in step with the rest of the pot, than it would on a stone bat.[151] However, the fine slip of the Kommian bats would have reduced their porosity.

The curved slab fragments from Kommos are 0.025 to 0.030 m thick, and if they belonged to circular slabs they would have been about 0.65 m in diameter. They would have been much larger and thicker than the published Minoan bats, which are only 0.18 to 0.30 m in diameter and 0.019 to 0.023 m in thickness.[152] Bats with diameters of roughly 0.65 m are still used by traditional Cretan potters for the manufacture of large basins, or *lekanes* (Fig. 44), but would not have been needed to make any of the vessel shapes found in the kiln or dump at Kommos.[153] It has been tentatively suggested above that the large slabs from Kommos may have been bats for wheels with short vertical axles, set low to the ground (see above, p. 34). No wheelheads have been found at Kommos, but they may have been carried off after operations ended, or else they may have been made of wood. However, all this is a matter of conjecture until the rounded slab fragments can be further mended to show that they belonged to circular bats.

151. G. A. London (pers. comm.).

152. Evely 1988, p. 89.

153. Most bats shown in ethnographic studies have diameters ranging between 0.30 and 0.40 m (Hampe and Winter 1962, fig. 14; Fiandra and Pelagatti 1962, figs. 1, 3). Such were also the diameters of most bats observed by the author in a traditional workshop at Thrapsano in 1994. A bat used to support a pithos on the wheel, drawn by Hampe and Winter (1962, fig. 13), has a diameter of about 0.50 m. Bats of about 0.65 m in diameter have been observed by the author at Thrapsano supporting *lekanes* that were drying before being fired (Fig. 44).

Dark-on-Light Patterned Vases (62–70; Fig. 38)

Fragments of about 20 vases carrying dark-painted decoration on a lustrous light-colored surface were mixed in with the kiln dump pottery, and one was found inside the rubble mound on which the kiln had been built (**62**). About 15 of these vessels have unusual fabrics and seem to come from other areas of Crete (e.g., **67, 68, 69, 70**). The remainder resemble the kiln products in fabric, but are unlikely to have been fired in this kiln because each one is unique. It is possible that these vases were produced elsewhere at Kommos or in the Mesara, but our present knowledge of central Cretan fabrics is insufficient for determining their origin. Only those examples that shed light on the dating of the kiln material have been catalogued. They will be discussed below, pages 98–102. Fragments with simple linear designs or others that do not have known comparanda have been omitted.

Wasters (Figs. 38, 42)

A large number of wasters, 312 in all, have been recovered from the dump, and an additional 3 come from the kiln channels and the firing pit. Most wasters were quite evenly distributed throughout the strata of the dump, occurring in 56 out of 138, or in more than one out of three, excavation units.[154] However, several clusters numbering up to 37 wasters have been found in the red and dark brown strata, mostly in the vicinity of the firing pit (Figs. 28, 30).[155] Their distribution suggests that wasters are to be associated with the firing pit rather than with the firing chamber.

Most wasters have medium-coarse fabrics, and only 42 have fine fabrics. Identifiable shapes are 2 kalathoi, 3 or 4 collar-necked jugs, 8 ewers, 5 oval-mouthed amphoras, 2 pithoi, and perhaps 2 bridge-spouted jars and 3 basins (Figs. 38: C 10279; 42).[156] Some fragments have only partially turned into wasters, either at one of their edges (e.g., C 10138) or on one side only.

154. The following units from the dump include wasters: trench 87B, pails 80, 81, 82, 83, 93, 96, 104, 105, 105B, 106, 106B, 107A, 112, 112A, 112B, 112D, 114, 115, 116C, 118; trench 91B, pail 46; trench 95A, pails 68, 70, 71, 92, 95, 107, 109, 115, 119, 134, 136, 137, 138, 140, 143, 144, 146, 147, 148, 150, 153, 156, 157, 158, 160, 163, 169, 178, 179, 189, 191, 201, 205, 207; trench 95B, pail 173. Within the kiln: trench 87B, pail 90A; trench 95A, pails 111, 127.

155. Lower dark brown stratum, north of channels: trench 87B, pail 112A [17]; south of firing pit entrance: trench 95A, pail 71 [11]; north of firing pit: trench 95A, pail 148 [28]; on court of Building T, north of firing pit: trench 95A, pails 137 [14], 205 [23]; at west end of dump: trench 95A, pail 163 [6].

Red stratum, over channels: trench 87B, pail 81 [12]; at firing pit entrance: trench 95A, pail 156 [37]; south of firing pit entrance: trench 95A, pail 158 [7]; north of firing pit entrance: trench 95A, pails 138 [23], 140 [12], 144 [8], 150 [10]; on court of Building T, north of firing pit: trench 95A, pail 136 [6]; west part of dump: trench 95A, pail 160 [8].

156. Some have been inventoried: bridge-spouted jars(?) C 10608, C 10609; collar-necked jugs C 10602, C 10611; ewers C 10068, C 10300, C 10610; oval-mouthed amphoras C 10018, C 10069, C 10138, C 10295, and possibly C 10279, C 10607; pithos C 10283. Seven ewers have fine necks and medium-coarse bodies (e.g., Fig. 42: C 10300), but the eighth is medium-coarse throughout.

DATING

Even though the kiln produced light-on-dark patterned pottery, and there is no evidence that it ever fired vases decorated with dark-painted motifs on a lustrous buff ground, there are compelling reasons for dating its life-time to the advanced and final stages of LM IA, as they are now defined at Kommos.

THE THREE STAGES OF LM IA AT KOMMOS

Until recently, the LM IA phase at Kommos was poorly known through a few stratified contexts on the Hillside and Hilltop. In their publications of this material, Betancourt and Watrous divided LM IA into two stages: early LM IA, also called "Transitional MM III/LM IA," and late LM IA.[157] Since 1991, newly excavated stratified remains from Building T and House X have much expanded the number of known LM IA deposits, so that we now can propose the existence of three distinct LM IA stages at Kommos. These have been named early, advanced, and final LM IA, in order to retain the maximum flexibility of terminology and to allow for the elaboration of more stages in the future.[158] The evidence for this new LM IA chronology is largely unpublished, and will be presented by J. B. Rutter and the present author in an upcoming article on Kommian Neo-palatial chronology. In the following paragraphs, a short overview is given of the pottery characteristics of each LM IA stage at Kommos, and their correspondences with the LM IA stages identified at other sites. Subsequently, the advanced to final LM IA dating of the kiln will be argued on the basis of the kiln stratigraphy and of the stylistic correspondences shown by the kiln vases and their associated pottery with the ceramic assemblages

157. *Kommos* II, pp. 41–48; *Kommos* III, p. 1.

158. For a discussion of the new LM IA chronology at Kommos, see also Van de Moortel 1997, pp. 25–28. In choosing names for the three stages at Kommos, we have consciously avoided Warren's terminology for the two LM IA stages at Knossos ("MM IIIB–LM IA transition" and "mature LM IA"), and this for several reasons. First of all, we have distinguished at Kommos three as opposed to two stages, and it appears that two of our stages correspond to parts of Warren's MM IIIB–LM IA transition (see below, Table 9). The synchronisms between the Kommian and Knossian subdivisions need to be worked out further. Second, Warren's designation "MM IIIB–LM IA transition" strikes us as unnecessarily cumbersome and as too much tied up with the notion of a mixed dark-ground and lustrous dark-

on-light assemblage. Following the logic of Warren's terminology, we would need to name all three LM IA stages at Kommos "MM IIIB–LM IA transition," since all have substantial numbers of dark-ground vases in addition to lustrous dark-on-light ones. Third, while Warren (Warren and Hankey 1989, p. 61) was unable to differentiate between dark-ground pottery of MM IIIB and MM IIIB–LM IA transitional deposits, distinctions between MM III and LM IA dark-ground vases can be made at Kommos (see below), and thus there is for us no compelling rationale for retaining a hyphenated designation. In the light of these considerations, we have opted for a simpler terminology.

To the early LM IA stage at Kommos, as presently defined, are assigned some floor deposits from the Hilltop (SHT 23, SHT 24, and SHT 28: *Kommos* II, pp. 50, 124–129) as well

as from Building T. In addition, it is possible that a few floor deposits from the Central Hillside published by Wright (1996) were closed in early LM IA, but these need more study. In Room 42 of Building T, an early LM IA floor deposit was stratified below an advanced LM IA floor. To advanced LM IA can be dated one floor deposit from House X and some from Building T. In Rooms 20 and 22 of Building T, advanced LM IA fills were stratified below final LM IA floors. To the final stage are assigned a few floor deposits from Building T. The LM IA fill published by Watrous may also belong, at least in part, to this final stage (*Kommos* III, pp. 1–2). The LM IA material from House X and Building T as well as stray finds in the later Building P are as yet unpublished. I thank J. B. Rutter for allowing me to refer to these.

of the newly established LM IA stages. The mid to late LM IA dating of the kiln assemblage is supported also by specific ceramic links with "transitional" as well as "mature" LM IA pottery from other central Cretan sites and Akrotiri.

The criteria for the new early LM IA stage defined at Kommos are based solely on evidence from floor deposits, and they correspond to some degree to those outlined by Betancourt.[159] Thus we share with Betancourt the view that the earliest LM IA stage at Kommos is most appropriately marked by the first occurrence of lustrous dark-on-light patterned vases carrying motifs other than tortoise-shell ripple. These vases have unusual fabrics and appear to be nonlocal.[160] The locally made early LM IA pottery, as identified by its relatively soft, pale fabrics, continues the MM III tradition of light-on-dark patterning, but with some changes. Betancourt noted that, in contrast with earlier practice, the dark coating of early LM IA vases often has a dilute appearance and frequently has been fired red rather than the black or dark brown that was common in MM III. He also pointed out that conical cups with flattened rims (type B) are smaller than in MM III.[161] To Betancourt's criteria we add the disappearance of plain ledge-rimmed conical cups (type A) in early LM IA, the appearance of monochrome convex-sided conical cups (types P and Q), and the marked increase in popularity of type V and W cups decorated with retorted spirals.[162] Hooked retorted spirals appear for the first time and may represent a typical LM IA Kommian feature.[163] In addition, there is a distinct trend

159. *Kommos* II, pp. 42–46. Even though his criteria were based in part on pottery from mixed contexts (e.g., nos. 1973, 1974, 1976, 1984, 2022, 2023, 2025–2034), some were retained in the light of the new evidence. Two criteria—new variants of straight-sided cups, and the increased occurrence of bell cups—are not supported by the latest finds. Also, the changes in conical cups proved to be somewhat different from those Betancourt proposed (see below, note 161). The date of light-on-dark patterned "lyrical floral" motifs is still under investigation.

160. *Kommos* II, nos. 847, 848 from Southern Hilltop Room 24 and unpublished stirrup jar C 6654 from Building T (Van de Moortel 1997, fig. 81). The askoi are decorated with a crude crosshatching (no. 847) and running spirals (no. 848). Stirrup jar C 6654 has light-on-dark dot rosettes on the shoulder and a dark-on-light frieze of lunettes and solids on the shoulder, as well as a zone with a thick wavy band at the level of the body's maximum diameter. It may be dated early in LM IA. Elsewhere on Crete

the appearance of lustrous dark-on-light painted pottery with motifs other than tortoise-shell ripple also has been taken to mark the beginning of LM IA (Warren and Hankey 1989, p. 61).

161. For early LM IA examples, see *Kommos* II, nos. 836, 839, 840. These come from a floor deposit in Southern Hilltop Room 24, and were associated with the lustrous dark-on-light patterned imported vases cited in the previous note. In Building T, 6 small type B cups (C 6650, C 6651, C 6653, C 6656, C 6661, C 6680) have been found together with the lustrous dark-on-light patterned stirrup jar (C 6654) described in the previous note (Van de Moortel 1997, p. 51, fig. 7). Whereas Betancourt believed that straight-walled conical cups with flattened rims did not appear before LM IA, we now have several such examples from a good MM III context north of House X (Van de Moortel 1997, p. 40, fig. 6). The MM III examples are larger than their early LM IA successors, however.

162. Monochrome conical cups from good early LM IA contexts are

C 6648, C 9432, C 9434, and C 9648 from Building T. Cup no. 1899 illustrated by Betancourt (*Kommos* II, pl. 97) is not monochrome coated but carries remnants of white paint splashes on the interior, paralleling **17** from the kiln dump. Its context is mixed MM III–LM IA in date. For spiral-decorated conical cups from good MM III contexts, see *Kommos* II, nos. 564, 1617, 1619 (cf. Wright 1996). For examples from contexts datable to early LM IA according to the present criteria, see *Kommos* II, nos. 879, 1616, and unpublished C 9431, C 9646, and C 9647 from Building T. Many more have not been catalogued. Two cups dated by Betancourt to MM III and six dated to early LM IA in fact come from mixed MM III–LM IA contexts (*Kommos* II, nos. 1615, 1618, 1907, 1908, 1909, 1910, 1911, 1912). Of these, nos. 1907, 1908, and 1910 have the dilute dark coating characteristic of LM IA vases.

163. Hooked spirals are found on early LM IA cup C 9431 from Building T. For an illustration of such spirals, see **19**.

toward simplicity in the dark-ground decorative repertoire. Monochrome coated vases are much more frequent in early LM IA than before. Polychromy has become rare, and the range of light-on-dark motifs is much smaller, being largely restricted to thick retorted spirals. Auxiliary bands are fewer.[164]

The trends noticed in early LM IA continue in the second, or advanced, stage of LM IA, along with some changes. The most dramatic shifts are the disappearance of conical cups with flattened rims and the enormous popularity of type C cups with convex sides and straight or rolled-in rims (Fig. 32: 5–7; see above, pp. 66–67). These type C cups are smaller and thinner-walled than MM III and early LM IA type C cups and are produced in finer fabrics. The other unpainted conical cup types in this stage (D, E, F) likewise are thinner-walled and have finer fabrics than before. Straight-sided cups decline in popularity, being now only as frequent as teacups. There also are changes among the pouring vessels. New in advanced LM IA is the collar-necked jug, while the small, medium-coarse, and crudely fashioned bridge-spouted jar that was common at the site in MM III and early LM IA now disappears.[165] Light-on-dark patterned decoration is even simpler than in early LM IA. Polychromy is now entirely absent, and dark monochrome coating is even more prevalent than before, occurring on all straight-sided cups and on most teacups. White-painted designs are restricted to thick retorted spirals on all vases except on kalathoi, which often carry reed or arc patterns. Dilute dark paints, often fired to red hues, are found even more frequently than before. For the first time, lustrous dark-on-light painted designs appear on vases that have soft, pale fabrics resembling those of the kiln pottery.[166] The range of dark-painted motifs is small, consisting mostly of tortoise-shell ripple, running and retorted spirals, single horizontal wavy bands, and plant designs. Motifs are often arranged in multiple registers, but plant designs may be free-floating over the entire vessel surface. The new ornamental scheme replaces dark-ground schemes on fine bowls, and is popular on teacups as well. Other shapes continue to be decorated in the light-on-dark tradition. The well-executed, intricate dark-on-light patterns polished to a soft luster represent an increased labor investment in comparison to the simplified light-on-dark motifs.

In the final stage of LM IA, as shown by the stratified deposits, lustrous dark-on-light painted pottery has greatly increased in popularity, now being found also on bridge-spouted as well as tubular-spouted jars, jugs, and rhyta. Multiple-register arrangements are still common. The range of motifs has been expanded to include multiple horizontal wavy lines and running spirals with stems ending in blobs or with foliate stems. Unlike before, tortoise-shell ripple is rare. Dark-ground decoration now is limited to conical and straight-sided cups, and to a shrinking number of closed vases. A small but persistent change can be observed in the shape of type C conical cups. Convex-sided examples with rolled-in rims continue from advanced LM IA, but alongside these are many type C cups with straight-flaring walls and straight rims, much resembling type C cups of LM IB. In fact, these straight-flaring cups differ from LM IB type C cups only by their thicker walls and somewhat coarser fabrics. Straight-sided cups have

164. In all these respects, early LM IA pottery from Kommos is distinguishable from MM III pottery at the site and elsewhere. For general descriptions of MM III pottery characteristics, see Walberg 1983, 1987, 1992; for Kommos, see *Kommos* II; for Phaistos, see Pernier and Banti 1951, Fiandra 1973, Levi 1976, Levi and Carinci 1988. In my opinion, the bulk of phase III pottery at Phaistos is datable to MM III, even though a few pottery groups assigned to phase III might be stylistically later: see Van de Moortel 1997, pp. 386–400. It is difficult to draw more firm conclusions, however, until this material has been fully published.

165. For collar-necked jugs from House X and Building T, see above, note 115. For examples of small, crude bridge-spouted jars, see above, note 113.

166. It is possible that these vases were produced at Kommos or elsewhere in the western Mesara, but no provenance studies have yet been initiated in an attempt to demonstrate this.

almost disappeared in final LM IA, while teacups, now dark-on-light patterned as a rule, have much increased in frequency. Medium-coarse side-spouted cups and amphoras with stylized dark-on-light patterned plant designs make their first appearance in final LM IA, but stratified examples are rare.

There is some evidence for determining the relative length of the LM IA stages, as well as their degree of proximity to earlier and later pottery phases at Kommos. Frequent admixtures of MM III pottery in early LM IA deposits indicate that these were formed in the beginning of LM IA. Conversely, the mixing of final LM IA and LM IB pottery in several otherwise homogeneous deposits is suggestive of the close proximity of final LM IA to LM IB. The chronological position of the advanced stage of LM IA is less certain, however. Some abrupt changes, such as the total disappearance of the previously popular conical cup with flattened rim, or the sudden rarity of MM III material, suggest that it is somewhat removed in time from the early LM IA stage. On the other hand, shifts between advanced and final LM IA are gradual rather than abrupt, suggesting that the two stages are close in time. Taking as a guide the number of architectural phases at Kommos that can be assigned to each LM IA stage, one may suggest that the final stage, which includes two architectural phases in Building T, was about as long as the two earlier stages combined, each of which is represented by only one architectural phase.

The relative lengths of the Kommian stages proposed on the basis of stratigraphy are supported by their correspondences with the two LM IA stages defined by Warren for Knossos and many other sites on Crete and in the southern Aegean, and identified also at Akrotiri.[167] There is strong evidence linking both the early and the advanced LM IA stages at Kommos with Warren's MM IIIB/LM IA transitional stage. First of all, the impoverished range of polychrome and light-on-dark painted motifs in early LM IA at Kommos is comparable to that of Warren's transitional stage.[168] But more important, in both the early and the advanced LM IA stage at Kommos the most frequent motif among lustrous dark-on-light patterned vases is tortoise-shell ripple, a pattern that also is predominant in Warren's MM IIIB/LM IA transition.[169] All of the lustrous dark-on-light painted vases in early LM IA, and at least some of those in advanced LM IA, are thought to come from outside the western Mesara, thus reinforcing the link of the two Kommian stages to transitional MM IIIB/LM IA elsewhere (see above, pp. 90–91). Knossian dark-on-light painted vases exhibit a much larger variety of motifs than those of the advanced LM IA stage at Kommos, and they occur on shapes other than just bowls and teacups, but this may merely reflect the fact that lustrous dark-on-light patterning developed earlier at Knossos than it did at Kommos.

The final stage of LM IA at Kommos in many ways corresponds to Warren's mature stage as identified at Knossos and elsewhere.[170] In both stages, dark-ground decoration and tortoise-shell ripple patterns have become rare, and the range of lustrous dark-on-light motifs has been further expanded, running and retorted spirals being among the most popular motifs.[171] The straight-sided cup has almost disappeared in favor of the teacup,[172] and the collar-necked jug is a prominent variety among jugs.

167. Warren and Hankey 1989, pp. 61–65, 72–75; Warren 1991; Marthari 1990. LM IA material from Phaistos and Aghia Triada is relatively scarce and for the most part poorly published (Carinci 1989; D'Agata 1989; La Rosa 1977, 1984, 1985, 1986, 1989). For a discussion of its chronological problems, see Van de Moortel 1997, pp. 280–292, 386–400. For specific correspondences between the kiln pottery and pottery groups from Aghia Triada, see p. 100 below.

168. Cf. Popham 1984, pp. 155–156, pls. 128, 129, 141, 142, 144, 145; Warren 1991, pp. 321–332, figs. 5–10, pls. 76–80. For our use of Popham's designation "MM IIIB/LM IA," see note 89 above.

169. Warren 1991, pp. 331–332.

170. Warren and Hankey 1989, pp. 72–74; Popham 1977, pp. 194–195, pls. 30–31; 1984, pp. 156–157. The ca. 70 conical cups found in a stone-lined pit in Vano 50 at Phaistos have straight-flaring walls and straight rims as do the final LM IA type C conical cups from Kommos (Levi 1976, pp. 405–408, fig. 630, pl. 217:z–f′). However, similar wall and rim profiles continue among LM IB conical cups from Kommos. Until the Phaistian deposit is fully published, it is hazardous to assign it a firm date.

171. Cf. Popham 1984, pl. 143:9; *PM* II, figs. 253:E, 254; Catling, Catling, and Smyth 1979, fig. 31: V.225.

172. Popham 1984, p. 156.

TABLE 9. PROPOSED SYNCHRONIZATION OF LM IA STAGES AT KOMMOS, KNOSSOS, AND PALAIKASTRO

Kommos	Knossos (Warren 1991)	Palaikastro (Bernini 1995)
Early LM IA	MM IIIB/LM IA transition	MM IIIB
Advanced LM IA	MM IIIB/LM IA transition	LM IA?
Advanced LM IA	Interval of unknown duration	
Final LM IA	Mature LM IA	LM IA

The presence of a mature LM IA Knossian straight-sided cup with dark-on-light reed pattern in a final LM IA context at Kommos further supports the contemporaneity of the two stages.[173] In view of the chronological proximity of the advanced and final stages at Kommos, it is likely that advanced LM IA at Kommos would have overlapped at least in part with the interval between transitional MM IIIB/LM IA and mature LM IA at Knossos conjectured by Warren. The proposed synchronisms between the LM IA stages of Kommos and Knossos are summarized in Table 9.

It is more difficult to synchronize the Kommian LM IA subphases with the MM IIIB/LM IA phasing for Palaikastro proposed by Bernini.[174] Rejecting Warren's MM IIIB/LM IA transitional phase, this author instead assigns to MM IIIB pottery groups that contain both dark-ground and lustrous dark-on-light patterned pottery. Without accepting her phase terminology, it is possible, in spite of major stylistic differences, for us to draw rough parallels between Bernini's ceramic phases and those distinguished at Kommos.[175] Overall, it seems that Bernini's two MM IIIB deposits from Palaikastro correspond best to early LM IA deposits at Kommos. Assemblages at both sites include a mixture of light-on-dark and dark-on-light patterned pottery. Lunettes-and-solids as well as tortoise-shell ripple motifs occur at both sites, and the range of light-on-dark patterned motifs is limited, consisting mainly of spiral friezes.[176] In addition, two East Cretan vases datable to Bernini's MM IIIB phase have been found in early LM IA contexts at Kommos.[177] Dark-on-light patterned vases, however, make up 50% of the assemblage at Palaikastro, being much more noticeable than in the earliest LM IA stage at Kommos.

173. Cup C 6501 from the west end of Rooms 20/22 in Building T (trench 52A, pail 43, and trench 56A1, pail 92).

174. Bernini 1995.

175. Bernini does not give any stratigraphical evidence and little stylistic reason for assigning these deposits to MM IIIB rather than to an early stage of LM IA. She merely states that her MM IIIB deposits are stylistically closer to the Protopalatial light-on-dark tradition than are her

LM IA deposits (Bernini 1995, p. 59). This is not a sufficient reason for abandoning Warren and Betancourt's excellent and unambiguous boundary marker for the beginning of LM IA, namely the appearance of lustrous dark-on-light painted schemes other than tortoise-shell ripple. I do agree with Bernini, however, that Warren's term "MM IIIB–LM IA transition" is cumbersome and potentially misleading (see above, note 158). Since it is in fact an early stage of LM IA, it would be

better to call it simply "early LM IA."

176. A stirrup jar (C 6654) decorated with lunettes-and-solids has been found in an early LM IA context in Building T (see note 160).

177. These are fine jug C 6632 with a dark-on-light frieze of lunettes and a light-on-dark frieze with a curvilinear pattern, possibly a spiral, from Room 19 of Building T, and medium-coarse jar C 10758 with a dark-on-light ripple pattern, from Space 16 in Building T.

Bernini's so-called LM IA pottery assemblage, on the other hand, agrees best with that of the final LM IA stage at Kommos and "mature" LM IA at Knossos. Dark-on-light patterning is now dominant at all three sites, and the widespread popularity of blob-centered spirals and foliate bands with central stalks at Palaikastro is paralleled at Knossos only in the "mature" stage, which corresponds to final LM IA at Kommos. Collar-necked jugs are prominent in this stage at the three sites.[178] However, a few characteristics of Bernini's LM IA deposits are still reminiscent of advanced LM IA at Kommos and Warren's MM IIIB/LM IA transitional stage at Knossos, either indicating regional differences or suggesting that Bernini's LM IA deposits fit early in final LM IA at Kommos. In both the LM IA phase at Palaikastro and advanced LM IA at Kommos, straight-sided cups are still important in number, but they have lost their painted ornament, being dark monochrome coated or unpainted instead. Tortoise-shell ripple still is a popular motif in both these stages as well, as it is in the transitional MM IIIB/LM IA stage at Knossos. In the final LM IA stage at Kommos and mature LM IA at Knossos, straight-sided cups are much in decline, and tortoise-shell ripple decoration has almost disappeared. A tentative synchronization of Bernini's Palaikastro phases with the LM IA stages of Kommos and Knossos also is presented in Table 9.

CHRONOLOGY OF THE KILN

Dates for the construction and operation of the kiln are based on stylistic as well as stratigraphical evidence. Both the kiln output and its associated lustrous dark-on-light patterned pottery closely correspond in shape and decoration with stratified advanced and final LM IA remains excavated in Building T and House X. What is more, many vases from those stratified contexts, being identical to kiln pottery in fabric, surface finish, and other technical details, must be kiln products themselves. Thus there is no doubt about the contemporaneity of the kiln dump and those stratified advanced and final LM IA pottery groups. The pottery from Building T and House X is currently being prepared for publication by J. B. Rutter.

The stratigraphical sequence to which the kiln dump itself belongs places its date in LM IA, and rules out an earlier dating. A *terminus ante quem* for the kiln's abandonment is provided by the large LM IIIA2/B fill covering the kiln and dump (Fig. 8; see above, pp. 9, 28). A *terminus post quem* for its construction is given by the pottery associated with the debris of the ruined South Stoa of Building T, which was stratified below the kiln dump (Fig. 8; see above, pp. 8, 31).[179] This pottery will be published shortly as well. It can be readily distinguished from the dump material by its much poorer state of preservation and by the absence of wasters and coarse red slabs. Apart from some Protopalatial sherds, this stoa pottery contains mendable vases and fragments of MM III and early LM IA date. It includes a few dark-on-light patterned sherds with lustrous surfaces that postdate the MM III phase.[180] Their decorative patterns (tortoise-shell ripple, spirals) would be at home in the early part of LM IA. A post–MM III dating is likewise suggested by the presence of conical cups of types P and Q, as well as by the absence of polychrome-decorated vases and the

178. Two East Cretan vases have been found in final LM IA contexts at Kommos: a jug (C 7621) with dark-on-light floral scrolls from the west end of Rooms 20/22, and dark-on-light patterned oval-mouthed amphora C 11077 with illegible decoration from the sottoscala area (Space 5B) of Building T (from the part formerly known as Building J: trench 36A, pails 21, 22, 24, 26, and part of 18).

179. Since excavations usually stopped when pre-kiln levels were reached, little stoa debris has been recovered from below the dump. Most of the studied stoa pottery comes from the areas east and west of the dump. Below the dump: trench 95A, pails 199, 200 (Fig. 8: section D–D). In all, 76 sherds weighing 2 kg. East of the dump: trench 84A/B, pail 49; trench 84C, pails 51, 52. Total of 499 sherds, weighing 4 kg. West of the dump: trench 95C, pails 84, 171, 177, 183, most of 186, 190, 192, 209, 210, 211, 212, 213, 214, 215. Total of 1,201 sherds, weighing 8.8 kg. In trench 95C, pail 186 also contained a few LM IB and later fragments. Some stoa debris was mixed in with the lower pails of kiln dump pottery over its entire area: trench 87B, pails 112, 115, 116, 116B, 116C, 116D, 116E, 117, 118, 118A, 120; trench 95A, pails 178, 182, 184, 201, 203, 206; trench 95C, pail 168.

180. These dark-on-light fragments were found in trench 95C, pails 177, 183, 192, 211, and 215.

very limited repertoire of white-painted motifs, which consists of retorted spirals and a single reed pattern (on a kalathos). Specifically diagnostic of the early LM IA phase at Kommos are the presence of small local conical cups with flattened rims (type B), as well as the fact that all dark-on-light patterned fragments with lustrous surfaces are of unusual, and presumably nonlocal, fabrics.[181] All this stoa pottery and destruction debris was found thoroughly mixed and is thought to have been deposited as a single mass in early LM IA, when the stoa was reduced to ruins.

A sounding (3.20 × 1.00 m to 1.50 × 1.50 m) done below the stoa debris just west of the kiln dump has revealed that at this location it was stratified on top of MM III and MM IIB strata. This sounding uncovered a shallow MM III foundation trench, roughly a meter wide and running adjacent to and below Building T's south wall. This foundation trench has been exposed over a length of 3.20 m. It had been dug into a MM IIB pebble floor belonging to the stoa of Building AA, Building T's predecessor, and was subsequently filled with soil containing Protopalatial and MM III pottery fragments. Below the trench a deep MM IIB stratum was uncovered, which extended north below the remains of Building AA's pebble floor. Thus at this location the stoa debris formed part of a tight stratigraphical sequence. Directly on top of this stoa debris was some kiln dump material mixed with stoa pottery. More important, the discovery elsewhere of pure kiln dump pottery stratified over stoa debris brings the kiln pottery in a direct stratigraphical relationship to the MM IIB–MM III–early LM IA sequence found in this sounding.[182]

A *terminus ad quem* for the construction of the kiln is given by the latest pottery from the mound on which the kiln had been built (see above, pp. 8, 31). Very little has been excavated of this kiln mound, and its material is poorly known.[183] For the most part its pottery resembles that of the stoa, and it is possible that stoa debris was used to construct the mound. However, the presence of a dark-on-light patterned, in-and-out bowl with a lustrous surface and a soft, pale fabric (**62**), found in a small sounding next to and below the level of the kiln wall on the east side, shows that the construction of the kiln mound postdates the earliest stage of LM IA and must have taken place in the advanced stage. For it has been pointed out above (p. 91) that the combination of such soft, pale fabric—which presumably is local—and a dark-on-light decorative scheme with a lustrous ground does not occur before the advanced stage of LM IA at Kommos. Also, the ledge rim of **62** is paralleled on an advanced LM IA bowl from House X (C 9675), and several of its motifs (fine tortoise-shell ripple,

181. Van de Moortel 1997, pp. 238–239.

182. The unit of mixed kiln dump material and stoa pottery at this location was excavated with pail 168 of trench 95C. The underlying pure stoa debris was excavated with pails 171, 177, and 183 of trench 95C. Pail 183 included a dark-on-light patterned fragment with lustrous surface and

nonlocal fabric, datable to LM IA (see above). The MM III foundation trench found below it was found with pails 1, 2, 3, and 4 of trench 97A, and the underlying MM IIB strata with trench 97A, pails 6, 7, 8, 9, 10, and 14. This sounding will be included in the forthcoming publication of the Kommian civic buildings. Its stratigraphy has only recently been studied and is incorrectly

shown in Fig. 8.

183. The kiln mound has been sampled in a sounding east of the kiln (trench 87B, pails 91, 119, 120), as well as in a narrow strip just north of the firing pit (trench 95A, pail 185). In total, 202 sherds were excavated, weighing 1.9 kg.

running spirals) are typical for the advanced stage.[184] Its foliate band with stubby leaves thus far has not been attested before final LM IA. However, since the earliest pottery from the kiln dump is datable to the advanced LM IA stage, the kiln could not have been built after this stage. The foliate band of bowl **62** might be indicative of a date late in advanced LM IA.[185]

The pottery from the kiln and the dump is stratified on top of the destruction debris of the South Stoa, deposited in early LM IA, and of the kiln mound, built in advanced LM IA. It is associated with lustrous dark-on-light patterned vases (**63–70**) datable to the advanced and final stages of LM IA, as they have been identified in stratified deposits elsewhere at Kommos, and it has itself clear stylistic affinities with both these stages. Thus it appears that the kiln's lifetime straddled these two stages.

Even though the kiln output is predominantly decorated in the light-on-dark scheme, and does not appear to include the small amounts of lustrous dark-on-light painted pottery found in association with it, the kiln vases cannot be dated stylistically to the MM III phase as this has been defined at Kommos. Unlike at other Cretan sites, the MM III pottery horizon at Kommos is well known, consisting of 27 homogeneous or largely homogeneous deposits that have yielded close to 500 inventoried vases.[186] The kiln pottery lacks a number of ceramic features that typify MM III pottery assemblages at Kommos, such as conical cups with flattened rims, crude bridge-spouted jars, pitharakia, and polychrome-on-dark patterned decoration. In terms of dark-ground motifs, the kiln pottery lacks nearly the entire range typical for MM III pottery at Kommos, such as groups of diagonal lines, dotted circles, dotted lozenges, crosshatching, wavy lines, scale patterns, chevrons, quirks, arched half-foliate bands, thin

---

184. With its squat body shape and ledge rim as well as its exterior decoration of tortoise-shell ripple and bands, bowl **62** also closely resembles in-and-out bowls from Palaikastro and the Zakros Pits, as reported by Bosanquet (Bosanquet and Dawkins 1923, p. 24, fig. 14). This bowl variety is not discussed by Bernini (1995), and seems to be not more closely datable than the LM IA phase in the East Cretan sequence. With their emphasis on tortoise-shell ripple, the bowls fit Bernini's MM IIIB (= Warren's transitional MM IIIB/LM IA) as well as her "LM IA" phase (see above, p. 93, Table 9). The Zakros Pits, according to Warren, are likely to date to the MM IIIB/LM IA transition, but may be as late as his "mature" stage of LM IA (Warren and Hankey 1989, pp. 77–78).

185. Also at Knossos and elsewhere, horizontal foliate bands may not appear

before the "mature" stage of LM IA. A tiny jug fragment with this motif was found in the upper level of the Magazine of the Tripod, dated by Warren to an early LM IA stage postdating the MM IIIB/LM IA transition (Popham 1977, p. 193, pl. 29:c.3; Warren and Hankey 1989, pp. 72–73, table 2.5). However, this foliate band, consisting of paired, stubby leaves without central stalk, is a twin to a band found on a final LM IA teacup from House X (C 9775; Van de Moortel 1997, fig. 13). This and the small size of the fragment suggest it could well be a mature LM IA intrusion. A cup fragment with a foliate band from a transitional MM IIIB/LM IA level south of the Unexplored Mansion is likely to be intrusive as well (Popham 1984, p. 155, pl. 133:a). In other words, no examples of horizontal foliate bands come from unimpeachable transitional MM IIIB/LM IA contexts at Knossos. Among

the imported Minoan pottery at Akrotiri, foliate bands do not appear before mature LM IA (Marthari 1990, pp. 61, 66), and at Palaikastro, the first occurrence of horizontal foliate bands clearly postdates the appearance of lustrous dark-on-light patterned motifs other than tortoise-shell ripple (Bernini 1995, fig. 6; see Table 9).

The in-and-out bowls continue to be a popular patterned shape in final LM IA and LM IB at Kommos, and in mid to final LM IA at nearby Seli (*Kommos* III, pp. 112, 114–115; Cucuzza 1993, p. 69). At Knossos they are rare in mature LM IA (Popham 1984, p. 157), but they clearly continue into LM IB with a Marine Style example (Mountjoy 1984, p. 188, no. 98; *contra* Macdonald 1996, p. 19).

186. *Kommos* II, pp. 37–41; Wright 1996; Van de Moortel 1997, pp. 225–235, 867–869.

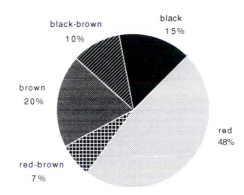

Figure 45. Frequencies of dark paint colors noted on an estimated 317 vases

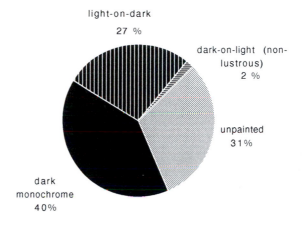

Figure 46. Decorative schemes on 365 cups and pouring vessels from the kiln and dump, excluding conical cups, bell cups, and side-spouted cups

running or retorted spirals, and pictorial, or "finicky," motifs. Instead, its dark-ground decorative repertoire is limited to white-painted thick re-torted spirals and an occasional reed or arc pattern.

In contrast, there are plenty of convincing positive stylistic correspon-dences placing the morphological and decorative repertoire of the kiln vases in the LM IA phase, and more precisely in the advanced and final stages of that phase. The presence of hooked spirals as a decoration on conical cups (**19**) and a bowl (**26**) from the kiln assemblage is consistent with a LM IA dating, and has never been attested in a MM III context (see above, p. 90). The dark paint of the kiln vases, whether it is used for ground coating or for motifs, often is fired to a dull red color (Fig. 45), consistent with that of other LM IA vases at Kommos, whereas in MM III dark paint usually was fired to black or brown. A date after early LM IA for the deposit is indicated beyond a doubt by the absence of conical cups with flattened rims and the predominance of type C cups (**1–7**; Fig. 40). Also the appearance of the collar-necked jug (**38–45**) and the absence of small, crude bridge-spouted jars place the deposit in either of the two stages after early LM IA. Type D, E, and F cups produced in the kiln have thinner walls and finer fabrics than do early LM IA examples, and fit an advanced or final LM IA date as well (**8–10**). The absence of polychromy, and the reduction of the range of motifs to thick retorted spirals, apart from reed and arc patterns on kalathoi (**32–36**), also accords well with a post–early LM IA date (see above, p. 91).

Most of the dump pottery should be assigned to the advanced rather than to the final stage of LM IA. The large majority of type C cups are convex-sided with rolled-in rims (see above, pp. 66–67), and the teacups (20), with their baggy, almost carinated bodies and short everted rims, most closely resemble advanced LM IA teacups from House X (see above, note 89). In terms of the decorative repertoire, the proportion of mono-chrome to light-on-dark patterned vases is much higher than in early LM IA contexts (Fig. 46). Light-on-dark patterned decoration still is used on a wide variety of shapes, except on fine bowls, which are absent from the dump, and on straight-sided cups. Also several lustrous dark-on-light pat-terned vase fragments associated with the kiln dump pottery (63, 65–70) fit an advanced LM IA date. Several have soft, pale fabrics similar to those of the kiln pottery (63, 65–66), and their motifs—frequent tortoise-shell ripple, some running and retorted spirals, plant motifs on closed shapes—are those of advanced LM IA vases. The combination of dark-on-light patterning and a soft, pale fabric is found only on fine bowls, teacups, and bridge-spouted jars, which also fits better an advanced than a final LM IA date.

It is possible to refine the initial date of the kiln even more, placing it toward the end of the advanced LM IA stage. Such a date was already suggested by the band of stubby leaves on bowl 62 from the kiln mound, which dates the construction of the kiln and has only final or mature LM IA comparanda at Kommos and elsewhere (see above, pp. 95–96). The surprising rarity of dark-ground teacups and straight-sided cups in the dump likewise accords with a date close to final LM IA, when straight-sided cups will all but disappear and all teacups will have lustrous dark-on-light patterning. The high frequency in the dump of dark-ground closed vessels, such as bridge-spouted jars and jugs, does not contradict a date late in advanced LM IA, because such vessels remained popular in final LM IA.

There are several indications that the kiln continued to be used into final LM IA. It has been argued above (p. 28) that the pottery found in-side the kiln seems to represent part of the last firing load. This pottery differs in some respects from the bulk of the dump material, and these differences seem to have chronological significance. All type C cups from within the kiln and some from the dump have straight flaring walls and straight rims, representing a variety that is typical for final LM IA (pp. 66–67). Furthermore, medium-coarse side-spouted cups (25) and ampho-ras with dark-on-light painted plant motifs, which have been found inside the kiln as well as in the dump, have only final LM IA comparanda. The side-spouted cups are much more frequent in the red and light brown strata—which also may represent final kiln debris—than they are in the dark brown stratum. Also, the fine bridge-spouted jars from inside the kiln differ in several respects from the majority of those found in the dump. They are smaller in size, are provided with handles with circular section instead of grooved strap handles, and lack patterned decoration. No such bridge-spouted jars have been found in stratified contexts elsewhere at Kommos, but comparanda at other Mesara sites are datable to mature LM IA, thus suggesting a final LM IA date for the Kommian examples (see above, p. 75). Finally, several lustrous dark-on-light patterned vases asso-

TABLE 10. POTTERY DATES FOR THE DUMP AND FOR THE FINAL USE OF THE KILN

Vessel Shape	Dump	Kiln
Conical cups		
type C	**Adv – fin LM IA**	**Final LM IA**
type D	LM IA	Absent
type E	**Adv/fin LM IA**	Absent
type F	**Adv/fin LM IA**	Absent
type P	LM I	LM I
type Q	LM I	LM I
type V	LM IA	LM IA
Teacups	**Advanced LM IA**	Absent
Straight-sided cups	**Advanced LM IA**	Absent
Bell cups	LM IA	LM IA
Side-spouted cups	**Final LM IA**	**Final LM IA**
Convex-sided bowls	LM IA	Absent
Conical bowls	Neopalatial	Neopalatial
Kalathoi,		
fine	LM IA	Neopalatial
medium-coarse	**Adv/fin LM IA**	**Adv/fin LM IA**
Bridge-spouted jars,		
fine	**Adv/fin LM IA**	**Final LM IA**
medium-coarse	Neopalatial	Neopalatial
Collar-necked jugs	**Adv/fin LM IA**	**Adv/fin LM IA**
Ewers	LM IA	LM IA
Rhyta	LM IA	Absent
Oval-mouthed amphoras,		
plant motifs	**Final LM IA**	**Final LM IA**
others	LM I	LM I
Basins	Neopalatial	Neopalatial
Large jars	LM I	Absent
Pithoi	LM I	LM I

The most precise dates are in boldface.

187. E.g., final LM IA teacups C 9481 and C 9499 (Van de Moortel 1997, p. 260, fig. 13). See also p. 91 above.

ciated with the kiln dump (**64, 68, 70**) show close similarities to mature LM IA vases from other sites, lending support to a final LM IA date for the demise of the kiln (see below).

It seems unlikely that the kiln was used until the very end of LM IA, however, because lustrous dark-on-light motifs, such as blob-stemmed running spirals or multiple thin wavy lines, which appear for the first time in final LM IA at Kommos, do not occur among the fragments associated with the kiln dump.[187] Moreover, all of the rope designs on the pithoi of the dump are of the molded and impressed variety, and none is in the form of raised, incised bands, as are commonly found elsewhere in mature LM IA and LM IB (see above, p. 84). We thus may conclude that the kiln's lifetime spanned only parts of the advanced and final stages of LM IA. The stylistic dating evidence for the lifetime of the kiln is summarized in Table 10.

If we are correct in assuming that the final LM IA stage at Kommos was twice as long as the earlier two stages, the kiln would have been in use from before the middle of LM IA to sometime in its latter half. Depending on the duration of the LM IA phase—estimates in the literature range from 50 to about 120 years—the kiln may have been operational for as few as 5 to 10 years to as many as 50 or 60 years.[188]

COMPARANDA FROM CENTRAL CRETE AND AKROTIRI

The kiln pottery and the stratigraphically associated lustrous dark-on-light vases that are unlikely to have been produced in this kiln show links with specific LM IA deposits from other Mesara sites as well as from Knossos and Akrotiri, supporting its mid to late LM IA date. Two published pottery groups from Aghia Triada dated by their excavators to the MM IIIB/LM IA transition show a much more restricted range of lustrous dark-on-light patterned motifs than do contemporary Knossian deposits, and closely resemble the dark-on-light painted vases associated with the kiln dump. One of these groups is the destruction material from the House of the Alabaster Threshold.[189] This group resembles the kiln dump in that it contains a majority of light-on-dark patterned pottery. It may be somewhat earlier in date than the dump, however, given the presence of some polychromy on teacups and straight-sided cups, and the use of light-on-dark decoration on bowls—features that do not occur anymore in the dump at Kommos.

Closer in date to the kiln dump may be the small pottery group from level IV in Room Delta at Aghia Triada.[190] Its teacup HTR 123 closely resembles in shape and decoration our teacup **63** as well as other advanced LM IA teacups from Kommos. The fragmentary bridge-spouted jar from level IV carries tortoise-shell ripple, as does **65**, and it has a register of multiple wavy lines. The latter motif does not appear before final LM IA at Kommos, so perhaps the jar from Aghia Triada belongs rather late in the transitional stage. Finally, the reed-decorated rhyton HTR 197 from level IV may be considered to be an example of the plant style, which is represented in the dump by **66** and **69**. In view of these correspondences it seems that the absence of light-on-dark patterned pottery in level IV re-

188. Popham as well as Warren is of the opinion that LM IA must have taken about three generations to complete. Popham assigns it 75 years (Popham 1990, p. 27), and Warren 100 to ca. 120 years (Warren and Hankey 1989, p. 169). On the other hand, Furumark saw LM IA as lasting only 50 years (Furumark 1972, p. 110; cf. Cadogan 1978, p. 210, table 1). In his most recent chronological study, Manning does not rule out any of these estimates but favors a duration between 50 and 100 years, with about 25 to 50 years for the latest, post-Theran stage of LM IA (Manning 1995, pp. 217, 220).

It is hazardous to venture an esti-mate of the kiln's life span based on the size of the kiln dump, because we have evidence that an unknown part of the dump was removed in LM IA (see above, p. 41), and in the absence of sufficient roof remains we cannot estimate with much precision the number of vases the kiln could fire in a single session, nor do we know the breakage rate of vases fired in Minoan channel kilns. A minimum life span of 5 to 10 years would allow for the appearance of the few stylistic changes noticeable in the pottery record (see above).

189. D'Agata (1989, pp. 94–96) has suggested the possibility that this group postdates the transitional MM IIIB/LM IA stage because of the presence of two nonlocal Vapheio cups with spiral motifs over single rows of dots, an advanced form of decoration not yet found on Vapheio cups from the Minoan Unexplored Mansion. However, more recently, Warren has encountered a fragmentary Vapheio cup with a similar combination of motifs in his transitional MM IIIB/LM IA deposit at the Stratigraphical Museum Extension site, and thus there is no longer any reason for dating the material from the House of the Alabaster Threshold later than the transitional MM IIIB/LM IA stage at Knossos (Warren 1991, p. 330).

190. La Rosa 1986, p. 83, fig. 36:e–g; 1989, pp. 83–84.

flects the earlier disappearance of this decorative scheme at Aghia Triada rather than indicating that the deposit would postdate the kiln dump.

A large deposit belonging to the latter part of LM IA has been found in the Volakakis house at Seli di Kamilari.[191] Its pottery is comparable to that of final LM IA at Kommos, and appears to postdate the abandonment of the kiln. Some of its dark-patterned motifs—running and retorted spirals, as well as the rare tortoise-shell ripple—resemble those of the dark-on-light painted pottery associated with the kiln dump. An especially close correspondence exists between fine bridge-spouted jar XXI-3 from Seli and teacup **64**, which carry registers with identical decorative motifs.[192] However, the general preponderance of dark-on-light patterning at Seli, found not only on all teacups and fine bowls but also on most fine closed shapes, suggests a date later than that of the kiln.[193] In particular, the use of blob-stemmed running spirals among the Volakakis pottery supports this later date, because this motif appears to postdate the Kommos kiln (see above, p. 99).

Several deposits from Knossos and Akrotiri offer specific comparanda to vase shapes and decorative motifs produced in the Kommos kiln. These have been discussed above in the morphological analysis (pp. 66–84), so only the most important ones need be recalled here. Teacups from the kiln have comparanda only in the transitional MM IIIB/LM IA stage at Knossos.[194] On the other hand, bell cups, fine bridge-spouted jars with round-sectioned handles, and large ewers with neck rings are paralleled in both LM IA stages at Knossos.[195] Comparanda for collar-necked jugs and amphoras with simple, dark-painted plant motifs may come only from mature LM IA deposits at Knossos, Akrotiri, and elsewhere.[196] The fact that the Knossian comparanda for the kiln vases date to the transitional MM IIIB/LM IA stage as well as to mature LM IA corroborates our advanced to final LM IA dating for the kiln's life span.

Also, the lustrous dark-on-light patterned vases associated with the kiln dump have comparanda in both Knossian stages. Their decorative repertoire overall fits best the transitional MM IIIB/LM IA stage at Knossos (see above, p. 92). However, close comparanda come exclusively

191. Cucuzza 1993, p. 78.

192. Cucuzza 1993, pp. 66–67, pls. 6, 16.

193. Cucuzza 1993, pp. 65, 68.

194. Warren 1991, fig. 10:B; Popham 1984, pl. 141:5.

195. For bell cups, see Warren 1991, fig. 9:N, O; Popham 1984, pl. 141:15, 16; 1977, fig. 31:a–c. A mature bell cup from Acropolis Deposit F (Catling, Catling, and Smyth 1979, fig. 35: V.240) lacks a handle, as does **23**. Macdonald has proposed downdating Deposit F to LM IB (Macdonald 1990, p. 87), but it seems to me that most of the pottery, except for stirrup jar V.225, fits a mature LM IA date. For Knossian fine bridge-

spouted jars with round-sectioned handles and their dates, see above, note 111. For large ewers or hydriae with neck rings, see Warren 1991, p. 322; *PM* I, fig. 404:f. The last example comes from the Temple Repositories, dated by Evans to MM III but downdated by Warren to mature LM IA (Warren and Hankey 1989, pp. 73–74). For comparable mature LM IA ewers from Akrotiri, see note 125 above.

196. For collar-necked jugs, see *PM* II, figs. 253:B, 349:i; Popham 1967, pl. 76:c. These Knossian examples with their rather short collars, lateral lugs, and single strap handles are quite close to the ones from the

Kommos kiln. For mature LM IA examples from Akrotiri and Gournia, see Niemeier 1980, fig. 27:1, 2, 5. The collar-necked jugs from Building 3 at Palaikastro, recently dated by Bernini to her LM IA phase, are roughly contemporary with the volcanic destruction at Thera (Bernini 1995, pp. 63–64, figs. 5:D, 11:29; for a discussion of Bernini's LM IA phase, see above, p. 94). The dating of amphoras with dark-painted plant motifs from the South-West Basement at Knossos and from Akrotiri comparable to those from the kiln dump is discussed above, note 130.

from mature LM IA contexts. This also applies to comparanda from Akrotiri. Closed vessel **68** with its double-linked blob-centered spiral frieze compares closely to a vase from the Room of the Chancel Screen at Knossos, dated to mature LM IA.[197] The probable absence of foliate bands at Knossos before the mature stage supports our proposed dating late in advanced LM IA for the foliate band of bowl **62** from the kiln mound, providing a *terminus ad quem* for the kiln construction (see above, pp. 95–96). Furthermore, a teacup from the Room of the Lilies at Akrotiri closely resembles teacup **63**, and crocus clumps as found on **66** also occur on a stirrup jar from the volcanic destruction level at Akrotiri.[198] Fragment **69** may belong to a fine reed jug similar to those found in Acropolis Deposit F.[199] And stirrup jar(?) **70** resembles an oval-mouthed amphora from the Temple Repositories, as well as stirrup jars from Acropolis Deposit F and from the volcanic destruction level at Akrotiri.[200] All are squat in shape, and many carry registers of tortoise-shell ripple. Jar **70** may even have a shoulder decoration of dark-painted concentric arcs similar to that of the Acropolis jar.

In sum, the kiln's output and its associated dark-on-light patterned pottery have comparanda at other central Cretan sites as well as at Akrotiri that support the conclusion reached on the basis of stratigraphical and stylistic evidence from Kommos, namely that the kiln began its operation near the end of the advanced LM IA stage at Kommos and went out of use sometime before the end of final LM IA. Importantly, this means that the abandonment of the Kommos kiln is likely to have taken place within a generation or so of the volcanic eruption of Thera—either not long before or at roughly the same time—since it has now been convincingly demonstrated that the Theran eruption also predated the end of the LM IA phase.[201]

LM IA POTTERY PRODUCTION AT KOMMOS

VASE SHAPES

The range of shapes fired in this kiln and their relative frequencies in this deposit are summarized in Table 4 and Figure 39 (pp. 43 and 67). Conical cups take up 56%, and other cup types and bowls an additional 15%. Pouring vessels represent 20% of the kiln output. These include bridge-spouted jars, jugs, and a few rhyta. Oval-mouthed amphoras take up 6% of the deposit, and large basins, closed jars, pithoi, and fine pedestaled vases the remaining 3%. With few exceptions, the percentages of the functional categories correspond remarkably well to those found in domestic deposits at Kommos and Seli,[202] and thus it appears that the kiln produced pottery primarily to meet household needs. More specific information on the distribution of kiln pottery in consumer contexts at Kommos will be available after completion of the study of contemporary floor deposits from House X and Building T.[203]

Apparently only cooking pots, lamps, and braziers were never fired in this kiln. Oval-mouthed amphoras, on the other hand, occur about twice as often in the dump as they do in domestic contexts (ca. 3%). Either they

197. Macdonald 1996, pl. 5:c.

198. For the teacup, see *Thera* IV, pl. 77:b. Tortoise-shell ripple is rare in the volcanic destruction level at Akrotiri, however (Marthari 1990, p. 61). For the stirrup jar decorated with crocus clumps, see *Thera* V, pl. 61:a.

199. Catling, Catling, and Smyth 1979, fig. 31: V.223.

200. Temple Repositories: *PM* I, fig. 404:g. Acropolis Deposit F: Catling, Catling, and Smyth 1979, p. 44, fig. 31: V.224. Akrotiri: *Thera* III, pp. 56–57, figs. 40, 41; *Thera* IV, pl. 79; *Thera* VI, pl. 72:c.

201. For discussions of the ceramic date of the Thera eruption, see Manning 1995, pp. 201, 220; Davis and Cherry 1984, p. 158; Lolos 1987, pp. 537–540. Davis and Cherry have argued that the latest stage of LC I was not present at Akrotiri, and Lolos has demonstrated the same for the latest stage of LH I.

202. Roughly contemporary domestic assemblages come from House X (unpublished) and from the Volakakis house at Seli (La Rosa 1972–1973; Cucuzza 1993). Domestic assemblages from the Central Hillside at Kommos dating to MM III and perhaps early LM IA have been published by Wright (1996; see note 158 above).

203. This study is currently being conducted by J. B. Rutter.

broke more frequently during firing than did other vases, or else more were produced than were needed for domestic use; since Kommos was a port town it is conceivable that these surplus amphoras were destined for trade. Medium-coarse kalathoi also are more frequent in the dump (6%) than in MM III and LM IA domestic contexts (max. 3%). However, these vases have tightly curving bodies and, to judge by their compression ridges, underwent a great deal of stress when thrown on the wheel (see above, pp. 73–74). It is possible that they broke more readily during firing than other vases. There is currently not enough evidence to indicate that a surplus of kalathoi had been produced for other than domestic needs.

A few morphological and decorative varieties appearing in the dump have not been identified elsewhere at Kommos. These are: oversized unpainted straight-sided cups (**22**), handleless bell cups (**23**), medium-coarse convex-sided bowls with wide, everted rims and flaring, pseudo-pedestaled bases (**26**), unpainted, fine bridge-spouted jars (**34**), and fine pedestaled bases perhaps belonging to chalices or fruitstands (**59**). All are sufficiently rare in the dump, however, to allow for the possibility that their absence from other contexts at Kommos is merely due to chance.

Unexpectedly absent from the kiln and the dump are tumbler-shaped, semi-ovoid, and semiglobular conical cups with dark-dipped ledge rims, types that are common in MM III and LM IA domestic assemblages at the site.[204] Since these cup types are roughly similar in shape, wall thickness, and fabric to the conical cups of the kiln dump, it is unlikely that they would have been more resistant to firing breakage than those other conical cups. It thus must be assumed that they were not fired in the kiln, or at least not during those stages of its operation that are represented by the kiln and dump remains.

Also missing are ribbed Vapheio cups, but only two examples (C 9678, C 9754) are known from an advanced LM IA deposit (from House X) and none from a final LM IA context at Kommos, and so this straight-sided cup variety may have been rare. It is unclear whether narrow-necked jugs or juglets were fired in the kiln. The kiln dump contained a few fragments of two large medium-coarse narrow-necked jugs with knobs around the neck (C 10594) as well as an almost intact unpainted juglet (C 10045), but not a single juglet fragment. Even though all these remains have fresh surfaces, they were considered to be too rare in the dump to be accepted as kiln products.[205] Also absent from the kiln and dump are pithoid jars, including those with collar-necks, which appear elsewhere in Crete and at Akrotiri in mature LM IA.[206] They have not been encountered elsewhere at Kommos in LM IA, nor have they been reported from Aghia Triada, but the LM IA deposits at that site have not yet been fully published. It is therefore still too early to conclude that collar-necked pithoid jars were not known in the Mesara in LM IA.

PRODUCTION TRADITION

The kiln in the South Stoa at Kommos and the adjacent dump represent the first excavated context in which a large mass of Minoan pottery has been associated with its production facility. Such a find offers an unprec-

204. These are labeled types I and J in the Kommian typology (Van de Moortel 1997, pp. 46–47, 54, 61–62, 68–69, figs. 6–9). For more examples, see *Kommos* II, figs. 30: no. 631; 41: nos. 873, 874; 67: nos. 1955, 1966. Several advanced and final LM IA cups of these types, which are thought to be contemporary with the kiln, are still unpublished (C 8399, C 9088, C 9520, C 9676, C 9727). A single, largely complete, but worn conical cup of type I (C 9989) has been found at the outskirts of the dump (trench 91B, pail 45), but its context is mixed. Perhaps one other, fragmentary example comes from the kiln dump.

205. The juglet resembles an early LM IA example from Kommos (*Kommos* II, no. 828) as well as mature LM IA juglets from Knossos (Popham 1977, p. 195; 1984, p. 157, pl. 143:15–17; Catling, Catling, and Smyth 1979, fig. 35: V.237; Macdonald 1996, fig. 1:c). It even may have had a lug in the place of a handle, as do some of the Knossian juglets. While this shape is proposed by Popham as a possibly diagnostic type for the mature LM IA stage at Knossos, it definitely occurs earlier at Kommos.

206. Niemeier 1980, p. 57, fig. 32.

edented opportunity to document the technological as well as morphological and decorative features that are peculiar to the pottery made at this
specific locale. Idiosyncrasies of the manufacturing process might allow us
in the future to distinguish pottery produced at Kommos from that made
in other areas, even if fabrics were indistinguishable.[207] This would facilitate the study of the distribution of Kommian pottery elsewhere in Crete.
Comparisons with technological characteristics of earlier and later pottery
at Kommos may yield clues about the longevity of LM IA production
techniques and methods. If in the future kilns with their waste dumps
should be discovered at other sites, this avenue of research would provide a
means for defining more clearly the different pottery production areas in
Crete. The study of the interaction between such areas would in turn contribute to a better understanding of relations between the various geographical regions of Minoan Crete.

A comprehensive documentation of fabric use, vessel formation, surface finish, and decoration, as well as drying and firing practices, as evidenced by the kiln pottery, has not yet been carried out. Thus far, 57 fabric
samples, assumed to be representative of the normal kiln products, have
been analyzed; they have been assigned to fabric groups and have yielded
information on firing conditions (see below, Chapter 3). In addition, the
following observations regarding fabric use have been made for about 300
vases (including **1–59**), or over one-fourth of the estimated 1,158 pots
found inside the kiln and the surrounding dump. Fabric textures of the
examined vessels are remarkably constant, revealing good control by potter over fabric preparation and the purposeful use of different fabric textures for specific pottery shapes and parts of vases. Fine vases have inclusion densities ranging between 0% and 3%, and the bodies of most
medium-coarse vases have 10% inclusions. Collar-necked jugs (**40–45**)
stand out as a group among the medium-coarse vases because their fabrics
are almost fine, having only 5–7% inclusions. Basins and pithoi are made
out of coarse fabrics (20%–30% inclusions). Some spouts (**44**), handles
(**47**), and neck rings (**49**) of medium-coarse vases are made out of coarse
fabrics with 20%–25% inclusions, whereas many medium-coarse ewers of
medium size have necks made out of fine fabrics (p. 79). This specific
combined use of fine and medium-coarse fabric types for medium-sized
ewers in the kiln dump has not been attested elsewhere in LM IA and may
be typical for Kommian pottery in this phase.

Most vases from the kiln and dump are wheel-thrown. There are indications, albeit uncertain, that the potter used a low wheel with a large
clay bat (see above, p. 34). Compression ridges and minor stretch marks
found on a wide variety of vases are consistent in following a downward
counterclockwise direction, showing that the potter's wheel turned counterclockwise (e.g., Fig. 41; see above, pp. 73–74). A detailed study of potters' motor habits has not yet been done on the kiln pottery, but already a
peculiarity may be pointed out regarding the application of cup handles.
Toward their lower attachment these are consistently twisted to the right
of the viewer.[208] A similar feature has been noticed in the handles of many
MM IIB, MM III, LM IA, and LM IB cups from other contexts at

207. The technological approach to
pottery studies has been pioneered by
H. J. Franken and J. Kalsbeek (1969).
I thank W. D. Glanzman of the University of British Columbia at Van-
couver for introducing me to its possibilities. This approach was applied for
the first time to Minoan pottery by
Whitelaw et al. (1997), who used it in
combination with fabric analysis to
distinguish the products of different
ceramic traditions at EM IIB Myrtos
Fournou Korifi.

208. See bell cup **24** in Fig. 32.

Kommos, which conceivably are of local manufacture. More research is needed to determine whether this feature is limited to Kommos in these phases or has a wider geographical and chronological extent. Complex vessels consisting of several joined parts, such as bridge-spouted jars, jugs, oval-mouthed amphoras, or pithoi, are likely as well to yield insights into details of vessel formation that were particular to the working habits of the Kommos potter or potters. The techniques involved in coil-building amphoras, basins, and pithoi may also be expected to show idiosyncrasies.

Surfaces of kiln vases have been cursorily wet-smoothed. It is unclear whether the smoothing was intentional. Appendages sometimes have been well integrated, but at other times their join to the vase body has been left clearly visible. The dark paint employed on vases produced in this kiln has a dilute, dull appearance, and most often has been fired to bright red or brown hues (Fig. 45). White-painted motifs consist mostly of thick retorted spirals. These always run to the viewer's left. This direction is not unique to the kiln pottery, but is observed also for retorted spiral motifs on MM IIB, MM III, and early LM IA pottery at Kommos, and on Protopalatial and phase III pottery at Phaistos.[209] While thick retorted spirals running to the left appear to form part of the decorative tradition of both Kommos and Phaistos, the hooked spiral variety found on type V conical cups (**19**) as well as on medium-coarse convex-sided bowls (**26**) is unique to LM IA Kommos. It has been found both among the kiln pottery and in other LM IA contexts at the site. Firing conditions in this kiln are studied by Day and Kilikoglou (see below). Here it will be said only that the bright red coatings found on many of the vases (Fig. 45) show a lack of reduction during their last stage of firing. The brown coatings, on the other hand, are indicative of unsuccessful reduction.

It is not clear how many potters made use of this kiln. The evidence for a pottery-making facility in the vicinity of the kiln is ambiguous (see above, pp. 33–35), but workshops may have left few traces, and the presence of more than one facility in the area cannot be ruled out.[210] The size of the kiln cannot be taken as an indication of its use by multiple producers. Blitzer's study of traditional potteries at Koroni shows that a single potter with a few assistants can produce sufficient numbers of vases to supply a kiln with a capacity estimated to be about three times that of ours.[211] Neither has the Kommos kiln pottery itself revealed evidence for multiple manufacturers: the vases are quite homogeneous in their characteristics, and it is as yet not possible to distinguish subgroups in fabric, shape, decoration, or technology that would suggest the output of more than one potter or workshop. Rather, a few observed differences among the vases of the deposit can be explained chronologically (see above, p. 98). We have not found widespread use of potters' marks on the kiln pottery, by which multiple potters would have identified their individual products in a shared kiln. Even though the question of the number of producers using this kiln cannot be resolved without further study, we can assume for the time being, based on our preliminary observations, that each vase shape fired in this kiln belonged to a single technological tradition.[212]

209. For Kommos, see *Kommos* II. For Phaistos, see Pernier 1935; Pernier and Banti 1951; Levi 1976. No such information has been published for Aghia Triada.

210. Cf. London 1989b, pp. 224–225.

211. Blitzer 1990, pp. 679, 695. The Koroni potters produce for six to eight months a year.

212. Rye (1981, p. 5) uses the term "technological tradition" to refer to a body of recurring manufacturing practices. It is debatable whether a technological tradition needs to represent the work of a single potter or whether multiple potters trained in a similar fashion and working closely together could have produced a single tradition. For this reason it is perhaps best to attribute a technological tradition to a single "analytical individual," regardless of whether the vases were actually produced by one or more potters. The term "analytical individual" is not used by Rye, but is borrowed from Redman (1977, p. 44). Recently, both Morris (1993) and Thomas (1997) have argued that it is possible to identify individual potters by their motor habits. This aspect has not yet been studied comprehensively for the kiln pottery.

ORGANIZATION OF POTTERY PRODUCTION

The pottery of the Kommos kiln and dump presumably was produced at a single locale, and it is possible that it represents the output of a single potter (see above, p. 105). A production assemblage such as this offers us a good opportunity to make inferences about the scale and mode of production of dark-ground pottery in the advanced and final LM IA stages at Kommos. Scale of production, as defined by Rice, "refers to levels of labor and resources used and quantity of output."[213] Production mode relates to manufacturing technology as well as the practical organization of the production activity.

We cannot calculate the production rate per year, since in the absence of a well-preserved roof we can only make very rough estimates regarding the kiln's capacity; furthermore, we do not know the potter's stacking practices, and we have no way of knowing how often the kiln was fired in a year.[214] The size of the Kommos kiln gives some indication as to its importance, however. With an average east–west interior length of an estimated 2.80 m and a north–south length of 2.70 m, its firing chamber—the area where the vases were stacked before firing—would have been between 7 and 8 m² (Table 11). This is much smaller than the firing chambers of the LM I kiln at Aghia Triada and of the Neopalatial kiln at Vathypetro, but larger than that of the MM IIIA(?) kiln at Kato Zakros and than the equivalent area of the kiln found west of the West Court at Phaistos, recently redated by Tomasello to the end of MM IIB. The firing chamber of the Kommos kiln is substantially larger than those of Neopalatial kilns 1 and 2 from the Stratigraphical Museum Extension site at Knossos, and of the LM II/IIIa kiln near the House of the Monolithic Pillars, which has a channel length of only ca. 0.5 m.[215]

Inferences about the rate of production in the Kommos kiln can also be made from clues regarding the speed with which vases were manufactured. There are several indications that the pottery fired in the Kommos kiln was produced in a hurried fashion. All but the largest shapes were thrown on the wheel. The frequent presence of compression ridges, minor stretch marks, and heavy wheel ridges on vases already is indicative of hurried production.[216] It has been suggested that the occurrence of heavy wheel ridges signals the use of a fast-spinning wheel.[217] However, a recent study by Courty and Roux indicates that they rather are the result of uneven pressures applied to the clay during throwing.[218] Such pressures occur when the potter lifts the vessel walls quickly as the wheel is turning. Thus, it is the fast movement of the potter's hands rather than the speed of the wheel that causes heavy wheel ridges on a vase.

Because of this apparent concern with speed on the part of the potter, it is suggested here that the minimal effort spent on the finish and decoration of the kiln pottery is a result of similar considerations. Heavy wheel ridges or compression ridges are not smoothed out after the lifting of the vessel. Surfaces are wet-smoothed at the most, and appendages are not always well-integrated. Decoration is much more simplified than before. Cups or serving vessels, which in earlier phases were light-on-dark patterned, now are commonly unpainted or simply dark monochrome coated

213. Rice 1987, p. 180.

214. The range of estimates of the number of vases that may have been fired in a single session is very rough and should be used with caution. If we assume that this kiln had a domed superstructure with a height of about 1.0 to 1.5 m (see above, p. 24, note 35), one could estimate the volume of the firing chamber to have been roughly 4–7 m³. Since we do not know whether all shapes were fired together or whether they were fired separately by size or decorative scheme, it seems best to consider a typical firing load to have consisted of a mixture of shapes and sizes, roughly in the percentages in which they occur in the dump and in consumer assemblages (Table 4; Fig. 39; see above). The potter may have put the vases on top of one another, or he may have nested smaller vases to a greater or lesser degree in larger open vases, thereby increasing his load. Given these unknowns, it seems best for the sake of our hypothesis to merely estimate a range of the numbers of vases that may have been part of a typical firing load; extremes of 200 to 1,000 vessels seem reasonable.

215. Evely in press.

216. Heavy wheel ridges on, e.g., **5, 30, 34, 35, 37, 40, 45**. For a discussion of compression ridges on kiln vases, and a list of examples, see above, pp. 73–74.

217. E.g., Levi and Carinci 1988, p. 305.

218. Courty and Roux 1995, p. 30.

TABLE 11. APPROXIMATE SIZES OF FIRING CHAMBERS OF MINOAN CHANNEL KILNS

Kiln	Date	Size of Firing Chamber (in m²)	References
Phaistos, west of West Court	MM IIB	ca. 5.3	Tomasello 1996, pp. 30–32, figs. 3–5
Kato Zakros	MM IIIA(?)	ca. 6	Platon 1975; Evely in press
Kommos	*LM IA*	*ca. 7–8*	
Knossos, SME 1	Neopalatial	ca. 1.2	Warren 1981, pp. 75–79, figs. 6–9
Knossos, SME 2	LM I	ca. 3.1	Warren 1981, pp. 75–79, figs. 6–9
Vathypetro	Neopalatial	ca. 16	Marinatos 1960; Evely in press
Aghia Triada	LM I	ca. 16	Tomasello 1996, p. 29, figs. 1, 3–5

Calculated from measurements and plans given by authors.

Knossos SME 1 and SME 2 = kilns 1 and 2, respectively, of the Stratigraphical Museum Extension site.

(Fig. 46). Polychrome patterning on a dark ground is entirely absent, and white-painted motifs are limited on most vases to simple, thick retorted spirals. Different motifs (reeds, arcs) are found only on kalathoi, perhaps to emphasize their tectonic qualities. Auxiliary bands are much rarer than in early LM IA. The relative rarity and extreme simplicity of the decoration on kiln vases cannot be explained merely by their utilitarian character, since even utilitarian vases in earlier phases in the Mesara were more intricately patterned. All this represents the intensification of a trend that had already begun in MM III at Kommos and in phase III at Phaistos,[219] and together with the summary surface finish, is likely to reflect a deliberate and long-term effort on the part of the potter to save time and hence labor investment.[220] Simplifications in shape, such as the disappearance of flattened rims on conical cups, and the change from grooved strap handles to round-sectioned handles on fine bridge-spouted jars, may be viewed as further efforts to increase production speed in a variety of minor ways. This concern with speed on the part of the potter may reflect an effort to increase the rate of production and conceivably also its scale.

In the scholarly literature, an increase in the scale of production has been linked also to an increase in vessel standardization.[221] This link is not unequivocal, however, because standardization conceivably also can increase for reasons other than decisions made to streamline the manufacturing process and thereby increase output. For instance, increased standardization could reflect a response to a demand for more uniform vessels.[222] Furthermore, there are significant problems involved in interpreting perceived decreases in variability. For example, as noted by Blackman, Stein, and Vandiver, the degree of standardization also is a function of the number of potters producing a given body of pottery, and even of the number of episodes in which this pottery was made. Thus, standardization at a given time and place should be highest in the output of a single potter working during a single episode.[223] The more potters who were involved in the making of a group of pottery, the greater is the likelihood that they followed different practices with respect to standardization, and consequently

219. For MM III Kommos, see *Kommos* II, p. 38. For phase III Phaistos, see Levi and Carinci 1988, p. 305. For a more in-depth analysis of the trend observed in MM IIB–LM IA pottery production at Kommos and in other central Cretan sites, see Van de Moortel in press.

220. See Rice 1987, p. 203; Hagstrum 1985.

221. E.g., Rice 1987, p. 190; Feinman, Kowalewski, and Blanton 1984, p. 299.

222. For a discussion of the factors that may account for increases in standardization, see Blackman, Stein, and Vandiver 1993, p. 61.

223. Blackman, Stein, and Vandiver 1993, pp. 74–77.

the more blurring of the evidence is to be expected.[224] Since at Kommos we seem to have identified the material of the last kiln load, we are provided with a rare opportunity to study the degree of standardization of vases produced within a single production tradition, and perhaps by a single potter, over a relatively short period of time.[225] Thus we will be able to establish a reference base with which to compare the degree of standardization of other pottery assemblages.

The standardization of a pottery assemblage relates to various aspects of vases, such as fabric, shapes, dimensions, decoration, and manufacturing technology. A comprehensive study of the vases thought to represent the last kiln load has not yet been carried out, but it has been observed already that the 30 restored type C conical cups from within the kiln are much more homogeneous in fabric, shape, and surface treatment than those from the dump (cf. **1–3**; Table 8). They have identical fabrics, with a reddish yellow color (7.5YR 7/6) and 2% inclusions, similar straight-flaring body contours, straight rims, and surfaces covered with identical, very pale brown slips or self-slips (10YR 8/3–4). They also are more standardized in their dimensions than are type C cups from the dump.[226] Thus these results support Blackman et al.'s notions of standardization.

However, within the pottery assemblage from the dump we observe a high degree of homogeneity. In terms of fabrics, production apparently was limited to fine, medium-coarse, and coarse calcareous, and the percentages of inclusions in those three fabric groups were highly standardized within each vessel shape (see above, p. 104). There is no evidence that cooking pots, lamps, braziers, or large slabs, made out of coarse red, noncalcareous fabrics, were ever fired in the kiln. Their absence is the more remarkable because the kiln obviously was used to a large extent for the production of ordinary domestic pottery. Thus the kiln dump pottery may well be our first evidence for the specialized production of Neopalatial cooking pots, lamps, and braziers.

The kiln assemblage shows a decrease in morphological variability compared to earlier assemblages. Most shapes have been reduced to a few basic varieties. Among the conical cups, the small, unpainted type C cups take up 47%, and all other types except one have large, convex-sided bodies that are either semiglobular or ovoid in shape (Fig. 40). Fine, convex-sided bowls are not produced, and the output of teacups is small. Only two jug and rhyton types were certainly fired in the kiln. Among the bridge-spouted jars, the small, crude, medium-coarse examples that were common in MM III and early LM IA at Kommos have disappeared. These changes are not characteristic of just the kiln pottery, but are observed also among the dark-ground and plain pottery in contemporary residential deposits at the site, thus representing a broad trend in the advanced and final stages of LM IA. It is not clear, however, whether this decrease in morphological variability is due to a decrease in the number of potters distributing pottery at Kommos in advanced and final LM IA, or to an increase in the standardization of an individual potter's output.

Most significant are our observations regarding the dimensional standardization of the kiln pottery. The type C cups from the dump show a similar degree of dimensional standardization as those from contempo-

224. See Davis and Lewis 1985, p. 90.

225. Blackman, Stein, and Vandiver (see above, note 222) were able to conduct standardization studies on identical Early Bronze Age bowls from Tell Leilan, Syria, found stacked together as kiln waste. These are most likely to have been produced in a single episode. No such stacks have been observed in the kiln dump.

226. Van de Moortel 1997, pp. 251–253, 263–267, appendixes C–D.

rary consumer contexts at the site.[227] Both groups, even with advanced and final LM IA cups combined, are much more standardized in their dimensions than are conical cups of the MM III or early LM IA phases. This is the more meaningful because the advanced and final stages of LM IA are thought to represent a much longer timespan than does early LM IA. Since conical cups were simple mass-produced vessels, it is unlikely that the potter would have spent time trying to control their size with a measuring device. Rather, their decrease in metric variability may be seen as the result of improved motor skills, and it is commonly linked to a rise in routinization on the part of the potter.[228] This in turn may reflect an increase in the scale of production of this vase type, or it may be a result of increased product specialization. Both developments would have enabled the potter to produce vases of a particular type in fewer and longer episodes, which in itself already would have been conducive to a decrease in metric variation.[229]

It is interesting to place the observed trends within the broader context of LM IA pottery production. The perceived increase in labor-cutting measures and in the speed of production happened at a time when the light-on-dark decorative tradition was in decline, its vases being gradually replaced by pottery with dark-painted motifs on a lustrous light ground (see above, p. 91). The absence and near-absence in the dump of dark-ground fine bowls and teacups, respectively, appears to be symptomatic of this change, because the evidence from residential deposits at Kommos shows that these were the first shapes to adopt the new lustrous dark-on-light patterns. Vases painted in the new scheme are much better finished and more intricately decorated than the kiln products. They are likely to have formed an elite class of pottery.[230] The perceived time-saving measures in the production of kiln pottery therefore need not reflect an increase in the scale of production, but may instead be part of the potter's strategy to cope with the rise in popularity of the new decorative scheme, by specializing in utilitarian shapes, producing them faster and with less labor investment.[231] It is also possible that the potter simply was increasing his scale of production in response to an increase in demand for utilitarian

227. Van de Moortel in press; 1997, pp. 251–253, appendix D.

228. Balfet 1965, p. 170; Feinman, Kowalewski, and Blanton 1984, p. 299; Blackman, Stein, and Vandiver 1993, p. 61.

229. Cf. Blackman, Stein, and Vandiver 1993, pp. 74–76. Longacre, Kvamme, and Kobayashi (1988, pp. 108–109) point out that an additional factor introducing metric variability is the possible difference between the pottery classification imposed by the archaeologist and that applied by the producers of the pottery themselves. By unwittingly lumping two or more emic size classes together, the archaeologist may blur the evidence. However, in view of the distinctive characteristics of the conical cup types at Kommos in MM III and LM IA, it is unlikely that we have lumped emic classes.

230. Cf. Rice 1987, pp. 203–204. The term "elite" is used here to refer to the relatively high quality of the vases, and does not imply that their distribution was limited to an elite group of people. There is no evidence for a restricted distribution of LM IA elite pottery.

231. A similar explanation for the increase in dimensional standardization of LC II conical cups in Aghia Irini has been proposed by Davis and Lewis (1985, p. 89).

vessels caused by the switching of other potters to the new, and higher quality, lustrous dark-on-light pottery.

Seeing market strategies and profit motives as the cause of changes in LM IA pottery assumes that pottery production was part of a market economy, however, and that the potter was an independent producer, free to adjust his strategies to changes in demand.[232] This interpretation seems likely, given the apparently unrestricted distribution of LM IA pottery of all quality classes in the Mesara sites and at Knossos. However, such un-limited distribution still needs to be demonstrated for the products of this kiln. One should keep in mind that the kiln and the dump were located within the boundaries of Building T and its Protopalatial predecessor situated below it—both to all appearances official buildings. It remains to be seen whether the reused parts of Building T in the advanced and final stages of LM IA retained any official function. The possibility must be entertained that the potter or potters using the kiln were specialists attached to an official authority.[233] If this were the case, the changes observed in the dark-ground pottery of this period may have been dictated by this authority. Whatever his situation, it is clear that the Kommos potter did not lag behind other sites in the development of new vase shapes. This is exemplified by his production of the collar-necked jug, a new jug type that appears earlier at Kommos than at other sites (see above, p. 78).

FUTURE AVENUES OF STUDY

Thus far only a few examples of each vase shape produced in the kiln have been restored and studied. Because of the unique possibilities this deposit offers for defining the technological tradition of pottery production at Kommos, it would be worthwhile to continue the restoration process and carry out a detailed study of the techniques and methods used in each step of the manufacturing process, while looking for variations that may reveal the presence of more than one potter at the site. Such study also would allow us to determine if all the vases were produced in a hurried fashion, as apparently were the few that have been restored to date. More extensive analyses of the degree of fabric and shape standardization are needed, as well as a systematic investigation of the degree of dimensional standardization within each vessel type. These would give us a better understanding of the organization of pottery production at Kommos at the end of the light-on-dark tradition. A comparison of the kiln dump deposit with contemporary residential deposits at this and other sites could reveal patterns of consumption, which in turn might throw light on perceived changes in production strategies.

232. For discussions of independent versus attached producers, see Earle 1981, p. 230; Peacock 1982, pp. 10–13. See also Costin 1991, pp. 34–35; Clark 1995. For a recent discussion of independent versus attached pottery producers in Protopalatial central Crete, see Day and Wilson 1998; for Protopalatial Mallia and Myrtos Pyrgos, see Knappett 1997; for Proto- and Neopalatial central Crete, see Van de Moortel 1997; in press.

233. See Earle 1981, p. 230. For a discussion of archaeological correlates of attached production, see Costin 1991, p. 34. For independent versus attached pottery production in Neopalatial Crete, the reader is referred to Van de Moortel in press and the publications cited above, note 232.

CHAPTER 3

ANALYSIS OF CERAMICS FROM THE KILN

by Peter M. Day and Vassilis Kilikoglou

WORKSHOPS AND ANALYTICAL CONTROL GROUPS IN THE PREHISTORIC AEGEAN

Analytical research on prehistoric Aegean pottery has concentrated on questions of both provenance and technology, with notable success in its long history of work.[1] The study of Minoan ceramics has been an important component of this development, exploiting both elemental and, more recently, mineralogical techniques.[2]

Provenance studies have generally been based on comparison of the elemental composition of pottery of unknown origin with chemical control groups, sampled to be representative of the products of known centers of pottery production. In reality, however, there are very few locations of production whose existence in the past is certain, although some recent finds have revealed workshop installations.[3] Thus, the majority of chemical control groups comprised pottery assumed on *archaeological* grounds (in terms of both style and spatial distribution) to form a homogeneous group and to have been made in the vicinity of a major center of settlement.

We now know that the assumption that the majority of pottery at a given site is manufactured locally is often unfounded. Indeed, recent work has shown that the production of pottery in Minoan Crete was perhaps concentrated in a smaller number of centers and that distribution from

1. We would like to thank the 23rd Ephorate of Prehistoric and Classical Antiquities, the Conservation Division of the Ministry of Culture, and the American School of Classical Studies at Athens for permission to sample the material from the kiln for analysis. The analyses would not have been possible without the generous support of the Institute of Aegean Prehistory. Several people have made important contributions to this paper through their help and advice, some of whom are the coauthors of other work result-ing from the analyses. We would like especially to thank J. Buxeda i Garrigòs, E. Faber, A. Tsolakidou, E. Kiriatzi, and D. Bacon.

2. For an account of the history of analytical work on Aegean ceramics, see Jones 1986; also Day et al. 1999.

3. For the pottery workshop at Zominthos, see Sakellarakis 1989; for the LM III kiln complex at Gouves on the north coast of Crete, see Vallianou 1997; for kilns at Phaistos and Aghia Triada see Tomasello 1996.

TABLE 12. CATALOGUE OF SAMPLES FOR ANALYSIS FROM THE KILN

Sample	Excavation No.	Inv. No.	Context	Surface	Shape	Pottery Cat.	Group No.
95/1	K93A/87B/3:90A	C 10577	Kiln channel 1, 2, 3	UP	Basin	54	4
95/2	K93/87B/4:97	C 10534	Kiln dump	UP	Basin	55	2a
95/3	K95/97F/3:72	C 10533	Kiln channel 3	UP	Conical bowl	28	2a
95/4	K94/95A/3:172	C 10167	Kiln channel 2	UP	Side-spouted cup	25	2a
95/5	K93/87B/3:90A	C 10567	Kiln channel 1	UP	Bridge-spouted jar		1a
95/6	K94/95A/3:172	C 10168	Kiln channel 2	UP	Pithos	57	4
95/7	K94/95A/4:127	C 10566	Kiln firing pit	Mono	Bridge-spouted jar		1a
95/8	K95/97F/3:72	C 10530	Kiln channel 3	Mono	Conical cup P		1a
95/9	K95/97F/3:72	C 10531	Kiln channel 3	Mono	Conical cup P		1a
95/10	K95/97F/3:72	C 10055	Kiln channel 3	Mono	Conical cup P		1a
95/11	K93/87B/3:90	C 9917	Kiln channel 1	Mono	Conical cup P	13	1b
95/12	K93/87B/5:107C	C 9945	Kiln dump	UP	Conical cup E	9	1b
95/13	K95/97F/3:72	C 10528	Kiln channel 3	UP	Conical cup C		1b
95/14	K95/97F/3:72	C 10524	Kiln channel 3	UP	Conical cup C		1b
95/15	K93/87B/3:90	C 9915	Kiln channel 1	Mono	Conical cup Q	15	2a
95/16	K95/97F/3:72	C 10525	Kiln channel 3	UP	Conical cup C		1b
95/17	K95/97F/3:73	C 10514	Kiln channel 3	UP	Conical cup C		1a
95/18	K95/97F/3:72	C 10522	Kiln channel 3	DP	Bell cup		1a
95/19	K93/87B/5:107	C 9947	Kiln dump	UP	Bell cup	23	3
95/20	K93A/87B/4:96	C 10553	Kiln dump	LOD	Piriform rhyton		1a
95/21	K93/87B/7:115A	C 8979	Kiln dump	UP	Conical cup D		2a
95/22	K93/87B/6:111	C 9959	Kiln dump	UP	Conical cup C		1b
95/23	K93/87B/5:106C	C 9439	Kiln dump	LOD	Kalathos		1a
95/24	K94/95A/3:153	C 10301	Kiln dump	DOL	Cup		1b
95/25	K94/95A/3:152	C 10337	Kiln dump	LOD	Kalathos	33	2a
95/26	K94/95A/3:172	C 10601	Kiln channel 2	UP	Kalathos		1b
95/27	K94/95A/8:109	C 10072	Kiln dump	UP	Side-spouted cup		3
95/28	K94/95A/5:216	C 10272	Kiln dump	Mono	Ewer		2a
95/29	K94/95A/3:152	C 9930	Kiln dump	LOD	Kalathos	32	2a
95/30	K93/87B/5:106D	C 10499	Kiln dump	Mono	Collar-necked jug	45	2a
95/31	K93/87B/3:93A	C 10404	Kiln dump	LOD	Globular rhyton	50	1a
95/32	K93/87B/8:116B	C 10490	Kiln dump	LOD	Bridge-spouted jar		3
95/33	K93/87B/5:106C	C 10578	Kiln dump	UP	Pedestaled vase		1b
95/34	K93/87B/5:106C	C 10569	Kiln dump	UP	Pedestaled vase		3
95/35	K93/87B/4–7:108	C 8937	Kiln dump	Mono	Teacup	20	1b
95/36	K93/87B/5:106B	C 10583	Kiln dump	LOD	Bridge-spouted jar		1a
95/37	K93/87B/6:107	C 9985	Kiln dump	LOD	Convex-sided bowl	26	3
95/38	K93/87B/5:106D	C 10550	Kiln dump	LOD	Bridge-spouted jar	35	2a
95/39	K94/95A/3:165	C 10568	Kiln dump	Mono	Ewer	47	3
95/40	K93/87B/8:116B	C 8973	Kiln dump	Mono	Ewer	49	2a
95/41	K93/87B/6:111D	C 9934	Kiln dump	UP	Ewer(?)	46	1b
95/42	K94/95A/5:179	C 10420	Kiln dump	UP	Side-spouted cup		1b
95/43	K94/95A/3:285	C 10605	Kiln dump	Waster			2b
95/44	K94/95A/5:161	C 10138	Kiln dump	Waster	Basin		6
95/45	K94/95A/3:148	C 10286	Kiln dump	Waster	Kalathos		2a
95/46	K93/87B/6:111D	C 10554	Kiln dump	Mono	Ewer	48	2b
95/47	K94/95A/3:71	C 10018	Kiln dump	Waster	Oval-mouthed amphora		2b
95/48	K94/95A/4:127	C 10600	Kiln firing pit	DOL	Oval-mouthed amphora(?)		2b
95/49	K93/87B/5:106C	C 10602	Kiln dump	Waster	Jug		2b
95/50	K93/87B/7:112D	C 10603	Kiln dump	Waster			2b
95/51	K94/95A/3:107	C 10604	Kiln dump	Waster			2b

TABLE 12, CONT'D

Sample	Excavation No.	Inv. No.	Context	Surface	Shape	Pottery Cat.	Group No.
95/52	K93/87B/6:111	C 10597	Kiln dump	DOL	Oval-mouthed amphora	53	2a
95/53	K93/87B/4–7:108	C 9935	Kiln dump	LOD	Collar-necked jug	40	1b
95/54	K94/95A/3:147	C 10285	Kiln dump	CSE	Slab		5
95/55	K94/95A/3:100	C 10052	Kiln channel 3	CSE	Slab		6
95/56	K93/87B/7:115	C 10606	Kiln dump	CSE	Slab		6
95/57	K93/87B/8:116E	C 8971	Kiln dump	DOL	Oval-mouthed amphora	52	2a

UP = Unpainted   DOL = Dark-on-light
Mono = Monochrome   DP = Dipped
LOD = Light-on-dark   CSE = Coarse, unpainted

these was widespread even in the Early Bronze Age.[4] Such results, combined with renewed work to discriminate chemically between samples from different areas of Crete, have led to a need for new control groups, based either on a combination of stylistic and petrographic information or on the analysis of assemblages from pottery kilns of Minoan date.[5] What is clear is that many of the large excavated settlements once consumed large quantities of pottery, some of which was not made in the immediate vicinity.[6] This human-induced complexity in the ceramic picture—the wide distribution of ceramic vessels—compounds that introduced by natural factors. The latter include a general homogeneity of composition, which is due to the common use of similar Neogene gray clays throughout the island.

The discovery of the Kommos kiln provides an opportunity to analyze pottery that is definitely found at its *production* location, forming a certain "control group." Furthermore, it enables a different approach to the second major theme, that of ceramic technology. The most successful technological studies have concentrated on distinctive classes of pottery, on diachronic change in technology, or on the comparisons of different classes of one period within a site.[7] Examining a kiln assemblage, however, brings us nearer to the individual decisions made by potters within a specific location, in the context of the local environment, to their social and economic organization, and to the functional demands of the vessels produced. Matters of interest to us include the degree of standardization in such an assemblage, the variation in fabric recipes according to vessel func-

4. Day, Wilson, and Kiriatzi (1997) have argued for a restricted number of production centers in Early Minoan central and eastern Crete, with a wide distribution of their products. Such patterns have been documented in detail for the Mesara imports to Knossos in EM I–IIA (Wilson and Day 1994) and for the consumption of ceramics from different centers at the Early Minoan IIB hilltop hamlet of Myrtos Fournou Korifi (Whitelaw et

al. 1997). The pattern is similar in the Middle and Late Bronze Ages, with specific centers of production and the distribution of ceramics within local areas and beyond (Day 1995; Day and Wilson 1998).

5. Discrimination by chemical analysis within central Crete is often difficult (Jones 1986, pp. 256–257; Tomlinson 1991). Recent work has demonstrated the effect of technology on ceramic group composition in central

and eastern Crete (Day et al. 1999).

6. For a consideration on the movement of Kamares Ware between regions of central Crete see Day and Wilson 1998.

7. For studies of classes of pottery, see Betancourt 1979, 1984; Noll, Holm, and Born 1971; and Noll 1978. Work on variation between different wares and fabrics over one site was discussed by Maniatis, Perdikatsis, and Kotsakis (1988).

tion and morphology, and the adaptation of firing conditions for specific pot types. All these factors can provide insight into the skills, decisions, and organization of production of the potters at Kommos.

On a more detailed level, analytical work on the pottery of the kiln may lead to insights into how the kiln itself functioned. The design and use of the well-known Minoan channel kilns has long been a matter of debate, and analytical work such as that presented here can reveal much about the firing conditions within the kiln.[8]

THE ANALYTICAL PROGRAM

To take advantage of this opportunity, an integrated program of analysis was designed and executed using petrographic thin-section analysis (PE), scanning electron microscopy (SEM), neutron activation analysis (NAA), X-ray fluorescence (XRF), and X-ray diffraction (XRD). The study considered 57 samples selected as representative of the range of shapes and macroscopic fabrics present in pottery excavated inside and around the kiln structure (see Table 12). Excepting those sherds that are clearly wasters, the flawed products of drastic overfiring, it was assumed that much of this kiln dump was representative of the normal production of the kiln.

All samples were analyzed by each method, in order to produce a detailed account of the materials chosen, their manipulation in manufacture, and the relationship between the mineralogy and the chemistry of these ceramics. The pottery not only provided information on the technology of production at this site, as well as a petrographic and chemical control, but also led to substantive, unexpected implications for the methodology of physico-chemical analysis in general, and specifically of postburial alteration of ceramic composition. These aspects, including the results of XRF and XRD, will be published in detail elsewhere.

The general aims of the analytical program were as follows:

—To identify clay and temper sources exploited in the production of pottery at this kiln site.
—To collect information on the firing temperature and atmosphere used in the kiln.
—To characterize and group the pottery in mineralogical and chemical terms, relating this to stylistic groups.
—To investigate the reasons for any compositional variation within this kiln assemblage.

This section of the report will first summarize the petrographic fabric groupings, then assess the micromorphological characteristics of petrographic and stylistic groups by SEM. This will be followed by an account of chemical grouping of the material by NAA.

8. The LM I kiln at Aghia Triada that is so similar to the one at Kommos has been published by Levi and Laviosa (1986); that and other kilns are discussed in Tomasello 1996. The channel kilns from Knossos of uncertain function, excavated by Warren in the Stratigraphic Museum Extension excavations, are presented in Catling 1979. J. Soles and C. Davaras recently excavated a small channel kiln in what they interpret as an artisans' quarter at Mochlos (Soles 1997). S. Chrysoulaki has also excavated a channel kiln at Kokkino Froudi in the area of Sphaka, Zakros (Chrysoulaki 1996). The Aghia Triada, Mochlos, and Sphaka Zakrou examples seem to be related to ceramic production, whereas the specific function of those at Knossos and another at Kato Zakros appear to be less clear.

THIN-SECTION PETROGRAPHY

Thin-section petrography has been applied to a variety of ceramic assemblages within the Aegean and especially on the island of Crete, where a varied geology aids discrimination between raw material sources. The technique involves examination on the polarizing microscope of the minerals, rocks, and textures that are present in the ceramic. The characterization and consequent grouping of pottery samples in itself can be valuable in archaeological interpretation, especially in combination with typological information. The second source of interpretation is the technological information petrographic analysis provides, enabling in some instances the reconstruction of recipes for raw materials used. Finally, the combination of all data can sometimes lead to an ascription of provenance for the ceramic object.

On Crete, ceramic petrography has been exploited in the study of both provenance and technology. Riley carried out some of the first analyses, characterizing changes in raw material sources at Knossos over time[9] and demonstrating the exchange of coarse ceramics on the island.[10] Betancourt and Myer have taken the approach further, using petrography both to characterize the production of specific sites[11] and as part of multitechnique studies of specific ware groups.[12] More recently Day and coworkers have carried out a number of studies on both site-based and regional production and distribution patterns.[13]

These latter studies have used petrography in combination with chemical analysis, critically developing methodology for integrating mineralogical with chemical information.[14]

Thin-section analysis of the Kommos kiln assemblage produced a restricted number of fabric groups, characterized according to the texture of the ceramics, their mineral and rock content, and their optical activity. This last reflects their firing conditions. The fabrics are presented in summary here, whilst detailed description of the fabrics is presented in Appendix I.

The assemblage was divided into six petrographic groups, the first two of which have two subgroups. Almost all of the samples are closely related according to petrographic criteria.

1. A fine fabric, which can be divided between relatively high-fired and low-fired subgroups
2. Medium-coarse fabric with rounded sand inclusions, with an overfired subgroup
3. Medium-coarse calcareous fabric
4. Coarse fabric with sand inclusions
5. Siltstone/mudstone fabric
6. Coarse red fabric with schist

9. Riley 1983.

10. Riley (1981) analyzed coarse vessels at Knossos; these contained serpentine and therefore were not compatible with a local origin.

11. For Kommos, see Myer and Betancourt 1990; for Pseira, see Myer, McIntosh, and Betancourt 1995.

12. Betancourt and coworkers carried out integrated studies of two characteristic pottery wares from eastern Crete: Vasiliki Ware (Betancourt 1979) and White-on-Dark Ware (Betancourt 1984).

13. These studies cover Early, Middle, and Late Minoan ceramics: Day 1995, 1997; Day, Wilson, and Kiriatzi 1997; Day and Wilson 1998; Wilson and Day 1994.

14. Day et al. 1999.

GROUP 1A AND 1B

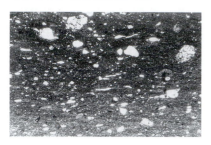

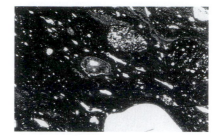

Figure 47 *(left)*. Photomicrograph of 95/10 to illustrate group 1a, XP. Horizontal dimension = 4mm

Figure 48 *(right)*. Photomicrograph of 95/22 to illustrate group 1b, XP. Horizontal dimension = 4mm

Fine-grained fabric   Figs. 47, 48

Low optical activity (high-fired): Kommos 95/5, 7, 8, 9, 10, 17, 18, 20, 23, 31, 36 (11 samples)

High optical activity (low-fired): Kommos 95/11, 12, 13, 14, 16, 22, 24, 26, 33, 35, 41, 42, 53 (13 samples)

A fine fabric with few aplastic inclusions. The micromass is generally yellowish orange and displays streaks of calcareous clay in a darker matrix, which is taken to indicate the mixing of clays in the preparation of the clay body.

The coarse fraction contains sandstone and serpentine, while the fine fraction includes carbonates, quartz, biotite and muscovite mica, chlorite, and clinozoisite. The micromass varies from being optically highly active to optically slightly active. This great difference bears witness to the use of a range of quite different firing temperatures to fire what is essentially the same clay body.

Figure 49 *(below, left)*. Photomicrograph of 95/29 to illustrate group 2a, XP. Horizontal dimension = 4mm

Figure 50 *(below, center)*. Photomicrograph of 95/52 to illustrate group 2a, XP. Horizontal dimension = 4mm

Figure 51 *(below, right)*. Photomicrograph of 95/46 to illustrate group 2b, XP. Horizontal dimension = 4mm

GROUP 2A

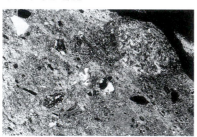

GROUP 2B

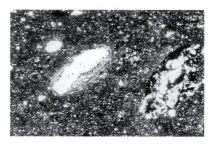

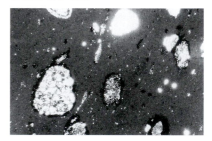

Medium-coarse fabric   Figs. 49, 50

Kommos 95/2, 3, 4, 15, 21, 25, 28, 29, 30, 38, 40, 45, 52, 57 (14 samples)

The medium-coarse fabric contains few to common inclusions. The micromass is as in group 1, with evidence of clay mixing. The coarse fraction of the aplastics comprises a variety of schists, amphibolite, volcanic rocks, and phyllites, as well as a range of sedimentary rock fragments. The fine fraction contains quartz, biotite, carbonates, amphibole, epidote, and clinozoisite. Most

examples of this fabric are optically slightly active, suggesting a generally higher firing temperature than group 1.

Medium-coarse, overfired   Fig. 51

Kommos 95/43, 46, 47, 48, 49, 50, 51 (7 samples)

This fabric is a higher-fired version of the group 2a fabric described above. Many of the aplastic inclusions have suffered alteration and bloating due the very high firing temperatures.

GROUP 3

Figure 52 *(left)*. Photomicrograph of 95/19 to illustrate group 3, XP. Horizontal dimension = 4mm

Figure 53 *(right)*. Photomicrograph of 95/39 to illustrate group 3, XP. Horizontal dimension = 4mm

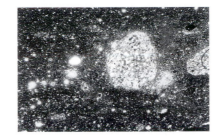 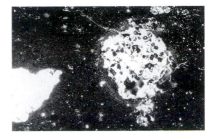

Medium-coarse calcareous fabric

Figs. 52, 53

Kommos 95/19, 27, 32, 34, 37, 39 (6 samples)

This medium-coarse fabric contains few inclusions in a micromass that is generally more clearly calcareous than examples of group 2. The coarse fraction includes sandstone and a lesser proportion of schist, siltstone, and polycrystalline quartz, displaying a slightly different variant from the main medium-coarse fabric. Nevertheless, there are still indications of clay mixing, although the matrix is more calcareous and the aplastics seem to indicate a somewhat different choice of materials.

Figure 54 *(below, left)*. Photomicrograph of 95/1 to illustrate group 4, XP. Horizontal dimension = 4mm

Figure 55 *(below, center)*. Photomicrograph of 95/54 to illustrate group 5, XP. Horizontal dimension = 4mm

Figure 56 *(below, right)*. Photomicrograph of 95/56 to illustrate group 6, XP. Horizontal dimension = 4mm

GROUP 4

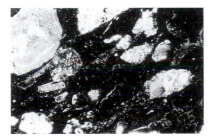

Coarse fabric with sand inclusions

Fig. 54

Kommos 95/1, 6 (2 samples)

This fabric is a coarser version of group 2, with aplastic inclusions similar in composition, which occur more frequently. The clay matrix displays less evidence of clay mixing than do the medium and fine equivalents.

GROUP 5

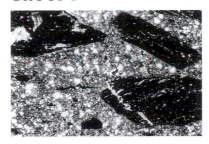

Siltstone fabric   Fig. 55

Kommos 95/54 (1 sample)

This fabric is characterized by the presence of large, elongate grains of fine-grained, dark brown siltstone rock fragments together with a range of generally elongate, low-grade metamorphic rock fragments in a quartz-rich red-firing clay. The optical activity of the matrix suggest a relatively low firing temperature.

GROUP 6

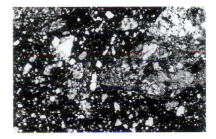

Coarse red fabric with schist   Fig. 56

Kommos 95/44, 55, 56 (3 samples)

This fabric is characterized by the presence of abundant low-grade metamorphic rock fragments of various types, with rare metamorphosed volcanic rock fragments. The clay is red-firing and appears noncalcareous. The aplastics of this fabric link it to groups 1, 2, and 4, but it appears not to be based on a marl clay matrix.

Raw Materials Used in the Manufacture of Pottery: The Evidence of Petrography

As a result of the petrographic analyses, several comments can be made that address the questions posed in this study.

First, the groups formed are relatively internally consistent and, in the case of groups 1–4, are closely related to each other. Groups 1–4 are based primarily on the same type of groundmass and therefore on the same clay raw materials. They are differentiated by grain size and proportion of their aplastic inclusions and, in the case of the two subgroups of group 1, by optical activity. They present clear evidence for clay mixing, both through a bimodality of the grain size distribution (see especially groups 1 and 4: Appendix I, pp. 139–141 and 148–150) and through their textural concentration features. As should be the case, groups 1–4 reflect different clay mixes that form, however, a consistent assemblage in terms of geological origins: they consist of recipe variants used by the potters of Kommos that were created from their chosen raw materials.

Through the evidence for clay mixing, it may be suggested that at least one clay has been used to form the basic paste. The analysis suggests that the mix includes a calcareous clay and a red, perhaps noncalcareous clay. The use of such a clay mix has been suggested for the Mesara previously and is common in eastern Crete.[15] Both Neogene calcareous and red alluvial clays are available in quantity within the locality of Kommos in the Mesara Plain and the surrounding foothills of the Asterousia.[16]

In petrographic terms, the aplastics of these groups are compatible with those of fabrics described in previous work in the area of the Mesara, with a general source in rocks of the ophiolite series and schist/gneiss.[17] These rocks are present in the foothills of the Asterousia Mountains on the south side of the Mesara Plain and in the foothills of the Psiloritis range to the north of the plain.[18] The gneiss outcrops just 4 km east of Kommos, around the villages of Sivas and Kouses. The altered basaltic rocks are especially characteristic of the Mesara and have been observed by one of the present authors in geological deposits and linings of modern kilns to the south of Kouses, on the southern edge of the Mesara.[19] The frequent, well-rounded sand grains appearing as dominant aplastics within a fine clay matrix are interpreted as sand temper added by the potter. This practice conforms to a long-lived tradition of paste formation in south-central Crete during the Bronze Age, which has its roots in Early Minoan I and even the Final Neolithic.[20] Similar fabrics are present throughout the Early, Middle, and Late Minoan periods in the Mesara as well as in the Early Minoan period in the Asterousia.[21] Although a characteristic of pottery from Kommos, sand tempering is not a feature exclusive to this site. In fact, Neopalatial fabrics throughout the plain, including those found at Aghia Triada and associated with the kiln at that site, were made with a similar general recipe.[22]

Group 3 differs slightly in its aplastics, in that it lacks the schists and amphibolites that link groups 1, 2, 4, and 6 to the gneiss of the Asterousia Nappe. Nevertheless it may be compatible with an origin in the Flysch or Vatos Schists east of Pitsidia.

15. For such clay mixing at Kommos, see Myer and Betancourt 1990; for eastern Crete, see Betancourt 1984.

16. Detailed geological maps of the area have been published (Bonneau, Jonkers, and Meulenkamp 1984; Davi and Bonneau 1985). Gifford has summarized the geology and geomorphology of the area (Gifford 1995) and Wilson and Day (1994, fig. 10) provide a summary map of the geology relevant to this chapter.

17. For previous work, see Myer and Betancourt 1990; Wilson and Day 1994, pp. 56–70, fig. 10.

18. For the Asterousia, see Davi and Bonneau 1985; for the Mesara Plain itself, the foothills to the south, including Pitsidia, Sivas, and Kouses, and the foothills of Psiloritis, see Bonneau, Jonkers, and Meulenkamp 1984.

19. Myer and Betancourt (1990: see especially pl. A) argue that these are characteristic of the Kommos area.

20. Sand temper was found in Mesara imports to Knossos in EM I (Wilson and Day 1994, esp. pls. 11:e and 11:f), while some Final Neolithic pottery from Phaistos is sand tempered.

21. Whitelaw et al. 1997.

22. The common presence of this type of fabric recipe was a factor that complicated early work on Neopalatial storage jar production (Day 1988). For sand tempering in the Mesara, see Wilson and Day 1994, p. 52.

Turning to the remaining groups: group 5 has no known exact parallels either in the literature or in other samples examined by the authors. It is not incompatible with low-grade metamorphic rock sources on the south side of the Mesara, but it may be an intrusive piece that was not produced in this kiln. Although group 6 is the only fabric that does not display a calcareous groundmass, it nevertheless is related to groups 1–4 in terms of its aplastics and possibly also through some of the constituents of its red clay component. These coarse slabs have refractory properties and so would not be unsuitable as kiln furniture.

Examination of petrographic fabrics from the kiln provides important comparative material for other archaeological pottery found both on Crete and outside the island. Perhaps one of the most striking similarities is between certain transport stirrup jars found elsewhere in central Crete and the oval-mouthed amphoras from the Kommos kiln. Further work will shed light on the materials exploited, the technology used, and the location of pottery production in the Mesara, although it is clear from this and other work that the Mesara holds a special place in the production of ceramics in Bronze Age Crete.

PETROGRAPHIC GROUPS, TECHNOLOGY, AND THEIR RELATIONSHIP TO STYLISTIC CRITERIA

In terms of the other questions outlined, consideration of petrographic group membership is revealing. Two clear patterns emerge. The first relates to the link between the paste used for the vessels and the size/shape of the pot. The second concerns the relationship between the optical activity of the groundmass (indicative of firing temperature) and the presence/absence of painted decoration.

Within the first fabric group, the samples belong mostly to small shapes: predominantly to cups (14 of 24), but also to other small vessels, such as bridge-spouted jars, rhyta, kalathoi, a jug, a ewer(?), and a pedestaled vase. The optically inactive, high-fired subgroup (1a) comprises mainly painted ceramics (9 of 11 samples) and the optically active, low-fired group (1b) predominantly unpainted examples (9 of 13). As might be expected, the medium-coarse vessels of groups 2 and 3 are mainly slightly larger vessels, such as jars, kalathoi, and ewers. Group 4 consists of a basin and a pithos, which matches their coarse nature, while group 5 is a pottery slab of indeterminate function. Finally, group 6 consists of a basin base and two pottery slabs.

The petrographic analysis, then, shows clearly the choice of different clay pastes according to the size of the vessel, with the larger vessels having a correspondingly coarser fabric. The clay matrices appear to be broadly similar in all cases, but with slight differences due to differential mixing of clays to form the body, as suggested by textural observations in thin section. The clear differences lie in the proportion and size of aplastics, according to the vessel size. With the exception of groups 5 and 6, such choices should be linked to the requirements of the forming, firing, and use of the vessel and reflect variations on a basic choice of raw materials and a repeated recipe (see also below, p. 131).

The optical activity of a vessel's micromass is a function of the degree of its vitrification, which depends on the firing temperature experienced by that vessel.[23] The groupings based on variation in the optical activity of the micromass suggest the existence of differences in the firing temperatures exploited for different vessel types at this single production site. Such groupings are not random, but rather they imply a correlation with whether the vessels were unpainted (low-fired examples) or painted. For a detailed investigation of this and other technological aspects, scanning electron microscopy is the technique that provides the most information.

SCANNING ELECTRON MICROSCOPY

Scanning electron microscopy is a well-established technique used for the characterization of ceramic technology. Examination of ceramics under the SEM provides information concerning their micromorphology and, more specifically, the degree of vitrification and the texture. When this information is combined with chemical analysis (energy dispersive x-ray analysis: EDAX), the type and treatment of raw materials, the firing parameters (temperature, atmosphere), and the quality of decoration can be assessed.

Freshly fractured surfaces, in cross-section, of all sherds were mounted on aluminum stages and examined. The samples were oriented in such a way that both the exterior and interior surfaces could be observed and analyzed. Firing temperatures were estimated from the assessment of degree of vitrification, using the vitrification stages established by Maniatis and Tite.[24] The firing atmosphere was determined from the color of the body and the decoration. For reddish/brown bodies without decoration an oxidizing atmosphere was assumed; for the same bodies but with black iron–rich decoration an oxidizing–reducing–oxidizing atmosphere was assumed; and for a buff or gray body a mixed or a reducing atmosphere was attributed. In the case of a reducing atmosphere, the firing temperature estimation was lowered by 50° C because of the advancement in vitrification from the presence of FeO, which acts as a flux.

In the Kommos material, however, there were marked difficulties in examination, due to the deposition of high amounts of secondary calcite. Secondary calcite is crystallized and deposited on ceramics, either during use or during burial, usually forming small crystals that fill voids. In the material studied it was present on the surface of most of the sherds as well as in the voids of the ceramic bodies (Fig. 57). For this reason, systematic examination of decorative materials and techniques was not possible, although some general observations are related in the account that follows. Table 13 contains information on the CaO levels in the ceramic body, firing temperature estimates from the level of vitrification, and data on the firing atmosphere used in production; however, due the problems of secondary calcite, there are no data on the painted layers.

A large proportion of the pottery excavated in the vicinity of the kiln and in the kiln channels consisted of conical cups. In order for sampling to be representative of the pottery excavated, 25% of the samples analyzed were unpainted or monochrome conical cups. All seven unpainted conical cups analyzed by SEM exhibited a remarkable consistency in microstruc-

Figure 57. SEM photomicrograph of paint layer of a painted conical cup (95/15). Formation of secondary calcite can be seen in the void between the paint and the body. Bar = 10μm

23. Whitbread 1995, p. 382.
24. Maniatis and Tite 1981. Their characterization of vitrification stages has been used in several papers dealing with technological studies of Cretan pottery: Maniatis 1984; Kilikoglou 1994; Floyd 1995.

TABLE 13. SCANNING ELECTRON MICROSCOPY RESULTS FOR THE KILN SAMPLES

Sample	Firing Atmosphere	Calcareous	Vitrification Body	Firing Temperature (°C)
95/1	O	high	NV	<750
95/2	O	medium	IV	750–800
95/3	O	medium	IV	750–800
95/4	O	medium	V_{C-}	800–850
95/5	O	medium	V_C/V_{C+}	1000–1080
95/6	O	high	V_C	850–1050
95/7	O–R–O	medium	V_C/V_{C+}	1000–1080
95/8	O–R–O		V_{C-}	800–850
95/9	O–R–O	medium	IV	750–800
95/10	O–R–O		V_{C-}	800–850
95/11	O–R–O	low	V_{C-}	800–850
95/12	O	medium	IV	750–800
95/13	O		NV	<750
95/14	O	medium	NV	<750
95/15	O–R–O	medium	V_{C-}	800–850
95/16	O	medium	NV	<750
95/17	O	medium	NV	<750
95/18	O	medium	V_C	850–1050
95/19	O	medium	V_C	850–1050
95/20	O–R–O	medium	V_C	850–1050
95/21	O	medium	NV	<750
95/22	O	medium	NV	<750
95/23	O–R–O		V_C/V_{C+}	1000–1080
95/25	O–R–O	medium	V_C	850–1050
95/26	O (FF*)	low	V_C	850–1050
95/27	O	high	V_{C+}	1050–1080
95/28	O–R–O		V_{C+}	1050–1080
95/29	O–R–O		V_{C+}	1050–1080
95/30	O	medium	V_{C-}	800–850
95/31	O–R–O	medium	V_{C-}	800–850
95/32	O–R–O	medium	V_C	850–1050
95/33	O	medium	IV	750–800
95/34	O	medium	V_C	850–1050
95/35	O–R–O	medium	V_{C-}	800–850
95/36	O	medium	V_C	850–1050
95/37	O–R–O	medium	V_{C+}	1050–1080
95/38	O–R–O		V_C	850–1050
95/39	O	high	V_C	850–1050
95/40	O–R–O		V_{C+}	1050–1080
95/41	O	medium	IV	<750
95/42	O	medium	V_C	850–1050
95/43		medium	TV	>1080
95/44		low	V_{C+}	1050–1080
95/45	O	medium	V_C	850–1050
95/46	O–R–O	medium	V_{C+}	1050–1080
95/47		medium	TV	>1080
95/48	O–R–O		TV-	>1080
95/49		medium	TV	>1080

TABLE 13, CONT'D

Sample	Firing Atmosphere	Calcareous	Vitrification Body	Firing Temperature (°C)
95/50		medium	TV	>1080
95/51		medium	TV	>1080
95/52	O–R–O		IV	750–800
95/53	O–R–O	medium	V_C	850–1050
95/54	O	low	IV	750–800
95/55	O	medium	IV	750–800
95/56	O	low	IV	750–800
95/57	O–R–O	low	V_C	850–1050

Firing temperature was estimated as a function of the vitrification state of the body, the level of Ca (calcareous), and the firing atmosphere.

Low = 3–6% CaO; medium = 6–10% CaO; high = >10% CaO
NV = no vitrification
IV = initial vitrification
V = extensive vitrification
TV = total vitrification
$_C$ = calcareous
* = Fast firing

ture, with no or very slight vitrification of clay (Fig. 58). This corresponds to a firing temperature of <750° C or around 750° C. Another feature worthy of note is the uniformity of the color of the ceramic bodies in all examples throughout the section. This indicates that even at such low temperatures, the oxidizing atmosphere of the kiln was complete and fully under control. This is unusual, as commonly the most predominant feature at these temperatures is a reducing atmosphere, which produces uneven coloring and often gray cores.[25] Similar consistency was observed in the microstructure of the *monochrome* conical cups, but for these, a slightly higher temperature (750–850° C) was employed consistently (Fig. 59).

In both conical cup groups the same type of calcareous clay was used and was fired in an oxidizing atmosphere, resulting in a pale red/brown color of the ceramic body. The black monochrome decoration of these cups was created by the application of a clay very low in calcium, finer than the body, and fired in a three-stage firing scheme: oxidation to the top temperature–reduction at the top temperature–oxidation during cooling. In this way the fine low calcareous clays vitrify in the reducing atmosphere and remain dark during the last oxidation stage, while the body, because of its porosity, re-oxidizes and turns red.[26] A typical microstructure of the paint layer of a conical cup is shown in Figure 57. The ca. 100° C difference in firing temperature between unpainted and monochrome conical cups seems intentional, because in order to achieve an intense color in the monochromes the temperature should reach the 800–850° C range. At such temperatures and in noncalcareous clays (slip clay), iron-oxide conglomerates increase and therefore the intensity of the red color increases too, which at the reduction stage produces dark gray/black colors.[27]

25. See Kilikoglou and Maniatis 1993 for discussion of this.
26. See Kilikoglou 1994.
27. Maniatis, Simopoulos, and Kostikas 1981.

Figure 58. SEM photomicrograph of an unpainted conical cup (95/14) showing no vitrification.
Bar = 10μm

Figure 59. SEM photomicrograph of a monochrome conical cup (95/11) with incomplete vitrification.
Bar = 10μm

Figure 60. SEM photomicrograph of a ewer(?) (95/41) exhibiting initial stages of vitrification.
Bar = 100μm

Figure 61. SEM photomicrograph of an unpainted kalathos (95/26) exhibiting extensive vitrification of calcareous clay.
Bar = 100μm

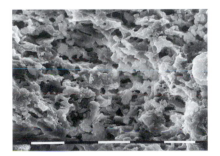

Figure 62. SEM photomicrograph of a monochrome ewer (95/46) with dense vitreous mass.
Bar = 100μm

The other thirteen unpainted vases examined were a bell cup, side-spouted cups, a kalathos, a conical bowl, a bridge-spouted jar, a ewer(?), basins, a pithos, and pedestaled vases. Firing temperatures in this group of samples vary from 750° C to 1080° C. This temperature range results in ceramic bodies exhibiting very little vitrification (<750° C) (Fig. 60) up to extensive vitrification (850–1050° C or a bit higher) (Fig. 61). They were all made of calcareous clays, which develop a very stable extensive micro-structure for a wide range of temperatures (850–1050° C). This is advantageous for the potter, for the quality of the pottery in terms of mechanical properties can be consistent even if the kiln temperature varies within this range.[28] Within this firing range, it is conceivable that higher firing temperatures may be more suitable for larger vessels, but the nature and numbers of our samples do not allow us to comment further.

The other seven monochrome vessels studied were four ewers, one bridge-spouted jar, one collar-necked jug, and a teacup. Four of them (three ewers and the bridge-spouted jar), bearing dark decoration, were fired at high temperatures (1000–1080° C) (Fig. 62); this is at the higher end, above the beneficial range of 850–1050° C, which produces good quality decoration.[29] At the 1000–1080° C range the ceramic bodies produced

28. Maniatis and Tite 1981.
29. Kilikoglou 1994.

Figure 63. SEM photomicrograph
of a high-fired light-on-dark
kalathos (95/25). Bar = 100μm

Figure 64. SEM photomicrograph
of a light-on-dark kalathos (95/23)
showing higher degree of vitrification than above. Bar = 100μm

have very high strength but the quality of the decoration is poor because of
bloating pores, which make the decorative surface friable and dull.[30] The
clay used for decoration is chemically similar to the one used for the conical cups. It seems that in these vessels good-quality decoration might not
have been the priority. The jug and teacup, coated with a red paint, were
fired below 850°C, a temperature at which a black color on a light back-
ground is not possible using the three-stage firing.

Ten samples bearing light-on-dark decoration were examined and
compared to the monochrome and unpainted vessels of similar shape.
Light-on-dark decoration was produced by the iron-reduction technique
using noncalcareous clays for the substance painted on the surface. Firing
was carried out in a reducing atmosphere to produce a black paint, and
then the atmosphere was changed to oxidizing to produce a light-color
body. The majority of the pottery studied was fired in the 850–1080°C
temperature range (Figs. 63, 64), with one at a lower temperature (800–
850°C).

Overall the SEM analyses of the Kommos kiln assemblage show that
the vessels underwent firing at a variety of temperatures. However, there
are several trends visible, notably the higher firing of the monochrome
conical cups compared to the unpainted ones and the high firing temperatures of all the light-on-dark and the majority of monochrome examples.
Such a temperature is necessary to produce an iron-reduction black finish.
The alteration of the firing atmosphere from oxidizing to reducing attests
to a built kiln of some sophistication. Desirable firing temperatures may
have been achieved by placing the pots at different positions in the kiln.
The two lower-fired, iron-rich, red monochrome vessels analyzed (95/30,
95/35) either accidentally or deliberately did not reach the desired temperature to produce a black finish, perhaps due to their position in the
kiln. However, although such differentiation by position in the kiln seems
plausible, all the temperature differences among the pottery pieces analyzed seem in excess of what might reasonably be assumed to be the result
of placement of pottery within one kiln firing.

30. For strength of ceramics, see
Kilikoglou, Vekinis, and Maniatis 1995.

Neutron Activation Analysis

Chemical characterization of archaeological pottery, for provenance determination, is based on the principle that ceramics made by different raw materials should exhibit different chemical patterns. In order for this principle to be applied, chemical control groups must be constructed for the areas and the particular types of pottery under investigation. This is the manner in which most pottery provenance work in the Aegean has been carried out (Jones 1986). However, as already mentioned in the introduction to this chapter, problems have arisen recently in reassessments of chemical control groups in central Crete, resulting mainly from the formation of questionable control groups. Therefore, this study is a unique opportunity to characterize a kiln group from Bronze Age Crete that comprises pottery clearly produced, rather than consumed, at the site. In this way a secure chemical group for the Kommos kiln will be established.

All samples were powdered, homogenized, and left overnight to dry at 120° C. A portion of about 150 mg from each sample was then weighed and heat-sealed in polyethylene vials. The same procedure was followed for the reference materials used, an International Atomic Energy Agency SOIL-7 and an in-house Lefkandi Brick. Samples and standards were irradiated in batches of ten (eight samples and two standards) at the swimming pool reactor of NCSR Demokritos at a thermal neutron flux of 3×10^{13} n.cm^{-2}.s^{-1}. Eight days after irradiation the samples and standards were measured for Sm, Lu, U, Yb, As, Sb, Ca, Na, and La, and twenty days later for Ce, Th, Cr, Hf, Cs, Tb, Sc, Rb, Fe, Ta, Co, and Eu.

The complete analytical data are presented in Table 14. An initial examination of the results reveals that there is a relative chemical homogeneity among the samples for most of the elements analyzed. This might perhaps be expected as they represent a series of cup/jug/jar shapes from one kiln structure, comprising fine or medium-coarse illitic calcareous clays. They do not include cooking vessels, which might be more likely to have been manufactured from another type of clay, especially a noncalcareous material. Additionally, we are dealing with pottery from a single production site where geologically similar clays have been used (see petrographic analysis results above). Some of the elements that display relative homogeneity are La, Th, Sc, and Fe; these have an overall 6.8%, 11.9%, 11.6%, and 10.8% standard deviation, respectively. However, some of the elements exhibit a variability that is much higher than normal levels. Besides some extreme values in Sb and Ta, which are attributed to the poor counting statistics, and in As, which is due to its inherent natural inhomogeneity, the elements that display anomalous variability are Na, Cs, and Rb. These three elements are alkalines, known in geochemistry to be relatively mobile, and we are probably dealing with variation induced by conditions prevalent in the burial environment—most probably due to the influence of the proximity of seawater, or the partial immersion of the site in seawater.[31] High variation in alkalines within archaeological pottery has been reported previously in the literature, and it is attributed to the atomic substitution of these elements.[32]

31. For marine transgression at the site, see Gifford 1995, pp. 71–80.

32. Picon 1991; Fillieres, Harbottle, and Sayre 1983.

TABLE 14. NEUTRON ACTIVATION ANALYSIS COMPOSITIONAL DATA (in PPM)

	Sm	Lu	U	Yb	As	Sb	Ca*	Na*	La	Ce	Th	Cr	Hf	Cs	Tb	Sc	Rb	Fe*	Ta	Co	Eu
95/1	4.67	0.31	1.96	2.40	7.0	0.2	5.3	0.675	23.75	55.19	9.31	397	3.57	4.60	0.40	20.49	45.02	5.932	0.82	37.05	0.76
95/2	3.95	0.33	1.42	2.14	7.1	0.6	7.1	0.791	22.05	65.73	8.16	472	2.90	4.47	nd	21.78	52.95	5.984	1.30	39.56	0.90
95/3	4.75	0.31	2.19	2.53	7.4	0.2	7.7	0.633	23.71	57.50	9.02	439	3.46	3.85	0.45	19.41	66.12	5.499	0.62	36.40	0.72
95/4	3.95	0.37	2.41	2.45	7.1	0.6	6.9	0.612	22.83	61.67	9.38	369	2.85	5.42	0.43	20.47	104.82	5.797	1.33	36.11	0.80
95/5	4.14	0.39	2.73	2.77	5.9	0.6	6.9	0.507	25.81	78.33	11.52	496	3.95	5.45	0.21	26.80	82.18	7.059	0.76	45.16	1.15
95/6	4.18	0.31	1.86	2.43	6.3	0.2	6.0	0.887	22.70	51.91	8.04	306	3.10	4.65	0.17	18.64	99.25	5.161	1.12	33.98	1.03
95/7	3.63	0.40	1.77	2.32	2.7	nd	6.2	0.737	23.14	61.67	9.46	386	2.81	7.15	nd	22.92	108.8	6.224	1.27	40.34	0.87
95/8	3.75	0.39	2.22	2.88	5.0	nd	5.3	0.419	24.34	63.03	11.05	527	4.13	4.23	nd	27.75	107.9	7.676	1.00	51.61	0.77
95/9	4.43	0.35	2.88	2.48	8.0	0.7	8.4	0.526	24.83	61.83	9.69	412	4.41	4.37	1.06	21.02	57.69	5.823	0.98	39.18	0.86
95/10	4.34	0.38	1.74	2.36	4.2	nd	7.7	0.412	24.17	61.05	10.98	472	3.65	2.01	nd	25.90	54.45	7.042	1.44	46.25	1.01
95/11	4.32	0.35	2.26	2.86	3.4	nd	4.7	0.408	25.75	66.44	11.32	563	3.96	5.51	nd	26.74	95.18	7.579	1.41	51.73	0.96
95/12	4.29	0.36	2.04	2.48	6.0	0.4	6.0	0.503	23.13	59.49	10.12	445	3.24	7.25	nd	24.50	119.5	6.576	0.92	41.12	0.86
95/13	3.78	0.33	1.92	2.08	13.4	0.5	4.6	0.561	23.12	62.88	9.11	310	3.23	6.68	0.12	19.30	93.47	5.483	0.49	33.53	0.74
95/14	3.52	0.35	1.50	2.20	9.7	0.5	5.3	0.478	20.79	55.55	8.82	314	3.62	6.27	0.29	19.65	66.56	5.560	1.42	34.74	0.93
95/15	4.55	0.31	1.93	2.45	7.6	0.6	7.8	0.713	24.08	73.53	9.40	431	4.14	6.93	0.44	21.09	78.29	5.706	1.05	38.73	1.06
95/16	3.52	0.32	2.65	2.33	6.6	0.2	3.6	0.554	20.58	58.01	9.49	323	3.85	10.06	0.42	19.92	137.3	5.646	1.00	37.10	0.97
95/17	3.77	0.33	2.55	2.67	4.0	nd	7.9	0.446	23.59	60.03	9.63	433	4.00	2.19	0.34	21.75	65.23	6.087	0.79	38.66	0.83
95/18	4.69	0.37	2.66	2.37	10.4	0.7	8.3	0.331	25.27	59.33	10.57	466	3.52	2.16	0.43	21.94	27.56	5.910	1.64	38.58	0.96
95/19	3.72	0.33	2.84	2.64	3.3	nd	9.6	0.521	23.25	57.53	9.71	416	3.55	5.53	0.46	22.24	85.35	6.270	0.59	41.29	0.96
95/20	4.01	0.39	2.62	2.60	7.6	0.6	9.6	0.390	24.53	62.26	9.91	406	3.46	3.79	nd	23.00	67.01	6.376	1.00	40.06	0.92
95/21	4.50	0.33	1.74	2.56	6.9	0.8	nd	0.624	21.84	77.25	10.78	429	3.96	8.60	0.52	24.18	108.2	6.688	0.77	43.78	1.00
95/22	4.18	0.32	2.17	2.13	5.7	0.5	6.1	0.738	22.05	68.70	8.83	397	3.46	8.30	0.86	20.43	116.6	5.635	0.76	37.94	0.65
95/23	4.61	0.37	2.19	2.18	6.4	0.6	7.5	0.743	24.31	57.33	9.47	431	3.12	6.40	0.17	23.48	105.2	6.138	1.20	41.03	0.98
95/24	3.28	0.32	2.74	2.12	5.9	0.2	7.1	0.888	19.68	49.27	7.06	303	3.08	5.16	0.38	18.23	68.48	4.986	0.24	32.26	0.73
95/25	4.35	0.38	2.69	2.38	5.8	0.5	7.5	0.737	24.16	57.15	9.80	423	2.35	4.62	0.30	23.13	86.75	6.170	0.74	40.75	0.91
95/26	4.24	0.34	1.86	2.25	6.4	0.6	3.1	0.597	21.96	57.48	9.29	358	2.88	11.15	0.16	22.59	141.9	5.925	0.66	40.73	1.07
95/27	4.12	0.35	3.12	2.12	5.1	nd	11.3	0.864	20.37	47.35	7.83	326	2.56	3.76	0.42	17.85	62.29	4.853	0.56	31.11	0.82
95/28	4.35	0.34	2.59	2.37	3.8	0.4	6.1	0.755	22.77	58.12	9.30	467	2.86	6.01	0.24	21.67	111.2	6.005	1.37	38.76	0.75
95/29	4.42	0.35	2.28	2.62	7.4	0.5	7.5	0.607	24.96	64.03	9.89	426	3.44	4.87	0.17	24.13	91.47	6.612	0.26	47.11	0.97
95/30	4.06	0.32	2.12	2.36	6.7	0.6	7.1	0.596	22.39	53.48	9.09	419	3.27	6.87	nd	21.41	112.4	5.720	1.14	36.97	0.93
95/31	5.21	0.40	1.68	2.43	5.5	0.8	5.6	0.737	26.13	65.74	9.95	488	3.19	6.19	nd	25.17	133.4	6.893	0.59	49.12	0.99
95/32	4.25	0.46	2.40	2.23	6.5	0.5	10.2	0.543	23.17	57.83	9.01	379	2.97	4.55	nd	23.06	106.6	6.313	0.82	42.32	0.75
95/33	4.71	0.38	2.45	2.59	7.4	0.6	7.8	0.656	24.38	62.13	10.02	367	2.92	6.27	nd	21.16	116.0	5.972	1.05	40.39	1.23
95/34	4.53	0.36	2.52	2.42	5.1	0.4	10.1	0.544	24.59	60.63	9.08	373	3.19	4.60	0.58	21.78	113.9	5.872	0.46	39.71	0.97
95/35	4.43	0.30	1.77	2.34	7.7	0.8	7.3	0.365	25.25	76.71	9.98	437	3.04	6.47	0.49	24.07	99.18	6.546	0.75	44.16	0.85
95/36	3.96	0.37	2.90	2.58	6.0	0.5	10.6	0.516	24.46	77.32	10.34	439	3.57	4.41	0.81	23.52	96.45	6.314	0.99	40.64	0.94

95/37	4.14	0.39	3.18	2.37	2.3	0.4	9.8	1.158	23.10	55.26	8.80	375	2.90	6.01	0.45	21.27	39.78	5.784	0.95	39.05	0.83
95/38	3.42	0.34	2.12	2.53	8.7	0.7	6.8	0.610	23.85	67.58	9.15	427	3.53	6.57	0.21	23.81	102.0	6.590	0.83	43.33	1.06
95/39	4.16	0.41	2.81	2.22	4.3	nd	9.9	0.671	22.94	56.31	8.73	359	2.97	6.12	0.37	20.73	117.1	5.744	0.75	35.75	1.03
95/40	4.53	0.44	3.27	3.13	6.9	0.6	4.2	0.728	26.74	70.71	10.30	400	4.24	3.39	0.58	21.05	84.87	6.486	1.56	38.78	0.98
95/41	4.57	0.39	3.21	2.83	10.2	0.6	5.4	0.636	24.16	61.83	10.41	396	3.92	6.49	0.77	23.06	162.7	6.604	1.15	42.28	0.86
95/42	3.91	0.31	2.01	2.43	6.2	0.6	5.0	0.638	23.41	70.93	9.33	441	3.47	6.63	0.56	23.44	113.7	6.131	1.48	40.42	0.89
95/43	4.53	0.36	2.12	2.18	3.4	0.3	7.1	0.806	22.36	56.54	9.11	345	2.81	5.75	0.62	22.43	86.91	6.180	0.48	40.03	1.00
95/44	4.82	0.41	2.26	3.12	4.8	0.7	3.5	1.314	26.62	71.71	8.83	339	4.96	5.58	0.93	21.04	110.6	5.661	1.10	33.59	1.27
95/45	4.27	0.34	2.04	2.41	7.2	0.7	8.6	0.739	24.39	74.18	9.34	490	3.53	5.17	nd	21.34	107.5	5.854	1.06	39.30	0.90
95/46	4.31	0.34	1.58	2.55	2.8	0.5	10.1	0.974	21.68	60.22	8.15	445	2.87	6.31	0.28	21.05	85.26	6.043	0.80	41.32	1.15
95/47	3.95	0.34	2.80	2.36	4.8	0.7	6.2	0.780	23.30	57.80	9.01	384	3.08	8.28	nd	22.10	110.0	5.970	0.30	40.12	0.91
95/48	3.63	0.36	1.89	2.11	2.7	0.3	7.3	0.763	22.07	54.76	8.17	323	3.32	6.10	0.10	19.04	93.45	4.996	0.71	33.01	0.72
95/49	3.57	0.29	1.86	2.33	3.1	0.5	8.6	1.109	21.73	62.81	8.84	403	3.30	5.43	0.42	21.76	52.45	5.936	0.56	39.75	1.14
95/50	4.65	0.30	2.28	2.33	3.4	0.8	11.0	1.041	22.99	62.16	8.24	353	3.47	5.01	nd	21.24	69.56	5.665	0.88	38.19	1.06
95/51	4.11	0.31	2.49	2.29	4.8	0.7	6.6	0.844	22.16	58.27	8.79	334	3.14	7.33	0.19	21.18	131.4	5.795	0.69	38.74	0.97
95/52	3.86	0.30	3.00	2.23	6.7	0.6	5.9	0.827	23.20	53.53	8.83	386	3.01	6.04	0.31	20.56	161.2	5.646	0.83	38.34	0.88
95/53	4.42	0.40	1.82	2.49	7.2	0.5	6.5	0.553	24.20	69.77	10.34	499	3.51	8.28	0.39	24.06	133.6	6.682	1.57	45.42	1.09
95/54	4.50	0.34	1.57	2.47	5.6	0.6	nd	0.800	23.39	58.37	8.60	362	5.02	4.13	0.30	16.34	82.03	4.914	1.15	29.84	0.86
95/55	4.65	0.36	1.86	2.90	1.8	nd	3.6	1.265	22.48	61.96	7.03	328	4.69	3.86	0.32	20.34	67.40	5.402	0.48	33.06	1.27
95/56	5.09	0.46	1.76	2.83	5.1	0.4	nd	1.313	22.43	61.36	6.94	401	3.84	3.22	0.76	20.89	68.87	5.381	0.80	31.75	1.26
95/57	3.74	0.33	2.70	2.62	6.3	0.5	4.4	0.450	25.94	66.96	9.93	561	3.07	5.08	0.33	23.53	101.2	6.527	0.93	42.19	1.17

Ca, Na, and Fe are measured as percentages.

TABLE 15. CHARACTERISTIC VECTORS LOADINGS

Element	Characteristic Vector 1	Characteristic Vector 2
Sm	-0.022 (0)	-0.027 (0)
Lu	0.024 (0)	-0.025 (0)
U	0.098 (1)	-0.031 (0)
Yb	0.020 (0)	-0.011 (0)
Na	-0.813 (66)	0.085 (1)
La	0.093 (1)	-0.020 (0)
Ce	0.117 (1)	0.039 (0)
Th	0.256 (7)	0.017 (0)
Cr	0.266 (7)	-0.038 (0)
Hf	0.024 (0)	-0.068 (0)
Cs	-0.085 (1)	0.687 (47)
Sc	0.191 (4)	0.027 (0)
Rb	0.166 (3)	0.711 (51)
Fe	0.202 (4)	0.022 (0)
Co	0.229 (5)	0.046 (0)
Eu	-0.060 (0)	0.018 (0)
% of total variance	25.2	36.8

Figure 65 *(opposite page, above)*. Dendrogram using all elements except As, Sb, Ta. The three major clusters are marked, while cluster 4 contains samples 16, 26, and 21, and cluster 3 contains samples 10 and 18.

Figure 66 *(opposite page, below)*. Dendrogram as in Figure 65 but without the affected elements (Na, Cs, Rb)

In order to understand the contribution of each element to the overall data variation, the characteristic vectors of the variance-covariance matrix of the whole dataset were calculated using the statistical program ADCORR.[33] It is known that the vectors with the highest characteristic values follow the direction of the highest variability within the data set.[34] In the present case study the characteristic vectors with the two top characteristic values, accounting for 36.8% and 25.2% of the total variability, were mainly loaded by Na, Cs, and Rb, as can be seen in Table 15. This indicates that indeed Na, Cs, and Rb behave differently from the rest of the elements, and therefore these elements should not be automatically included in the formation of the control groups and the reference compositions for the Kommos kiln pottery.

As a next step, cluster analysis was performed on the neutron activation data using all the above elements as log-ratios over the concentration of La. The use of log-ratios was preferred as a means of compensating for all the perturbations that may occur in the data and are due to anthropogenic reasons (tempering, purification, firing, etc.) and natural alterations.[35] The square mean euclidean distance was used as an intersample distance, and the centroid clustering algorithm was employed on the distance matrix. In the dendrogram produced, five clusters can be identified (Fig. 65). The first cluster contains the majority of the samples analyzed (40 out of the 56), coming from all the stylistic groups, and therefore its chemical composition represents the fingerprint of the Kommos kiln pottery. This cluster contains most of the samples of petrographic groups 1, 2, 3, and 4. The second, the fourth, and the fifth clusters have been separated because of the Na, Cs, and Rb anomalies, and they contain the rest of the samples of the petrographic groups 1, 2, 3, and 4 that are not included in the first cluster. The third cluster contains samples with relatively low Ca and cor-

33. Sayre 1977. Detailed accounts of the interpretation of the Kommos kiln NAA data are presented elsewhere (Buxeda i Garrigòs, Kilikoglou, and Day in press).

34. J. C. Davis 1986.

35. This is not to say that the chemical variations induced by anthropogenic activity are not valid categories in themselves in archaeological terms. However, in trace element provenance studies (that is, finding the *geological* or *spatial* provenance of a ceramic) it is desirable for the data to be as free as possible of perturbations induced by tempering with aplastics and those resulting from loss-on-ignition or post-burial alteration (Buxeda i Garrigòs 1999). If such correction is not made for such potential alteration, then two ceramics made with the same clay, but tempered or altered to a greater or lesser degree, will appear to have different chemical compositions. The interpretation of such differences in terms of geological or spatial provenance will consequently be incorrect.

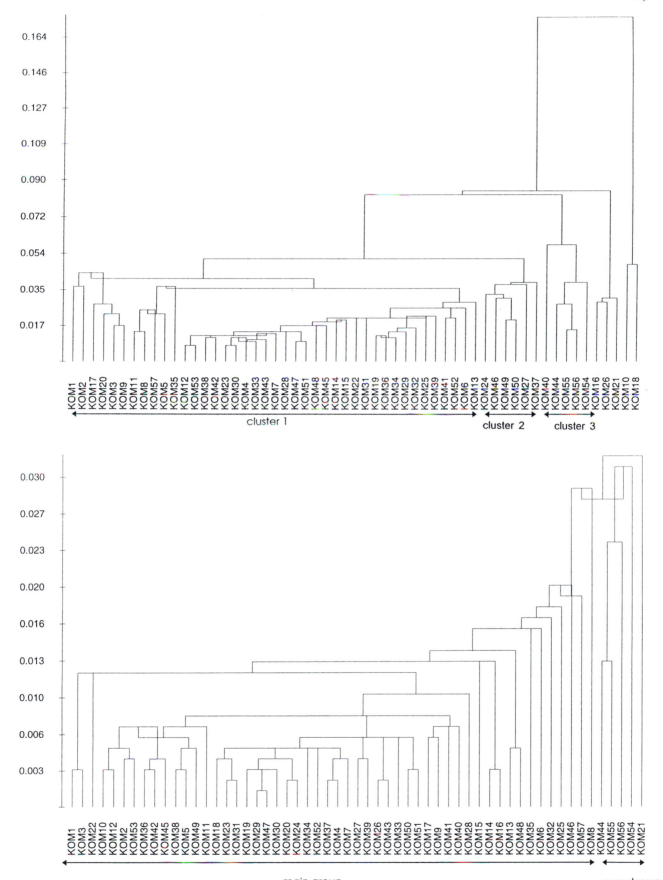

TABLE 16. ELEMENTAL COMPOSITION OF THE KILN MAIN GROUP

Na	0.62	(21.9)	La	23.7	(5.1)
Ca	7.1	(23)	Ce	62.6	(11.1)
Sc	22.3	(9.5)	Sm	4.18	(9.3)
Cr	418	(15.2)	Eu	0.92	(14.3)
Fe	6.14	(9.2)	Tb	0.41	(58)
Co	40.4	(10.8)	Yb	2.43	(8.6)
As	6.3	(33)	Lu	0.35	(10.3)
Rb	99.9	(26)	Hf	3.35	(13.1)
Sb	0.5	(29)	Ta	0.9	(33)
Cs	5.69	(22)	Th	9.51	(8.1)

Measured in ppm. Numbers in parentheses are group standard deviations (%).

responds to the petrographic groups 5 and 6. This last cluster is in chemical terms clearly incompatible with the main population of the Kommos kiln pottery and contains samples made from other clays. Finally, cluster analysis was repeated without the concentrations of Na, Cs, and Rb and using exactly the same conditions as the first time. It can be seen in Figure 66 that the dendrogram now appears "compressed" by comparison; the maximum distance is about 0.033 units while in Figure 65 it is about 0.17 units. The low calcareous fabrics (petrographic groups 5 and 6) are separable at the lower end of the dendrogram. The rest of the samples belong broadly to the same chemical group. If we are to seek a control group to fingerprint from the Kommos LM IA kiln, then the first group of the dendrogram of Figure 66 corresponds to the main group. The average chemical compositions of all elements determined are given in Table 16.

PREVIOUS WORK ON NAA AT KOMMOS

Chemical analysis of Middle Minoan pottery from Kommos has been carried out by Hancock and Betancourt, with the aim of characterizing and, if possible, discriminating between the predominant fabrics.[36] The pottery analyzed was categorized macroscopically into coarse red, fine buff, and tempered buff. The investigators concluded that the coarse red fabric is clearly separable from the other two, which are chemically very close to each other. The results of their study are in a broad sense quite similar to the ones presented here. The fine buff fabric corresponds to our petrographic group 1, and the tempered buff to groups 2 and 4. Their coarse red (low calcareous) group corresponds to petrographic group 6 in the present study. However, their interpretation of the tempered buff and fine buff as chemically different seems to be problematic, since the average concentrations do not differ significantly and the predominant clay characteristics are feldspars and amphiboles, which are present in both fabrics, only in different grain sizes.[37] These two groups, although not chronologically contemporary with the Kommos kiln material, in chemical terms correspond to the main chemical group of the present work, which has been shown to be internally uniform.

36. Hancock and Betancourt 1987. Unpublished analyses were also carried out by J. Tomlinson in his doctoral thesis (Tomlinson 1991).

37. The putative group discrimination is presented in Hancock and Betancourt 1987, table 1.

SYNTHESIS OF ANALYTICAL RESULTS

In the light of the combined results presented here, the questions posed at the commencement of the program can now be discussed.

IDENTIFICATION OF CLAY AND TEMPER SOURCES EXPLOITED FOR POTTERY OF THE KOMMOS KILN

The clay paste recipes exploit raw materials, both plastic and aplastic, that are readily available in the southwestern Mesara Plain. Both Neogene clays and red noncalcareous clays are available in the area, certainly within a radius of ca. 5 km from the site of Kommos. As noted above, this recipe based on tempered calcareous clays has been found in ceramic products with similar pastes found in several locations within the western Mesara. As a result, it appears that such a composition may have been shared by a number of production locations, including the Aghia Triada kiln, which is broadly contemporary. The red fabric used for the clay slabs (group 6) appears similar to that used in cooking vessels from Kommos. The aplastics present in group 3 appear to have a slightly different geological origin from those in groups 1, 2, 4, and 6, while still being compatible with the local area.

It is also worth noting that the tempered, calcareous fabric in the Mesara has a history stretching back at least to the beginning of the Early Bronze Age. It seems unlikely, therefore, that the construction of pottery kilns in settlement areas in LM I, and in this case in a space that was previously public/ceremonial, reflects an influx of potters unrelated to the existing pottery tradition of the area.

THE RELATIONSHIP BETWEEN ANALYTICALLY DETERMINED GROUPS AND MORPHOLOGICAL/STYLISTIC ATTRIBUTES OF THE KILN ASSEMBLAGE

There is a very clear correlation between the different clay pastes observed in the analysis and the size of the ceramic vessel. The larger vessels, which were subject to greater mechanical stresses, have a higher proportion of aplastic inclusions, as might be expected.[38]

In addition, there appears to be a correlation, most evident in the conical cups, between firing temperature and the decoration of the vessels analyzed. The painted examples in general seem to have been fired at temperatures adequate to complete vitrification of the paint layers and retain a black color upon re-oxidation. Such differences in temperature seem systematic and reflect a high degree of control by the potters, who either fired different types of vessels in different firing episodes or, more likely, placed pottery in appropriate areas of the kiln that reached different relative temperatures.

38. Kilikoglou et al. 1998.

THE FIRING CONDITIONS USED IN THE KILN AND THE IMPLICATIONS FOR OUR UNDERSTANDING OF KILN DESIGN AND FUNCTION

The details provided by SEM and PE analyses of the samples from the Kommos kiln give us valuable evidence regarding the design and use of the kiln. We know that the kiln was capable of firing to high temperatures, and of allowing both close control of temperature (with the obvious exceptions of those episodes that resulted in the wasters found in the kiln dump) and control of the atmosphere in the firing chamber.

The iron-rich black finish produced in the painted pottery required the kiln to reach a minimum temperature of 800–850°C in order to achieve vitrification of the decoration. Moreover, it would have required a highly reducing atmosphere at that temperature and then the complete re-oxidation of the pottery. It is clear from the core color of the fabrics examined that the re-oxidation was in most cases complete, while even the low-fired examples are completely oxidized. This indicates a control of atmosphere that only a built kiln with a built upper structure can provide. Whether the superstructure was permanent is another matter, but it was clearly designed in such a way as to create a *completely* reducing atmosphere and then to facilitate the complete re-oxidation of the firing chamber. This suggests an efficient use of portals or apertures that could be blocked and opened at different stages of the firing process.

A strongly reducing atmosphere is difficult to produce in an open up-draft kiln, but easier in a cross-draft or down-draft kiln. It is apparent that even during the Early Bronze Age in this area, special products were made that exploited sophisticated kiln technology to produce an even reduction firing. Such kilns were most likely not of simple up-draft technology.[39] The Kommos kiln was also of sophisticated design. Cross-draft kilns like the one under study, when provided with a domed upper structure and a channel bed sloping up toward an outlet, are more efficient in their use of the heat generated by burning fuel, as heat is reflected down again into the firing chamber. They are, therefore, capable of higher firing temperatures. Gaimster has discussed recently a kiln tantalizingly similar in design to the Minoan channel kilns, which has a steeper uphill slope of 20° in its channels.[40]

We may hypothesize as to how different firing temperatures observed within the assemblage analyzed might result from the differential placement of vessels within the kiln. It is conceivable that the temperature was lower at the eastern end of the kiln, perhaps near an aperture or chimney that drew the draft to the end of the kiln. The different depths of the channels may themselves have had an effect on the establishment of a variety of firing temperatures within the kiln. Since channels obviously played an important role in the circulation of air and heat within the kiln, and since the control of both was sophisticated, the channels would certainly not have been filled with vessels to be fired. They were probably temporarily bridged by pots having a diameter larger than the channels, or by slabs or large sherds that formed a temporary floor to support the ceramic load in the kiln.

39. It is difficult to conceive how the even reduction that produces the silver finish of Fine Gray Ware of EM I–IIA in Crete could be produced without a cross-draft or down-draft technology (see Wilson and Day 1994).

40. Gaimster (1997) discusses the case of a German kiln of the 14th century A.C., which has a horizontal channel design and a stoking chamber on a lower level. The introduction of this kiln design created the ability to reach the higher firing temperatures required for stoneware.

Finally, without some kind of baffle separating the stoking pit and the western end of the chamber itself, it appears that firing mishaps such as those that produced our wasters would be frequent, as the pottery at the western end of the kiln would be more susceptible to the deleterious effects of sudden temperature fluctuations.

FORMING CONTROL GROUPS: REASONS FOR COMPOSITIONAL VARIATION WITHIN THE KILN ASSEMBLAGE

The NAA and PE results have furthered our characterization of pottery from this area of Crete, which is so important for our understanding of Minoan pottery technology. The NAA main group has been related to that of pottery products previously analyzed from Kommos, while the compositions of the ceramic slabs (samples 95/55 and 95/56) are compatible with those of the common cooking pot fabric from the site.[41]

In forming this control group from the pottery of the Kommos kiln, variations in chemical and mineralogical composition were found that correlate with selective alterations during burial. The finding that such alteration was relative to clay type and firing temperature has important implications for provenance methodology and is discussed at further length elsewhere.[42]

41. For cooking pot fabrics at Kommos see Myer and Betancourt 1990, p. 11.

42. Buxeda i Garrigòs, Kilikoglou, and Day in press.

CHAPTER 4

CONCLUSION

Recent excavations of a number of pottery kilns throughout Crete have increased substantially our knowledge of the variations in their design during the Minoan period. The LM IA kiln at Kommos belongs to one of the most familiar of these types and one which seems to be linked particularly to the Neopalatial period: the channel kiln. The Kommos example is oval in shape, consisting of a stoking pit on the western (seaward) side of the structure that leads to a firing chamber with four parallel channels running to the back wall of the kiln. Its oval shape and the in-sloping wall of the firing pit suggest that there was probably a domelike roof. The heat from the fuel would have been drawn upward and through the kiln, perhaps with the aid of an aperture on the east side of the kiln, with heat also flowing through the channels beneath the pottery.

The pottery within and outside the kiln constitutes a rare, rich source of information about a Minoan production center. It dates the kiln's operation to parts of the advanced and final stages of LM IA at Kommos, roughly corresponding to the end of the "Transitional MM IIIB/LM IA" stage and part of the mature LM IA stage elsewhere on Crete. Viewed in a broader context, production at the kiln appears to have ended either not long before, or at about the same time as, the volcanic eruption of Thera. In terms of its decoration, the kiln pottery belongs to the last throes of the light-on-dark tradition.

There are only tentative clues as to the location of a potter's workshop or the tools used in pottery production. However, the pottery itself provides us with the first opportunity in Minoan ceramic studies to characterize the output of a local potter or potters and to understand more about the nature of ceramic production in Neopalatial Crete. Even though only about one-quarter of the some one thousand kiln vases have been investigated in detail, this first ceramic study of the material, presented above in Chapter 2, already points to some decorative and technical characteristics of the pottery that may help to identify the kiln's products in residential contexts at Kommos as well as in the assemblages of other sites. The potter or potters made ordinary vases for household use, and perhaps also amphoras for trade, but there is no convincing evidence in the kiln for the manufacture of cooking pots, lamps, or braziers, nor do these potters seem to have engaged in the production of high-quality pottery. Thus we have for the first time evidence for product specialization in Neopalatial pottery production.

In addition, the kiln products testify to the standardization of vessel shapes and fabrics, with a conscious selection of specific fabrics for different vessel types and even for different parts of the same vessel. The raw material recipes to produce such fabrics are familiar from the area of the Mesara, essentially being based on the tempering of a calcareous base clay with greater or lesser amounts of sand. This characteristic procurement and manipulation of raw materials, which are available relatively locally to the site of Kommos, place those responsible for pottery production at the kiln within a fabric tradition stretching back until at least the Early Bronze Age.

The way in which the coarseness of fabric is varied according to size and functional criteria seems to have been matched by the variation in firing conditions to fit with the demands of decorated and nondecorated pottery. In fact, while the quality of the iron-rich black slip produced was not the highest, the control of both firing atmosphere and temperature seems to reflect a relatively sophisticated kiln design. Such a detailed image of the complexity of the production sequence is supplemented by indications of an increase in the speed and efficiency of production processes, but the reasons for these changes and their relationship to the decline of the light-on-dark tradition are not yet clear. Future research will focus on documenting in more detail the characteristics of the local technological tradition, analyzing the dynamics of pottery production and consumption at Kommos, and determining its wider economic implications.

This study incorporates an array of evidence from the design of the kiln structure through to stylistic, technological, and physico-chemical attributes of the pottery that result from unconscious and conscious aspects of craft practice in the Mesara at the beginning of the Late Bronze Age. Kiln structure and ceramic products are often addressed in terms of the information they provide on a practical and functional level. However, the picture emerging does not deal solely with the demands of materials themselves in acts of production and transformation. It also reveals a more human aspect, in building an image of pottery as part of a ceramic tradition. Recently, the reproduction and manipulation of ceramic paste recipes have been shown in several instances to be indicative of craft traditions,[1] and it is suggested that the same may apply in the Kommos case. But this should also apply to the structures excavated. Just as kiln design in the earlier 20th century on Crete reveals information about different traditions of potters, especially those intrusive to Crete,[2] so might our firing structures of the Bronze Age reward such social interpretations. As much as the channel kiln of Kommos appears to be representative of production in the Mesara during the Neopalatial period, it also appears in stark contrast to the design of kilns on the contemporary Greek mainland and of those firing structures we know from the LM III period.

1. For the social meaning of ceramic pastes recipes in 20th-century Crete see Day in press; for the same in modern Peru see Sillar 1997.

2. Unroofed, circular up-draft kilns are used by potters from both Kentri and Thrapsano in Crete, with the kilns of the former frequently being smaller than those of the latter. However, the kilns of the potters from Nochia in western Crete normally had domed roofs. Potters from Siphnos in the Cyclades who came to work in the town of Aghios Nicholaos, east Crete, during the mid 20th century built their characteristic rectangular barrel-vaulted Cycladic-style kilns.

With this in mind, we suggest that integrated studies of ceramic production sites, such as in this monograph, have the potential to reveal a detailed picture of the process of pottery manufacture. But they can also do much more, providing valuable information about the everchanging economic and social relations revealed by this most fruitful class of archaeological material.

THE KOMMOS LM IA KILN:
PETROGRAPHIC FABRIC DESCRIPTIONS

by Louise Joyner and Peter M. Day

These descriptions use a modified version of the system outlined by Whitbread.[1]

GROUP 1A AND 1B: FINE-GRAINED FABRIC

This fabric class can be divided into two subgroups based on the optical activity of the micromass: probably representing a high-fired group and a low-fired group.

Low optical activity (high-fired): Kommos 95/5, 7, 8, 9, 10, 17, 18, 20, 23, 31, 36

High optical activity (low-fired): Kommos 95/11, 12, 13, 14, 16, 22, 24, 26, 33, 35, 41, 42, 53

MICROSTRUCTURE

There are few to very few voids. Rare mega vughs and few macro vughs and meso vughs. There are very few planar voids, mainly macro planar voids. These and the elongate vughs have a long axes orientation parallel to the vessel margins. The aplastic inclusions appear to be randomly oriented for the most part. The micromass, however, appears to have a crude orientation parallel to the vessel margins.

GROUNDMASS

Homogeneous to heterogeneous, depending on the section. There is some differentiation in color in the groundmass, where there is evidence of clay mixing, which appears as streaks of either calcareous clay in a red clay or vice versa. The streaks appear to be orientated with the vessel margins. The color in PPL is generally orange and in XP yellow-orange (×40). The micromass varies from being highly optically active in the low-fired samples to optically slightly active in the high-fired samples.

INCLUSIONS

c:f:$v_{10\mu m}$ ca. 10:80:10 to 20:75:5
Coarse fraction = 3.5 mm to 0.2 mm (granules to fine sand)
Fine fraction = 0.2 mm or less (fine sand and below)

The inclusions appear to have a bimodal size distribution consisting mainly of coarse sand-sized inclusions and above, and a fine sand-sized

1. The method used here for the description of ceramic thin sections is based on that developed and detailed by Whitbread (1986; 1989; 1995). The system of description has been applied to a wide variety of locations and time periods in the Aegean and Mediterranean. To express mineralogical and textural features, their frequency, shape, and size, standard terminology used is as described by Whitbread (1995, pp. 379–388).

fraction. There are some grains that fall between these two fractions but they are few in number. They are moderately to poorly sorted.

COARSE FRACTION

Common:

Sandstone, quartzarenite: composed of moderately to well-sorted quartz grains of very fine sand to coarse silt size. Matrix of biotite mica. Seems to grade into siltstones with increasing matrix content and decrease in quartz grain size. Generally elongate, sr-r. Size = 0.8 mm or less, mode = 0.5 mm.

Calcimudstone: grades into a micritic sandstone with sparse inclusions of monocrystalline quartz. Equant. Generally slightly elongate, sr. Size = <0.75 mm, mode = 0.5 mm.

Quartz-biotite schist: generally elongate, sr-r. Size = generally <1.7 mm, mode = 0.5mm

Polycrystalline quartz: varies from equigranular to inequigranular. Some with opaques. Equant. Size = 1.25 mm, mode = 0.5 mm.

Very few:

Altered volcanic rock fragments: composed of plagioclase laths and biotite mica, forming a decussate texture, contains clinozoisite; other fragment that is porphyritic, plagioclase laths set in a devitrified groundmass. Size = <1.45 mm.

Rare:

Slate: elongate, sa-sr. Size = <1.55 mm.

Mudstone: brown, with some calcitic veins (sheared). Elongate, sr. Size = 2.1 mm.

Very rare:

Intergrowth of quartz and alkali feldspar: displaying granophyric texture. Elongate, sa. Size = 0.4 mm.

Alkali feldspar: with sieve texture. Elongate. Size = 0.8 mm.

Microfossils: Microcalcitic shells, from ostracods rarely with organic black deposit inside shell. Size = 0.5 mm.

Metamorphic rock fragment: composed of an intergrowth of chlorite and an opaque mineral. Elongate. Size = 1.1 mm. Another composed of amphibole and biotite, amphibole possibly retrogressing to biotite.

Shelly limestone fragment: with calcitic cement and occasional quartz grains. Size = <0.3 mm.

Serpentinite?: very weathered. Size = 0.42 mm.

FINE FRACTION

Common to few:

Carbonate rock fragments: micrite, grading into sparite. sa, generally equant. Mode = 0.1 mm.

Monocrystalline quartz: equant, a-sa. Mode = 0.1 mm.

Few to very rare:

Biotite mica.

Rare:

Polycrystalline quartz: equant, sr. Size = <0.2 mm.
Microfossils: ostracods, shells, and foraminifera.

Very rare:

Plagioclase feldspar: laths.
Muscovite mica.
Chlorite: laths and pseudomorphs.
Clinozoisite.
Opaques.
Clinozoisite/biotite/quartz metamorphic rock.

Amorphous Concentration Features

Very few to very rare. Sr-r. Clear to diffuse boundaries, high optical density, usually equant, discordant with the micromass. Orange-brown color in PPL, reddish orange in XP (×100). Possible signs of clay mixing through visible streaking of the clay matrix.

Comment

This fabric group is characterized by a fine-grained groundmass with sparse, coarse sand inclusions. The inclusions are well-rounded, comprising sandstone/siltstones, altered volcanic, and low-grade metamorphic rock fragments. Clinozoisite in the altered basalt also indicates low-grade metamorphism. There are two different clays, which appear to have been mixed—clearly visible in Kommos 95/5—red and calcareous clay, but also coarse-grained inclusions (third clay?) mixed in. Both the clay mixing and the presence of altered basalt rocks have been recorded previously in pottery from Kommos.[2] Calcareous, fine Neogene clays are abundant in the area, with fine gray clays having been sampled by the authors in the Miocene deposits south of Sivas. These clays were used by modern potters working in Matala and Sivas as recently as the 1970s. Red clays are also available in alluvial form and associated with the gneiss deposits to the west of Kommos.[3]

GROUP 2A: MEDIUM-COARSE FABRIC

Kommos 95/2, 3, 4, 15, 21, 25, 28, 29, 30, 38, 40, 45, 52, 57

Microstructure

There are few to rare voids in this fabric group. Few to very rare macro vughs and macro planar voids, and very rare mega vughs; common to rare meso vughs and meso planar voids; rare meso channel voids. The voids are single- to open-spaced. Some of the samples show crude, long axes orientation of the voids parallel to the vessel margins, particularly of the planar voids, while in others there is a more random orientation of the voids. The orientation of the aplastic inclusions is generally random.

Groundmass

Generally homogeneous throughout the section. There is evidence of clay mixing in some of the samples, appearing as color differences

2. Myer and Betancourt 1990, pp. 6–10, pl. A.

3. The Asterousia Nappe (Bonneau, Jonkers, and Meulenkamp 1984).

within the micromass, which varies in color from orange-brown to yellow gray-brown in PPL (×25) and is dark red-brown to orange-brown, through yellow-brown, to gray-brown in XP (×25). It varies from crystallitic, through optically slightly active, to optically active.

INCLUSIONS

c:f:v$_{10\mu m}$ ca. 15:80:5 to 25:65:10
Coarse fraction = 3.5 mm to 0.1 mm (granules to very fine sand)
Fine fraction = 0.1 mm or less (very fine sand and below)

The inclusions are generally poorly sorted and appear to have a bimodal grain-size distribution.

COARSE FRACTION

This fabric class is characterized by a wide range of coarse aplastic inclusions. However, the variation is not always represented within individual samples. The range and frequency of rock and mineral inclusions do overlap among the samples of this group, forming an overall continuum. Therefore it is not possible to give percentage estimates of the frequency of individual inclusions as these vary from being common to, in some cases, entirely absent.

The following inclusions are present within this fabric class:

Quartz-biotite schist: variable grain size and texture. Most have an overall alignment of the biotite mica laths, some have developed schistosity (biotite-rich and quartz-rich layers). Some contain calcite as well as biotite and quartz; some exhibit folding. Also comprise quartz-biotite-muscovite schist, biotite-clinozoisite schist, chorite-biotite-quartz schist, and greenschist.

Quartz-biotite phyllite: fine-grained, with a phyllitic texture sometimes showing crenulation cleavage.

Amphibolite: containing anthophyllite and plagioclase feldspar and/or quartz. No alignment of the minerals is discernible. Possibly some amphibolites undergoing retrogressive metamorphism to form biotite schists.

Slate: fine-grained and aligned chloritic material. Later growth of small rectangular ore minerals that cross-cut the slate texture. Grades into quartz-chlorite-biotite schist, with ore mineral growth cross-cutting the metamorphic texture. Some show a development of green amphibole laths.

Fine-grained volcanic rock fragments: porphyritic with laths of feldspar set in a red-brown devitrified glassy matrix, probably of basic composition. The feldspar is often partially altered. Textures include variolitic, decussate, trachytic. Usually well-rounded grains.

Polycrystalline quartz: sometimes with micaceous inclusions (biotite). Usually straight extinction, but some undulose. Sometimes display conserted texture.

Sandstone: quartzarenite to sublitharenite, composed of moderately well sorted quartz grains set in either a clay-rich matrix or a fine-grained quartz-rich matrix. Fairly well rounded. Some are partially metamorphosed, with quartz grains breaking down to form poly-crystalline quartz (consertal boundaries) and the clay matrix recrystallized to form biotite mica. Packing varies from well-packed to fairly loosely packed.

Siltstone, two types: (a) orange-red color in PPL and XP, consisting of quartz and mica (biotite and muscovite) in a red clay matrix. Fairly well sorted, well-rounded. Grade into fine-grained schists/phyllites, with the alignment of the biotite mica laths. (b) pale brown in PPL and dark gray-brown in XP, has tuffaceous characteristics. Sparse quartz and biotite mica laths set in a very fine-grained/glassy matrix, possibly volcanic tuff. Rounded, with alignment/lamination, grades into slate.

Chert: can have an irregular muddy appearance. Possibly grading into cherty mudstone, with occasional radiolaria tests. Well-rounded.

Calcimudstone: (micrite), rounded to subrounded grains, sometimes with irregular shapes.

Mudstones: almost the same brown-orange color as the micromass. Can show faint polygonal cracking. Also purple-brown mudstones.

Plagioclase feldspar: showing polysynthetic twinning.

Chlorite: pseudomorphs. Fibrous texture, well-rounded, with iron-staining.

Spinel: dark brown in PPL and isotropic.

Biotite mica.

Monocrystalline quartz.

Serpentinite?: pale yellow to orange in color in PPL.

Opaques: possibly iron-oxide.

Clay concentration features: bright orange.

FINE FRACTION

The fine fraction varies from being almost absent to fairly well packed. The aplastic inclusions in the fine fraction include:

Dominant to common:
　　Monocrystalline quartz.

Common to very few:
　　Biotite mica.

Common to very rare:
　　Amphibole.

Few:
　　Polycrystalline quartz.
　　Calcimudstone (micrite).

Few to rare:
　　White mica: laths.

Very rare:
　　Biotite-quartz schist.
　　Chert.

Plagioclase feldspar.
Sandstone: quartzarenite.
Calcite.
Epidote.
Opaques.
Alkali feldspar.
Clinozoisite.

TEXTURAL CONCENTRATION FEATURES (Tcfs)

Tcfs are few to rare, sr-r with clear to diffuse boundaries, high optical density, usually equant, discordant with the micromass. There are three types. The first type is red-brown in both PPL and XP (×100), with no inclusions (amorphous concentration features). These are generally very fine-grained, mode = 0.04 mm. The second type are a dark brown in PPL (×40) and dark red-brown in XP (×40). They contain sparse fine-grained inclusions of monocrystalline quartz; size = 1.35 mm. The third type appears to have a neutral optical density and is concordant with the micromass, having a similar distribution of mono-crystalline quartz inclusions; size = 0.85 mm.

There are crystalline concentration features (Kcfs) developed around calcimudstone rock fragments within some of the samples, and also in-fill the planar voids in some of the samples. Kcfs also form hypocoatings around the voids and aplastic inclusions in some of the samples.

COMMENT

This fabric group is characterized by the occurrence of a range of medium to large and well-rounded aplastic inclusions that do not all occur within a single sample. They comprise: volcanic rock fragments, generally fine-grained and porphyritic, although they can grade into more equigranular textures; metamorphic rock fragments, generally biotite-quartz schist, phyllite, and rare amphibolites, which appear to grade into each other; and siltstones, two types, one with a red matrix and the other having a gray tuffaceous appearance. The base clays used in this wide fabric class are also very variable, with a continuously overlapping sequence. Some of the clays appear very calcareous, while some can be seen to be mixtures of red and calcareous clays in various proportions. Evidence of clay mixing is seen, with streaks of red clay in a more calcareous yellow-brown base clay, and calcareous clay streaks within an essentially red base clay. Some samples show a mottled appearance. In some samples, the base clays appear to be very micaceous, with very fine-grained flakes of biotite mica present within the clay, having a long axes alignment parallel to the margins of the vessel. The biotite mica is likely to have its ultimate origin in rocks such the Asterousia Nappe Gneiss.[4] Such variability within fabrics has been observed in many classes of material that have their origin in the Mesara Plain, most notably within Neopalatial storage jars and in Early Minoan pottery.[5] This variability most likely has its origin in the mixing of different clays to form the base clay matrix and in the selection of sand of variable mineralogy to act as temper.

4. Bonneau, Jonkers, and Meulenkamp 1984.

5. For Early Minoan sand-tempered vessels, see Wilson and Day 1994, p. 52, and Day et al. 1999.

GROUP 2B: MEDIUM COARSE, OVERFIRED

Kommos 95/43, 46, 47, 48, 49, 50, 51

This fabric is a higher fired version of the group 2a fabric described above. It is characterised by the occurrence of a range of fairly large and well-rounded aplastic inclusions, which do not all occur within a single sample. They consist of volcanic rock fragments and low-grade metamorphic rock fragments, together with some siltstones and calcimudstone (micrite). The inclusion range is similar to group 2a, but many of the aplastic inclusions have suffered alteration and bloating due to the very high firing temperatures. In addition to the inclusions listed above there are calcareous siltstones present in some of these samples. Many of the coarse inclusions have a dark rim around them, possibly a result of the high firing temperature and conditions of reduction. The grain-size distribution is bimodal, and the coarse fraction comprises large, well-sorted sand-sized grains. The micromass is optically inactive, suggesting extensive vitrification. The micromass varies in color from a dark red-brown to dark gray-brown in PPL, and from dark red-orange to dark brown-gray in XP (x40). There tend to be more voids due to the bloating of the fabric in these samples. Evidence of clay mixing is still visible in the form of different colored clay streaks and a mottled effect.

These examples are quite clearly very overfired examples and were classified macroscopically as wasters.

GROUP 3: MEDIUM-GRAINED CALCAREOUS FABRIC

Kommos 95/19, 27, 32, 34, 37, 39

MICROSTRUCTURE

There are very few to very rare voids present in this fabric group. Rare to absent macro vughs, few meso vughs and micro vughs. Planar voids are much less common than the vughs; there are rare macro planar voids and few meso planar voids. Some of the voids in samples 95/19, 27, 37, and 39 are filled or partially in-filled with microcalcitic material. There tends to be a crude long axes orientation of the elongated voids parallel to the vessel margins. The micromass also appears to be aligned parallel to the vessel margins, while aplastic inclusions tend toward a random orientation.

GROUNDMASS

Heterogeneous in samples 95/32, 37, and 39, where there are distinct signs of clay mixing, with streaks of fine red firing clay within a calcareous base clay. The other samples in this fabric group are composed of a calcareous clay, which resembles the base clay in groups 1 and 2. The micromass is generally a yellow-brown in PPL and a yellow-gray in XP (x40) and varies from being optically slightly active to optically inactive, suggesting a relatively high firing temperature.

INCLUSIONS

c:f:v$_{10\mu m}$ ca. 7:88:5 to 15:80:5

Coarse fraction = 2.35 mm to 0.1 mm (granules to very fine sand)
Fine fraction = 0.1 mm or less (very fine sand and below)

The aplastic inclusions are poorly sorted and sparsely distributed, size = <2.35 mm, mode = 0.1 mm long diameter. The grain-size distribution appears bimodal.

COARSE FRACTION

Common:

Sandstone rock fragments: composed of angular grains of monocrystalline quartz, polycrystalline quartz, and occasional plagioclase feldspar and schist set in a matrix of clay minerals and opaques: quartzarenite. Elongate grains, a-sa. Size = <2.35 mm long diameter, mode = 0.8 mm long diameter. Some examples grade into quartzites, with consertal boundaries between the quartz grains, possibly indicative of mechanical compaction of the sediment. Some sandstones have a fine-grained, carbonate mud matrix with less densely packed inclusions of monocrystalline quartz, polycrystalline quartz, and possibly chamosite/limonite grains.

Few:

Quartz-biotite schist rock fragment: elongate with the direction of schistosity, a. Size = <0.94 mm long diameter.
Siltstone: composed of fine-grained monocrystalline quartz grains with rare biotite mica in a clay-rich matrix. Red-brown in PPL and XP (×100). Elongate with the lamination, sr-r. Size = <1.2 mm, mode = 0.5 mm long dimension. Variable packing of the inclusions, from well-packed to sparsely packed. Grading into sandstone, and some have been affected by a very low-grade metamorphism, with the clay-matrix recrystallized to biotite mica laths.
Polycrystalline quartz: approximately equant, consertal boundaries between the grains, inequigranular, sa-sr.

Few to very rare:

Calcimudstone (micrite): approximately equant, sr-r. Size = <1.3 mm, mode = 0.4 mm long dimension. Possibly grading into calcareous sandstone?
Monocrystalline quartz: sa. Mode = 0.2 mm long dimension.

Rare:

Phyllite: chlorite? and quartz. Elongate with crenulation cleavage, r. Size = 0.66 mm long dimension.

Very rare:

Alkali feldspar: turbid appearance in PPL. Simple twinning. Saussuritized. Approximately equant, a-sr. Size = 0.65 mm.
Plagioclase feldspar: tabular. Polysynthetic twinning. sr. Size = 0.2 mm long dimension.
Calcareous mudstone: with polygonal cracking.
Red mudstone.
Biotite mica: laths.

FINE FRACTION

Frequent:

Monocrystalline quartz: equant, sa-sr. Mode = 0.01 mm long dimension.

Biotite mica.

Frequent to absent:

Calcimudstone (micrite): 95/19 and 39, and especially 27. Approximately equant. Mode = 0.04 mm.

Few to absent:

Calcite: only in 95/27.

Very few:

Polycrystalline quartz: elongate, sa-sr. Mode = 0.06 mm long dimension.

Quartz-biotite schist rock fragments: elongate, sr. Mode = 0.08 mm long dimension.

Rare:

Opaques.

TEXTURAL CONCENTRATION FEATURES

There are very few to absent Tcfs in these samples, which are generally sr. Clear to diffuse boundaries, slightly higher optical density than the micromass, equant to slightly elongate, discordant with the micromass. They are brown in PPL and red-brown in XP (×100), contain sparse inclusions of quartz and/or calcite. These are probably clay pellets. Kcfs occur in some samples around voids and calcite grains. Microcrystalline calcite can also be seen to in-fill planar voids in some of the samples.

COMMENT

This fabric is characterized by a yellow calcareous base clay with relatively sparsely distributed, coarse aplastic inclusions in a very fine-grained base clay. The aplastic inclusions comprise sandstones, siltstones, and quartz-biotite schists. The optical inactivity of the micromass of most of these samples indicates a high firing temperature. There is evidence for clay mixing, as red clay appears to have been mixed into a calcareous base clay (e.g., streaks of the red clay visible in the calcareous base clay in 95/32, 39). A mottled effect is seen in some samples, e.g., 95/19. Although this fabric lacks the schists, amphibolites, and altered igneous inclusions of group 2, it is nevertheless compatible with the varied local raw material resources. The differences in aplastic mineralogy, however, do seem real, and they may have their geological origin in the Flysch and Vatos Schists around Pitsdia, Sivas, and Kouses, rather than in the gneiss of the Asterousia Nappe.

GROUP 4: COARSE FABRIC WITH SAND INCLU-SIONS

Kommos 95/1, 6

MICROSTRUCTURE

There are common voids in this fabric group, common mega and macro vughs, and mega and macro planar voids. Meso vughs and meso planar voids are rare. The voids are single- to double-spaced with a crude long axes orientation of the voids parallel to the vessel margins, particularly of the planar voids in both samples. The orientation of the aplastic inclusions is generally random.

GROUNDMASS

Homogeneous throughout the section. The color of the micromass is orange-brown in PPL (×25) and red-brown in XP (×25). The micromass is optically slightly active to optically active.

INCLUSIONS

c:f:v$_{10\mu m}$ ca. 20:65:15 to 30:60:10
Coarse fraction = 3.5 mm to 0.1 mm (granules to very fine sand)
Fine fraction = 0.1 mm or less (very fine sand and below)

The inclusions are moderately sorted and have a bimodal grain-size distribution. The coarse grains are more common, and there are very few grains in the fine fraction.

COARSE FRACTION

This is a coarser version of group 2 and as with that group, this is characterized by a wide range of coarse aplastic inclusions, and variation within the fabric class is not always represented within individual samples. However, the range and frequency of rock and mineral inclusions do overlap between the samples of this group, forming an overall continuum. It is therefore not possible to give percentage estimates of the frequency of individual inclusions as these vary from being common, to in some cases being entirely absent.

The following inclusions are present within this fabric class:

Quartz-biotite schist: variable grain size and texture. Most have an overall alignment of the biotite mica laths, some have a developed schistosity (biotite-rich and quartz-rich layers). Some contain calcite as well as biotite and quartz and some exhibit folding.
Quartz-biotite phyllite: fine-grained, with a phyllitic texture.
Amphibolite: possibly undergoing retrogressive metamorphism to form biotite schists.
Slate: fine-grained and aligned chloritic material. Later growth of small rectangular ore minerals, which cross-cut the slate texture. Grades into quartz-chlorite-biotite schist, with ore mineral growth cross-cutting the metamorphic texture.
Fine-grained volcanic rock fragments: porphyritic, with laths of feldspar set in a red-brown devitrified glassy matrix. The feldspar is often partially altered. The rock is probably of basic composition

and usually has well-rounded grains. Textures seen include variolitic, decussate, and trachytic.

Polycrystalline quartz: sometimes with micaceous inclusions (biotite). Usually straight extinction, but some undulose extinction, sometimes with a consertal texture.

Sandstone: quartzarenite to sublitharenite, composed of moderately well sorted quartz grains set in either a clay-rich matrix or a fine-grained quartz-rich matrix. Some have a calcareous matrix. Some are partially metamorphosed, with quartz grains breaking down to form polycrystalline quartz (consertal boundaries) and the clay matrix recrystallized to form biotite mica. Packing varies from well-packed to fairly loose packing. Fairly well-rounded.

Siltstone, two types: (a) orange-red color in PPL and XP, consisting of quartz and mica (biotite and muscovite) in a red clay matrix. Can be seen to grade into fine-grained schists/phyllites, with the alignment of the biotite mica laths. Fairly well sorted and well rounded. (b) pale brown in PPL and dark gray-brown in XP, tuffaceous? Sparse quartz and biotite mica laths set in a very fine-grained/glassy matrix. Has an alignment/lamination; grades into slate.

Chert: can have an irregular muddy appearance. Possibly grading into cherty radiolarian mudstone; well-rounded.

Calcimudstone (micrite): grains, sometimes with irregular shapes. r-sr.

Mudstones: brown-orange color similar to the micromass. Some display faint polygonal cracking. Also purple-brown mudstones.

Chlorite: pseudomorphs. Fibrous texture, well-rounded, with iron-staining.

Quartz-feldspar rock fragment.

Monocrystalline quartz.

Biotite mica.

Opaques: possibly iron-oxide.

FINE FRACTION

The fine fraction varies from being almost absent in the samples with a bimodal distribution, to being quite well-packed in samples with a unimodal grain-size range. The samples without a fine-grained fraction of inclusions may result from levigation of the raw clay, prior to the addition of temper, with a fairly large grain size. The aplastic inclusions in the fine fraction include:

Dominant to common:
 Biotite mica.

Common to very few:
 Monocrystalline quartz.

Few:
 Calcite.

Very rare:
 Calcimudstone (micrite).
 Opaques.

TEXTURAL CONCENTRATION FEATURES

Tcfs are rare, sr-r with clear to diffuse boundaries, high optical density, usually equant, discordant with the micromass. They are a dark brown in PPL (×40) and dark red-brown in XP (×40). They contain sparse fine-grained inclusions of monocrystalline quartz.

COMMENT

This fabric group is characterized by the occurrence of a range of fairly large and well-rounded aplastic inclusions, which do not all occur within a single sample. They comprise a range similar to those found on group 2 and appear to form a coarser version of that fabric. These inclusions comprise: volcanic rock fragments, generally fine-grained and porphyritic; metamorphic rock fragments, generally biotite-quartz schist and phyllite, which appear to grade into each other. Also present are siltstones, one possibly tuffaceous. The base clay shows little evidence of clay mixing. The groundmass is fairly micaceous, being rich in biotite mica. The geological origin of the material is as that described for group 2.

GROUP 5: SILTSTONE FABRIC

Kommos 95/54

MICROSTRUCTURE

There are common voids in this sample. Rare mega vughs, few macro vughs, and few meso vughs. The planar voids vary from very few mega, to common macro and meso. Some of the voids are curvilinear; they have a very crude long axes orientation parallel to the vessel margins, as do the aplastic inclusions.

GROUNDMASS

Homogeneous throughout the sample. The micromass varies from a red-brown margin to a mid brown core in PPL and is from an orange-red margin to yellow-brown in XP (×40). It is optically active.

INCLUSIONS

c:f:v$_{10\mu m}$ ca. 30:60:10
Coarse fraction = 4.2 mm to 0.2 mm (small pebbles to fine sand)
Fine fraction = 0.2 mm or less (fine sand and below)

The inclusions appear to have a bimodal grain-size distribution. They are poorly sorted overall, with a moderately sorted, fine-grained groundmass.

COARSE FRACTION

Common:

Siltstones, grading into **mudstones**: very dark brown in PPL (×40). Composed of sparsely distributed very fine sand–sized (ca. 0.02 mm) inclusions of monocrystalline quartz and muscovite mica in a clay-rich matrix. Some of these siltstones appear to grade into slates with low-grade metamorphism. Some have irregular areas rich in carbonate (microcrystalline calcite?). Elongate, a-sa. Size = <4.2 mm long dimension. Lamination is visible in some of the grains.

Few:

Metamorphic rock fragments: range includes metaquartzites, phyllite, quartz-biotite schist, actinolite-quartz schist, amphibolite, greenschist, and marble(?) with quartz inclusions. Low to medium-grade metamorphism. Slightly elongate to elongate, sa-sr. Variable grain sizes. Size = <1.55 mm long dimension.

Very few:

Limestone: varies from sparite to micrite (calcimudstone) even within the same grain. Approximately equant. Size = <0.5 mm long dimension.

Coarser-grained siltstones: different from those described above. Composed of more densely packed larger quartz grains set in a clay rich matrix; appear to grade into quartz-biotite schists. Elongate. Size = 0.8 mm long dimension.

Polycrystalline quartz: equant, sa-sr. Inequigranular. Size = <0.48 mm long dimension.

Rare:

Sandstone: quartzarenite, fairly well sorted with a small amount of clay-rich matrix. Elongate. Size = 1 mm long dimension. Another type has fairly well rounded quartz grains set in a calcite cement.

Alkali feldspar: slightly elongate. sr. Size = <0.5 mm long dimension. Some saussuritization along cleavage traces.

Very rare:

Plagioclase feldspar: very fresh. Polysynthetic twinning, sa. Slightly elongate. Size = 0.26 mm long dimension.

Chlorite pseudomorph: possibly after olivine? Fibrous. Equant. Size = 0.34 mm.

Opaques.

Clinozoisite: crystal. Elongate, a. Size = 0.3 mm long dimension. Tabular.

Quartz-alkali feldspar rock fragment: consertal boundaries between the grains. Possibly metamorphosed, or pressure solution effect?

Biotite mica pseudomorphs: fibrous. r.

Monocrystalline quartz: slightly elongate, sa-sr. Size = 0.47 mm long dimension.

FINE FRACTION

Frequent:

Monocrystalline quartz: equant, a-sa. Mode = 0.1 mm. Mainly straight extinction, rarely undulose.

Very few:

Amphibole: actinolite? Slightly elongate. Mode = 0.1 mm.

Muscovite mica.

Rare:

    Biogenic fragments.

    Polycrystalline quartz.

    Opaques.

    Metamorphic rock fragments: same range as above.

Very rare:

    Chalcedonic quartz.

    Epidote.

    Clinozoisite.

    Biotite mica.

    Plagioclase feldspar.

TEXTURAL CONCENTRATION FEATURES

Tcfs are a rare component of this fabric. They are wr-r, have clear boundaries, high optical density, equant, discordant with the micromass. Dark red-brown in PPL and dark red in XP (×100). They contain poorly sorted inclusions of monocrystalline quartz and alkali feldspar, which are fairly sparsely distributed. Size = 0.38 mm.

COMMENT

This fabric class is characterized by the presence of large, elongate grains of fine-grained dark brown siltstone rock fragments, together with a range of principally generally elongate, low-grade metamorphic rock fragments in a quartz-rich red-firing clay. The siltstones are composed of moderately to well-sorted quartz grains of very fine sand to coarse silt size. Some have a matrix of biotite mica, others seem to grade into siltstones with increasing matrix content and decrease in quartz grain size. Textural concentration features are rare; there are no obvious signs of clay mixing. It is possible that the base clay was derived from a metamorphic source with the large siltstone rock fragments added as a temper. The optical activity of the matrix suggests a relatively low firing temperature. The fabric is not diagnostic of origin, but siltstones and mudstones occur in the flysch deposits that lie 2 km east of the kiln.

GROUP 6: COARSE RED FABRIC WITH SCHIST

    Kommos 95/44, 55, 56

MICROSTRUCTURE

There are few to common voids in these samples. They vary from very rare mega vughs to few macro and common meso vughs, very rare mega planar voids, common macro planar voids, and few meso planar voids. They are double- to open-spaced and tend to have an overall random distribution, with localized areas of parallel orientation. The aplastic inclusions tend to have a random orientation.

GROUNDMASS

Mainly homogeneous throughout each of the samples; however, samples 95/44 and 55 have areas of finer-grained clay matrix, suggesting either that heterogeneous clays were used or that clay mixing may have taken place. The micromass is optically slightly active in all the samples, and almost inactive in 95/44. Color in PPL ranges from dark brown in 95/44 to orange-brown in 95/55 and 56 (×40). In XP the color varies from dark red-brown in 95/44 to red-brown in 95/55 and 56 (×40).

INCLUSIONS

$c:f:v_{10\mu m}$ ca. 30:65:5 to 35:60:5
Coarse fraction = 5.5 mm to 0.5 mm (small pebbles to medium sand)
Fine fraction = 0.5 mm or less (medium sand and below)

The aplastic inclusions are moderately to poorly sorted, <5.5 mm, mode = 0.1 mm long diameter. Initially appears to be bimodal, but the seriate range of grain sizes indicates that it is more probably a unimodal grain-size distribution, perhaps from one raw material source.

COARSE FRACTION

Dominant:

Metamorphic rock fragments: there are a number of different types of metamorphic rock fragments that appear to grade into each other. They are low-grade metamorphics for the most part, with a few medium grade. The metamorphic rock fragments include: **quartz-biotite schist**, which with a decrease in grain size grades into quartz-biotite phyllite. Schistosity is developed, usually parallel with the elongation direction of the grain. In some of the grains, biotite replaces amphibole (cores of amphibole remain, amphibole habit is preserved). **Biotite schist**: some seem to have developed from the metamorphism of mudstone/siltstone (primary lamination preserved by the biotite mica laths) and sandstone (matrix metamorphosed, but larger grains of quartz, and less commonly plagioclase feldspar, are relatively unaffected). Some appear to have a relict volcanic texture, indicating metamorphism of volcanic rocks (feldspar laths have been pseudomorphed by epidote). **Feldspar biotite schist**: rare. **Quartz-biotite-muscovite schist**: not very common, as is **quartz-biotite-epidote schist**. **Quartz-clinozoisite granulite**: textured metamorphic rock fragment with minor amounts of biotite and muscovite mica. **Quartz-biotite clinozoisite feldspar schist**: rare. **Clinozoisite-epidote rock fragment**: rare. **Quartz tremolite biotite feldspar iron ore schist**: rare. **Slate** with occasional grains of sandstone included: very rare. These metamorphic rock fragments represent a sequence of metamorphosed mudstones and sandstones, and rare metamorphosed volcanic rock fragments. Usually elongate in the direction of the schistosity, sa-r. Size = <5.5 mm, mode = 0.75 mm long diameter.

Few:

Polycrystalline quartz: inequigranular, consertal boundaries between the constituent grains. Usually elongate, sa-sr. Size = <1.5 mm, mode = 0.75 mm long diameter.

Sandstone: well-sorted, composed mainly of monocrystalline quartz grains in a clay-rich matrix, occasionally with a calcareous component. Other grains include plagioclase feldspar, polycrystalline quartz, and biotite mica. Some show evidence of the beginnings of low-grade metamorphism: sedimentary texture is well preserved. With an increase in the proportion of plagioclase feldspar present, the quartzarenite grades into subarkose/arkose. Usually equant to slightly elongate, sa-r. Size = <3.2 mm, mode = 1 mm. Can grade into greywackes with a increase in matrix component.

Chert: slightly elongate, a-sa. Size = <0.7 mm long diameter.

Rare:

Chlorite: pseudomorphs composed of chlorite laths. Elongate. Size = 0.54 mm long diameter.

Micrite (calcimudstone): slightly elongate, sr. Size = 0.5 mm long diameter.

Feldspar: partially sericitized. Elongate, sa. Size = 1.1 mm long diameter. Possibly a perthite/antiperthite?

Altered volcanic rock fragment: Feldspar laths have a decussate texture (random orientation) with a devitrified groundmass. Slightly elongate, sr. Size = 0.64 mm long diameter.

FINE FRACTION

Dominant:

Monocrystalline quartz: Equant, sa-sr. Mode = 0.06 mm long diameter.

Common to few:

Low-grade metamorphic rock fragments: same range as described above. Usually elongate, sa-r. Mode = 0.2 mm long diameter.

Biotite mica: laths.

Few:

Polycrystalline quartz: inequigranular, sa-sr. Mode = 0.14 mm long diameter.

Plagioclase feldspar: laths, either as single laths or in aggregates.

Alkali feldspar.

Opaques.

Rare to very rare:

Chert: sa.

Very rare to absent:

Chlorite: lath. Size = 0.35 mm long diameter.

Clinozoisite: size = 0.4 mm long diameter.

Garnet: idiomorphic. Equant. Size = 0.3 mm.

Titanite (sphene)?

Epidote.

Perthite/antiperthite.

Muscovite mica.

TEXTURAL CONCENTRATION FEATURES

There are rare to very rare Tcfs in this fabric class. They are sa-r, with clear to diffuse boundaries, high optical density, equant to slightly elongate, concordant with the micromass. Contain sparse inclusions of monocrystalline quartz and occasional biotite mica and low-grade metamorphic rock fragments. Mode = 0.4 mm long diameter. Dark brown color in PPL and red-brown in XP (×40): probably clay pellets as they resemble the clay matrix in terms of clay and inclusion composition.

There are rare crystallitic concentration features that form partial hypocoatings around occasional vughs. The majority of the voids are unaffected.

COMMENT

This fabric is characterized by the presence of abundant low-grade metamorphic rock fragments of various types. They represent the metamorphism of a sedimentary sequence of mudstones and fine-grained sandstones, and this is reflected in the mineralogy and texture developed. Rarely metamorphosed volcanic rock fragments occur, which seem to have their origin in the ophiolite series which is present around the villages of Sivas and Kouses. The clay is red-firing, and appears noncalcareous. In samples 95/44 and 55 there is evidence of heterogeneity in the clay fabric where areas of finer-grained clay occur within the overall medium-grained clay. This may reflect either the use of a heterogeneous clay deposit or the intentional mixing of two different clays, one being finer-grained than the other. It seems likely, however, that this fabric has its origin in noncalcareous, coarse red clays associated with the Asterousia Nappe deposits that have their nearest occurrence ca. 4 km east of the kiln.

REFERENCES

Balfet, H. 1965. "Ethnographical Observations in North Africa and Archaeological Interpretation: The Pottery of the Maghreb," in F. R. Matson, ed., *Ceramics and Man*, Chicago, pp. 161–177.

Bernini, L. E. 1995. "Ceramics of the Early Neo-Palatial Period at Palaikastro," *BSA* 90, pp. 55–82.

Betancourt, P. P. 1979. *Vasilike Ware: An Early Bronze Pottery Style in Crete* (SIMA 56), Göteborg.

———, ed. 1984. *East Cretan White-on-Dark Ware* (University Museum Monograph 51), Philadelphia.

———. 1985. *The History of Minoan Pottery*, Princeton.

———. 1986. "The Chronology of Middle Minoan Plain Cups in Southern Crete," in *ΦΙΛΙΑ ΕΠΗ εἰς Γεώργιον Ἐ. Μυλωνᾶν*, part A, Athens, pp. 284–292.

Bikaki, A. H. 1984. *Ayia Irini: The Potters' Marks* (Keos IV), Mainz.

Blackman, M. J., G. J. Stein, and P. B. Vandiver. 1993. "The Standardization Hypothesis and Ceramic Mass Production: Technological, Compositional, and Metric Indexes of Craft Specialization at Tell Leilan, Syria," *AmerAnt* 58, pp. 60–80.

Blitzer, H. 1984. "Traditional Pottery Production in Kentri, Crete: Workshops, Materials, Techniques, and Trade," in Betancourt 1984, pp. 143–157.

———. 1990. "ΚΟΡΩΝΕΪΚΑ: Storage-Jar Production and Trade in the Traditional Aegean," *Hesperia* 59, pp. 675–711.

———. 1995. "Minoan Implements and Industries," in *Kommos* I.1, pp. 403–535.

Bonneau, M., H. A. Jonkers, and J. E. Meulenkamp. 1984. *Geological Map of Greece 1:50,000, Timbakion Sheet*. IGME, Athens.

Bosanquet, R. C., and R. M. Dawkins. 1923. *The Unpublished Objects from the Palaikastro Excavations, 1902–1906* (*BSA* Suppl. 1), London.

Buxeda i Garrigòs, J. 1999. "Alteration and Contamination of Archaeological Ceramics: The Perturbation Problem," *JAS* 26, pp. 295–303.

Buxeda i Garrigòs, J., V. Kilikoglou, and P. M. Day. In press. "Chemical and Mineralogical Alteration of Ceramics from a Late Bronze Age Kiln at Kommos, Crete: The Effect of Firing Temperature," submitted to *Archaeometry*.

Cadogan, G. 1978. "Dating the Aegean Bronze Age without Radiocarbon," *Archaeometry* 20, pp. 209–214.

Carinci, F. 1989. "The 'III fase protopalaziale' at Phaestos: Some Observations," in Laffineur 1989, pp. 73–80.

Caskey, J. L. 1972. "Investigations in Keos, Part II: A Conspectus of the Pottery," *Hesperia* 41, pp. 357–401.

Catling, E. A., H. W. Catling, and D. Smyth. 1979. "Knossos, 1975: Middle Minoan III and Late Minoan I Houses by the Acropolis," *BSA* 74, pp. 1–80.

Catling, H. W. 1979. "Archaeology in Greece, 1978–79," *AR,* pp. 3–43.

Chatzi-Vallianou, D. 1995. "Μινωϊκὰ κεραμικὰ ἐργαστήρια: Μία ἐθνολογικὴ προσέγγιση μὲ νέα δεδομένα," in *Proceedings of the Sixth International Cretological Congress, A2,* Rethymnon, pp. 1035–1060.

Chrysoulaki, S. 1996. " Ἐργαστήρια στὴν περιοχὴ Σφάκας Ζάκρου," in E. Gavrilaki, ed., *Κεραμικὰ ἐργαστήρια στὴν Κρήτη ἀπὸ τὴν ἀρχαιότητα ὡς σήμερα. Πρακτικὰ Ἡμερίδας, Μαργαρίτες, 30 Σεπτεμβρίου 1995,* Rethymnon, pp. 13–23.

Clark, J. E. 1995. "Craft Specialization as an Archaeological Category," *Research in Economic Anthropology* 16, pp. 267–294.

Coldstream, J. N., and G. L. Huxley, eds. 1972. *Kythera,* London.

Costin, C. L. 1991. "Craft Specialization: Issues in Defining, Documenting, and Explaining the Organization of Production," in M. B. Schiffer, ed., *Archaeological Method and Theory* 3, Tucson, pp. 1–56.

Courty, M. A., and V. Roux. 1995. "Identification of Wheel Throwing on the Basis of Ceramic Surface Features and Microfabrics," *JAS* 22, pp. 17–50.

Cucuzza, N. 1993. *Materiali dell' insediamento neopalaziale di Seli* (thesis, Scuola archeologica italiana di Atene).

Cummer, W. W., and E. Schofeld. 1984. *Ayia Irini: House A* (Keos III), Mainz.

D'Agata, A. L. 1989. "Some MM IIIB/ LM IA Pottery from Haghia Triada," in Laffineur 1989, pp. 93–97.

Davaras, K. 1973. "Μινωϊκὴ κεραμεικὴ κάμινος εἰς Στῦλον Χανίων," *ArchEph,* pp. 75–80.

Davi, E., and M. Bonneau. 1985. *Geological Map of Greece 1:50,000, Andiskarion Sheet.* IGME, Athens.

Davis, J. C. 1986. *Statistics and Data Analysis in Geology,* New York.

Davis, J. L. 1986. *Ayia Irini: Period V (Keos V),* Mainz.

Davis, J. L., and J. R. Cherry. 1984. "Phylakopi in Late Cycladic I: A Pottery Seriation Study," in

J. A. MacGillivray and R. L. N. Barber, eds., *The Prehistoric Cyclades,* Edinburgh, pp. 148–161.

Davis, J. L., and H. B. Lewis. 1985. "Mechanization of Pottery Production: A Case Study from the Cycladic Islands," in A. B. Knapp and T. Stech, eds., *Prehistoric Production and Exchange,* Los Angeles, pp. 79–92.

Day, P. M. 1988. "The Production and Distribution of Storage Jars in Neopalatial Crete," in E. B. French and K. A. Wardle, eds., *Problems in Greek Prehistory,* pp. 499–508.

———. 1995. "Pottery Production and Consumption in the Sitia Bay Area during the New Palace Period," in M. Tsipopoulou and L. Vagnetti, *Achladia: Scavi e ricerche della Missione greco-italiana in Creta orientale, 1991–1993* (CNR/GEI), Rome, pp. 148–175.

———. 1997. "Ceramic Exchange between Towns and Outlying Settlements in Neopalatial East Crete," in R. Hägg, ed., *The Function of the Minoan "Villa"* (ActaAth 4 XLVI), Stockholm, pp. 219–228.

———. In press. "Marriage and Mobility: Tradition and the Dynamics of Pottery Production in Twentieth-Century East Crete," in P. Betancourt and C. Davaras, eds., *Pseira* VI: *The Archaeological Survey,* Philadelphia.

Day, P. M., and D. E. Wilson. 1998. "Consuming Power: Kamares Ware in Protopalatial Knossos," *Antiquity* 71, no. 274, pp. 350–358.

Day, P. M., D. E. Wilson, and E. Kiriatzi. 1997. "Reassessing Specialization in Prepalatial Cretan Ceramic Production," in Laffineur and Betancourt 1997, pp. 275–285.

Day, P. M., E. Kiriatzi, A. Tsolakidou, and V. Kilikoglou. 1999. "Group Therapy: A Comparison between Analyses by NAA and Thin Section Petrography of Early Bronze Age Pottery from Central and East Crete," *JAS* 26, pp. 1025–1036.

Di Vita, A., V. La Rosa, and M. Rizzo, eds. 1984. *Creta antica: Cento anni di archeologia italiana, 1884–1984,* Rome.

Earle, T. K. 1981. "Comment on Rice," *CurrAnthr* 22, pp. 230–231.

Evely, R. D. G. 1988. "The Potters' Wheel in Minoan Crete," *BSA* 83, pp. 83–126.

———. 1993. *Minoan Crafts: Tools and Techniques, An Introduction,* vol. I (SIMA 92:1), Göteborg.

———. In press. *Minoan Crafts: Tools and Techniques, An Introduction,* vol. II (SIMA 92:2), Göteborg.

Feinman, G. M., S. A. Kowalewski, and R. E. Blanton. 1984. "Modelling Ceramic Production and Organizational Change in the Pre-Hispanic Valley of Oaxaca, Mexico," in S. E. van der Leeuw and A. C. Pritchard, eds., *The Many Dimensions of Pottery,* Amsterdam, pp. 295–337.

Fiandra, E. 1973. "Skutelia MM a Festòs," in *Proceedings of the Third International Cretological Congress, Rethymnon 1971,* Athens, pp. 84–91.

Fiandra, E., and P. Pelagatti. 1962. "Vasai cretesi," *ArchCl* 14, pp. 13–22.

Fillieres, D., G. Harbottle, and E. V. Sayre. 1983. "Neutron Activation Study of Figurines, Pottery, and Workshop Materials from the Athenian Agora, Greece," *JFA* 10, pp. 55–69.

Floyd, C. R. 1995. "An Assessment of Minoan Slips from Pseira, Crete, Using Scanning Electron Microscopy," in P. B. Vandiver, J. R. Druzik, J. L. Galvan Madrid, I. C. Freestone, and G. S. Wheeler, eds., *Material Issues in Art and Archaeology* IV, Philadelphia, pp. 663–672.

Franken, H. J., and J. Kalsbeek. 1969. *Excavations at Tell Deir Alla: A Stratigraphical and Analytical Study of the Early Iron Age Pottery,* Leiden.

Furumark, A. 1972. *Mycenaean Pottery,* vol. II: *Chronology,* Stockholm.

Gaimster, D. 1997. "Stoneware Production in Medieval and Early Modern Germany," in I. Freestone and D. Gaimster, eds., *Pottery in the Making: World Ceramic Traditions,* London, pp. 122–127.

Gesell, G. C., L. P. Day, and W. D. E. Coulson. 1988. "Excavations at Kavousi, Crete, 1987," *Hesperia* 57, pp. 279–301.

Gifford, J. A. 1995. "The Physical Geology of the Western Mesara and Kommos," in *Kommos* I.1, pp. 30–90.

Gillis, C. 1990. *Minoan Conical Cups* (SIMA 89), Göteborg.

Glock, A. E. 1987. "Where to Draw the Line: Illustrating Ceramic Technology," *Newsletter, Department of Pottery Technology (Leiden)* 5, pp. 93–110.

Hagstrum, M. B. 1985. "Measuring Prehistoric Ceramic Craft Specialization: A Test Case in the American Southwest," *JFA* 12, pp. 65–75.

Halbherr, F., E. Stefani, and L. Banti. 1977. "Haghia Triada nel periodo tardo-palaziale," *ASAtene* 55, pp. 7–296.

Hampe, R., and A. Winter. 1962. *Bei Töpfern und Töpferinnen in Kreta, Messenien und Zypern,* Mainz.

Hancock, R. G. V., and P. P. Betancourt. 1987. "INAA of Minoan Ceramics from Kommos, Crete," *Journal of Radioanalytical and Nuclear Chemistry,* articles 114, no. 2, pp. 393–401.

Hardy, D. A., and A. C. Renfrew, eds. 1990. *Thera and the Aegean World* III.3, London.

Hood, M. S. F. 1958. "Archaeology in Greece," *AR,* pp. 3–25.

Jones, R. E. 1986. *Greek and Cypriot Pottery: A Review of Scientific Studies* (Fitch Laboratory Occasional Paper 1), Athens.

Kilikoglou, V. 1994. "Scanning Electron Microscopy," in Wilson and Day 1994, pp. 70–75.

Kilikoglou, V., and Y. Maniatis. 1993. "Technological Study of Neolithic Ceramics from Tharrounia and Psachna," in A. Sampson, *Skoteini, Tharrounia: The Cave, the Settlement, and the Cemetery,* Athens, pp. 438–441.

Kilikoglou, V., G. Vekinis, and Y. Maniatis. 1995. "Toughening of Ceramic Earthenwares by Quartz Inclusions: An Ancient Art Revisited," *Acta metallurgica et materialia* 43.8, pp. 2959–2965.

Kilikoglou, V., G. Vekinis, Y. Maniatis, and P. M. Day. 1998. "Mechanical Performance of Quartz-Tempered Ceramics, Part I: Strength and Toughness," *Archaeometry* 40, pp. 261–279.

Knappett, C. 1997. "Ceramic Production in the Protopalatial Mallia 'State': Evidence from Quartier Mu and Myrtos Pyrgos," in Laffineur and Betancourt 1997, pp. 305–311.

Koehl, R. B. 1981. "The Functions of Aegean Bronze Age Rhyta," in R. Hägg and N. Marinatos, eds., *Sanctuaries and Cults in the Aegean Bronze Age,* Stockholm, pp. 179–188.

Kommos I.1 = J. W. Shaw and M. C. Shaw, eds., *The Kommos Region and Houses of the Minoan Town,* Princeton 1995.

Kommos I.2 = J. W. Shaw and M. C. Shaw, eds., *The Kommos Region and Houses of the Minoan Town,* Princeton 1996.

Kommos II = P. P. Betancourt, *The Final Neolithic through Middle Minoan III Pottery,* Princeton 1990.

Kommos III = L. V. Watrous, *The Late Bronze Age Pottery,* Princeton 1992.

Laffineur, R., ed. 1989. *Transition: Le monde égéen du Bronze Moyen au Bronze Récent* (Aegaeum 3), Liège.

Laffineur, R., and P. P. Betancourt, eds. 1997. *TEXNH: Craftsmen, Craftswomen, and Craftsmanship in the Aegean Bronze Age. Proceedings of the 6th International Aegean Conference, Philadelphia, Temple University, 18–21 April 1996* (Aegaeum 16), Liège.

La Rosa, V. 1972–1973. "Saggio di scavo in contrata Selì di Kamilari," *ASAtene* 51, pp. 515–525.

———. 1977. "La ripresa dei lavori ad Haghia Triadha: Relazione preliminare sui saggi del 1977," *ASAtene* 55, pp. 297–342.

———. 1984. "Haghia Triada. Patrikies. Seli. Kamilari," in Di Vita, La Rosa, and Rizzo 1984, pp. 161–201.

———. 1985. "Le nuove indagini ad Haghia Triada," in Πεπραγμένα τοῦ Ε´ Διεθνοῦς Κρητολογικοῦ Συνεδρίου, ῞Αγ. Νικόλαος 1981, part A, Herakleion, pp. 190–198.

———. 1986. "Haghia Triada II: Relazione preliminare sui saggi del 1978 e 1979," *ASAtene* 57–58, pp. 49–164.

———. 1989. "Nouvelles données du Bronze Moyen au Bronze Récent à

Haghia Triada," in Laffineur 1989, pp. 81–92.

La Rosa, V., and N. Cucuzza. 2000. *L'insediamento di Selì di Kamilari nel territorio di Festòs,* Padua.

Lembesi, A. 1976a. "A Sanctuary of Hermes and Aphrodite in Crete," *Expedition* 18, pp. 2–13.

———. 1976b. " Ὁ οἰκίσκος τῶν Ἀρχανῶν," *ArchEph,* pp. 12–43.

———. 1979. " Ἱερὸ Ἑρμῆ καὶ Ἀφροδίτης στὴ Σύμη Βιάννου," *Prakt* 1976, part B, pp. 400–407.

———. 1990. " Ἱερὸ τοῦ Ἑρμῆ καὶ τῆς Ἀφροδίτης στὴ Σύμη Βιάννου," *Prakt* 1985, pp. 263–285.

———. 1991a. " Ἱερὸ τοῦ Ἑρμῆ καὶ τῆς Ἀφροδίτης στὴ Σύμη Βιάννου," *Prakt* 1984, part B, pp. 440–463.

———. 1991b. "Τὸ Ἱερὸ τοῦ Ἑρμῆ καὶ τῆς Ἀφροδίτης στὴ Σύμη Βιάννου," *Prakt* 1988, pp. 244–263.

———. 1994. "Τὸ Ἱερὸ τοῦ Ἑρμῆ καὶ τῆς Ἀφροδίτης στὴ Σύμη Βιάννου," *Prakt* 1991, pp. 306–330.

Levi, D. 1959. "La villa rurale minoica di Gortina," *BdA* 44, pp. 237–265.

———. 1961–1962. "La tomba a tholos di Kamilari presso a Festòs," *ASAtene* 39–40, pp. 7–148.

———. 1967–1968. "L'abitato di Festòs in località Chálara," *ASAtene* 45–46, pp. 55–166.

———. 1976. *Festòs e la civiltà minoica* I, Rome.

Levi, D., and F. Carinci. 1988. *Festòs e la civiltà minoica* II.2, Rome.

Levi, D., and C. Laviosa. 1986. "Il forno minoico da vasaio di Haghia Triada," *ASAtene* 57–58, pp. 7–47.

Lolos, Y. G. 1987. *The Late Helladic I Pottery of the Southern Peloponnesos and Its Local Characteristics,* Göteborg.

London, G. A. 1989a. "On Fig Leaves, Itinerant Potters, and Pottery Production Locations in Cyprus," in P. E. McGovern and M. D. Notis, eds., *Cross-Craft and Cross-Cultural Interactions in Ceramics* (Ceramics and Civilization IV), Westerville, Ohio, pp. 65–80.

———. 1989b. "Past Present: The Village Potters of Cyprus," *BiblArch* 52, pp. 219–229.

Longacre, W. A., K. L. Kvamme, and M. Kobayashi. 1988. "Southwestern Pottery Standardization: An Ethnoarchaeological View from the Philippines," *The Kiva* 53, pp. 101–112.

Macdonald, C. F. 1990. "Destruction and Construction in the Palace at Knossos: LM IA–B," in Hardy and Renfrew 1990, pp. 82–88.

———. 1996. "Notes on Some Late Minoan IA Contexts from the Palace of Minos and Its Immediate Vicinity," in D. Evely, I. S. Lemos, and S. Sherratt, eds., *Minotaur and Centaur. Studies in the Archaeology of Crete and Euboea Presented to Mervyn Popham,* Oxford, pp. 17–26.

MacGillivray, J. A. 1987. "Pottery Workshops and the Old Palaces in Crete," in R. Hägg and N. Marinatos, eds., *The Function of the Minoan Palaces,* Stockholm, pp. 273–278.

Maniatis, Y. 1984. "Firing Conditions of White-on-Dark Ware from Eastern Crete," in Betancourt 1984, pp. 71–74.

Maniatis, Y., and M. Tite. 1981. "Technological Examination of Neolithic–Bronze Age Pottery from Central and South-East Europe and from the Near-East," *JAS* 8, pp. 59–76.

Maniatis, Y., V. Perdikatsis, and K. Kotsakis. 1988. "Assessment of In-Site Variability of Pottery from Sesklo, Thessaly," *Archaeometry* 30, pp. 264–274.

Maniatis, Y., A. Simopoulos, and A. Kostikas. 1981. "Mossbauer Study of the Effect of Calcium Content on Iron-Oxide Transformations in Fired Clays," *Journal of the American Ceramic Society* 64, pp. 263–269.

Manning, S. W. 1995. *The Absolute Chronology of the Aegean Early Bronze Age,* Sheffield.

Marinatos, S. 1927. "Μεσομινωϊκὴ οἰκία ἐν κάτω Μεσαρᾷ," *ArchDelt* 9 (1924–1925), pp. 53–78.

———. 1952. " Ἀνασκαφὴ Μεγάρου Βαθυπέτρου Κρήτης," *Prakt* 1951, pp. 258–272.

———. 1956. " Ἀνασκαφαὶ ἐν Βαθυπέτρῳ Κρήτης," *Prakt* 1953, p. 298.

———. 1960. " Ἀνασκαφαὶ ἐν

Λυκάστῳ καὶ Βαθυπέτρῳ Κρήτης," *Prakt* 1955, pp. 306–310.

Marthari, M. 1990. "The Chronology of the Last Phases of Occupation at Akrotiri in the Light of the Evidence from the West House Pottery Groups," in Hardy and Renfrew 1990, pp. 57–70.

McLoughlin, B. 1993. *The Kilns of Ancient Greece: A Typology* (M.A. thesis, University of Sydney).

Mellaart, J. 1970. *Excavations at Hacılar,* Edinburgh.

Michaelidis, P. 1993. "Potters' Workshops in Minoan Crete," *SMEA* 32, pp. 7–39.

Morris, C. 1993. "Hands Up for the Individual! The Role of Attribution Studies in Aegean Prehistory," *CAJ* 3, pp. 41–66.

Mountjoy, P. A. 1984. "The Marine Style Pottery of LM IB/LH IIA: Towards a Corpus," *BSA* 79, pp. 161–219.

Myer, G. H., and P. P. Betancourt. 1990. "The Fabrics at Kommos," in *Kommos* II, pp. 1–13.

Myer, G. H., K. G. McIntosh, and P. P. Betancourt. 1995. "Definitions of Pottery Fabrics by Ceramic Petrography," in P. P. Betancourt and C. Davaras, eds., *Pseira* I: *The Minoan Buildings of the West Side of Area A,* Philadelphia, pp. 143–153.

Niemeier, W.-D. 1980. "Die Katastrophe von Thera und die spätminoische Chronologie," *JdI* 95, pp. 1–76.

———. 1997. "The Mycenaean Potter's Quarter at Miletus," in Laffineur and Betancourt 1997, pp. 347–352.

Noll, W. 1978. "Material and Techniques of the Minoan Ceramics of Thera and Crete," in C. Doumas and H. C. Puchelt, eds., *Thera and the Aegean World* I, London, pp. 493–505.

Noll, W., R. Holm, and L. Born. 1971. "Chemie und technik altkretischer Vasenmalerei vom Kamares-Typ," *Naturwissenschaften* 58, pp. 615–618.

Pantelidou-Gopha, M. 1991. "Κεραμεικὰ ἐργαλεῖα," *ArchEph* 130, pp. 1–13.

Papadopoulos, J. K. 1989. "An Early

Iron Age Potter's Kiln at Torone," *MeditArch* 2, pp. 9–44.

Peacock, D. P. S. 1982. *Pottery in the Roman World: An Ethnoarchaeological Approach,* London.

Pelon, O. 1966. "Maison d'Hagia Varvara et architecture domestique à Mallia," *BCH* 90, pp. 552–585.

———. 1970. *Fouilles exécutées à Mallia: Explorations des maisons et quartiers d'habitation (1963–1966),* III (EtCret 16), Paris.

Pernier, L. 1935. *Il palazzo minoico di Festòs* I, Rome.

Pernier, L., and L. Banti. 1951. *Il palazzo minoico di Festòs* II, Rome.

Picon, M. 1991. "Quelques observations complémentaires sur les alterations de composition des céramiques au cours du temps: Cas de quelques alcalins et alcalino-terreux," *Revue d'archeometrie* 15, pp. 117–122.

Platon, N. 1961. "Ἀνασκαφὴ μινωϊκῆς ἀγροικίας εἰς Ζοῦ Σητείας," *Prakt* 1956, pp. 232–240.

———. 1977. "Ἀνασκαφὴ Ζάκρου," *Prakt* 1975, pp. 343–375.

———. 1980. "Μεταλλουργικὸ Καμίνι στὴν Ζάκρο τῆς Κρήτης," *Proceedings of the Fourth International Cretological Congress,* pp. 436–446.

———. 1985. *The Discovery of a Lost Palace of Ancient Crete,* Amsterdam.

PM I = A. J. Evans, *The Palace of Minos at Knossos* I, London, 1921.

PM II = A. J. Evans, *The Palace of Minos at Knossos* II, London, 1928.

PM III = A. J. Evans, *The Palace of Minos at Knossos* III, London, 1930.

PM IV = A. J. Evans, *The Palace of Minos at Knossos* IV, London, 1935.

Popham, M. R. 1967. "Late Minoan Pottery: A Summary," *BSA* 62, pp. 337–351.

———. 1970. *The Destruction of the Palace at Knossos,* Göteborg.

———. 1977. "Notes from Knossos, Part I," *BSA* 72, pp. 185–195.

———. 1984. *The Minoan Unexplored Mansion at Knossos,* Oxford.

———. 1990. "Pottery Styles and Chronology," in Hardy and Renfrew 1990, pp. 27–28.

Poursat, J.-Cl. 1983. "Ateliers et sanctuaires à Malia: Nouvelles données sur l'organisation sociale

à l'époque des premiers palais," in O. Krzyszkowska and L. Nixon, eds., *Minoan Society,* Bristol, pp. 277–281.

———. 1992. *Guide de Malia au temps des premiers palais: Le Quartier Mu,* Paris.

Redman, C. L. 1977. "The 'Analytical Individual' and Prehistoric Style Variability," in J. N. Hill and J. Gunn, eds., *The Individual in Prehistory,* New York, pp. 41–53.

Rice, P. M. 1987. *Pottery Analysis: A Sourcebook,* Chicago.

Riley, J. A. 1981. "The Late Bronze Age Aegean and the Roman Mediterranean: A Case for Comparison," in H. Howard and E. L. Morris, eds., *Production and Distribution: A Ceramic Viewpoint* (BAR-IS 120), Oxford, pp. 133–143.

———. 1983. "The Contribution of Ceramic Petrology to Our Understanding of Minoan Society," in O. Kryszkowska and L. Nixon, eds., *Minoan Society,* Bristol, pp. 283–292.

Rutter, J. B. 1990. "Pottery Groups from Tsoungiza of the End of the Middle Bronze Age," *Hesperia* 59, pp. 375–458.

Rye, O. S. 1981. *Pottery Technology,* Washington, D.C.

Sakellarakis, J. 1989. "Ζώμινθος," *Ergon* 1988, pp. 165–172.

Sakellarakis, J. A., and E. Sapouna-Sakellaraki. 1991. *Archanes,* Athens.

Sayre, E. V. 1977. *Brookhaven Procedures for Statistical Analyses of Multivariate Archaeometric Data* (BNL Report 21693), New York.

Shaw, J. W. 1986. "Excavations at Kommos (Crete) during 1984–1985," *Hesperia* 55, pp. 219–269.

Shaw, J. W., and M. C. Shaw. 1993. "Excavations at Kommos (Crete) during 1986–1992," *Hesperia* 62, pp. 129–190.

———. 1999. "A Proposal for Bronze Age Aegean Shipsheds in Crete," in H. Tzalas, ed., *Tropis* V, *5th International Symposium on Ship Construction in Antiquity,* pp. 369–382.

Shaw, J. W., A. Van de Moortel, P. M. Day, and V. Kilikoglou. 1997. "A LMIA Pottery Kiln at Kommos,

Crete," in Laffineur and Betancourt 1997, pp. 323–332.

Shaw, M. C. 1990. "Late Minoan Hearths and Ovens at Kommos, Crete," in *L'Habitat égéen préhistorique* (*BCH* Suppl. 19), Paris, pp. 231–254.

Shepard, A. O. 1956. *Ceramics for the Archaeologist*, Washington, D.C.

Sillar, W. 1997. "Reputable Pots and Disreputable Potters: Individual and Community Choice in Present-Day Pottery Production and Exchange in the Andes," in C. G. Cumberpatch and P. W. Blinkhorn, eds., *Not So Much a Pot, More a Way of Life* (Oxbow monograph 83), Oxford, pp. 1–20.

Soles, J. 1997. "A Community of Craft Specialists at Mochlos," in Laffineur and Betancourt 1997, pp. 425–430.

Tadmor, M. 1992. "On Lids and Ropes in the Early Bronze and Chalcolithic Periods," in E. Stern and T. Levi, eds., *Eretz-Israel* (Archaeological, Historical, and Geographical Studies 23), Jerusalem, pp. 82–91, 149.

Tarling, D. H., and W. S. Downey. 1989. "Archaeomagnetic Study of the Late Minoan Kiln 2, Stratigraphical Museum Extension, Knossos," *BSA* 84, pp. 345–352 .

Terry, R. D., and G. V. Chilingar. 1955. "Summary of 'Concerning Some Additional Aids in Studying Sedimentary Formations,' by M. S. Shvetsov," *Journal of Sedimentary Petrology* 25, pp. 229–234.

Thera I = S. Marinatos, *Excavations at Thera. First Preliminary Report*, Athens 1968.

Thera II = S. Marinatos, *Excavations at Thera* II, Athens 1969.

Thera III = S. Marinatos, *Excavations at Thera* III, Athens 1970.

Thera IV = S. Marinatos, *Excavations at Thera* IV, Athens 1971.

Thera V = S. Marinatos, *Excavations at Thera* V, Athens 1972.

Thera VI = S. Marinatos, *Excavations at Thera* VI, Athens 1974.

Thomas, P. M. 1997. "Mycenaean Kylix Painters at Zygouries," in Laffineur and Betancourt 1997, pp. 377–386.

Tomasello, F. 1996. "Fornaci à Festòs ed Haghia Triada dall 'età' mediominoica alla geometrica," in E. Gavrilaki, ed., *Κεραμικὰ ἐργαστήρια στὴν Κρήτη ἀπὸ τὴν ἀρχαιότητα ὡς σήμερα. Πρακτικὰ Ἡμερίδας, Μαργαρίτες, 30 Σεπτεμβρίου 1995*, Rethymnon, pp. 25–37.

Tomlinson, J. 1991. *Provenance of Minoan Ceramics by Multivariate Analysis of Neutron Activation Data* (diss., University of Manchester).

Tomlinson, R. A. 1995. "Archaeology in Greece, 1994–95," *AR*, pp. 1–74.

Tzedakis, I. 1968. "Ἀρχαιότητες καὶ μνημεῖα δυτικῆς Κρήτης," *ArchDelt* 21 Β΄2 (1966), pp. 425–429.

———. 1969. "Ἀνασκαφὴ Καστελλίου Χανίων," *ArchDelt* 22 Β΄2 (1967), pp. 501–506.

Vallianou, D. 1997. "The Potters' Quarter in LMIII Gouves," in Laffineur and Betancourt 1997, pp. 333–344.

van As, A., and L. Jacobs. 1987. "Second Millennium B.C. Goblet Bases from Tell ed-Deir: The Relationship between Form and Technique," *Newsletter, Department of Pottery Technology (Leiden)* 5, pp. 39–53.

Van de Moortel, A. 1997. *The Transition from the Protopalatial to the Neopalatial Society in South-Central Crete: A Ceramic Perspective* (diss., Bryn Mawr College).

———. In press. "Pottery as a Barometer of Economic Change: From the Protopalatial to the Neopalatial Society in Central Crete," in Y. Hamilakis, ed., *Labyrinth Revisited: Rethinking Minoan Archaeology*, Oxford.

van Effenterre, H., and M. van Effenterre. 1976. *Fouilles exécutées à Mallia: Exploration des maisons et quartiers d'habitation (1956–1960)* IV (EtCret 22), Paris.

Voyatzoglou, M. 1974. "The Jar Makers of Thrapsano in Crete," *Expedition* 16, pp. 18–24.

———. 1984. "Thrapsano, Village of Jar Makers," in Betancourt 1984, pp. 130–142.

Walberg, G. 1983. *Provincial Middle Minoan Pottery*, Mainz.

———. 1987. *Kamares: A Study of the*

Character of Palatial Middle Minoan Pottery, 2d ed. Göteborg.

———. 1992. *Middle Minoan III: A Time of Transition,* Jonsered.

Warren, P. M. 1972. *Myrtos: An Early Bronze Age Settlement in Crete,* London.

———. 1980–1981. "Knossos: Stratigraphical Museum Excavations, 1978–1980, Part I," *AR,* pp. 73–92.

———. 1991. "A New Minoan Deposit from Knossos, c. 1600 B.C., and Its Wider Relations," *BSA* 86, pp. 319–340.

Warren, P. M., and V. Hankey. 1989. *Aegean Bronze Age Chronology,* Bristol.

Whitbread, I. K. 1986. "The Characteristics of Argillaceous Inclusions in Ceramic Thin Sections," *Archaeometry* 28, pp. 79–88.

———. 1989. "A Proposal for the Systematic Description of Thin Sections towards the Study of Ancient Ceramic Technology," in Y. Maniatis, ed., *Archaeometry: Proceedings of the 25th International Symposium,* Amsterdam, pp. 127–138.

———. 1995. *Greek Transport Amphorae: A Petrological and Archaeological Study* (Fitch Laboratory Occasional Paper 4), Athens.

Whitelaw, T. M., P. M. Day, E. Kiriatzi, V. Kilikoglou, and D. E. Wilson. 1997. "Ceramic Traditions at EMIIB Myrtos, Fournou Korifi," in Laffineur and Betancourt 1997, pp. 265–274.

Wiener, M. H. 1984. "Crete and the Cyclades in LM I: The Tale of the Conical Cups," in R. Hägg and N. Marinatos, eds., *Minoan Thalassocracy,* Stockholm, pp. 17–26.

Wilson, D. E., and P. M. Day. 1994. "Ceramic Regionalism in Prepalatial Central Crete: The Mesara Imports at EM I to EM IIA Knossos," *BSA* 89, pp. 1–87.

Wright, J. C. 1996. "The Central Hillside at Kommos, 2: The Middle Minoan Period," in *Kommos* I.2, pp. 140–199.

Xanthoudides, S. 1927. "Some Minoan Potter's-Wheel Discs," in S. Casson, ed., *Essays in Aegean Archaeology,* Oxford, pp. 111–128.

Index